CONDUCTING
HERMENEUTIC
RESEARCH

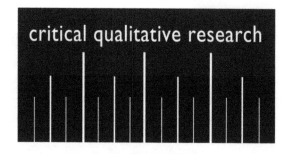

critical qualitative research

CRITICAL ISSUES FOR LEARNING AND TEACHING

Shirley R. Steinberg and Gaile S. Cannella
Series Editors

Vol. 19

The Critical Qualitative Research series is part of the Peter Lang Education list.
Every volume is peer reviewed and meets
the highest quality standards for content and production.

PETER LANG
New York • Bern • Frankfurt • Berlin
Brussels • Vienna • Oxford • Warsaw

Nancy J. Moules, Graham McCaffrey,
James C. Field, AND Catherine M. Laing

CONDUCTING HERMENEUTIC RESEARCH

From Philosophy to Practice

PETER LANG
New York • Bern • Frankfurt • Berlin
Brussels • Vienna • Oxford • Warsaw

Library of Congress Cataloging-in-Publication Data
Conducting hermeneutic research: from philosophy to practice /
Nancy J. Moules, Graham McCaffrey, James C. Field, Catherine M. Laing.
pages cm. — (Critical qualitative research; vol. 19)
Includes bibliographical references and index.
1. Hermeneutics. 2. Hermeneutics—Research. I. Moules, Nancy J.
BD241.C6235   001.4—dc23   2015003313
ISBN 978-1-4331-2733-5 (hardcover)
ISBN 978-1-4331-2732-8 (paperback)
ISBN 978-1-4539-1473-1 (e-book)
ISSN 1947-5993

Bibliographic information published by Die Deutsche Nationalbibliothek.
Die Deutsche Nationalbibliothek lists this publication in the "Deutsche
Nationalbibliografie"; detailed bibliographic data are available
on the Internet at http://dnb.d-nb.de/.

Index by INDEX-S

© 2015 Peter Lang Publishing, Inc., New York
29 Broadway, 18th floor, New York, NY 10006
www.peterlang.com

DEDICATION

To Dr. David W. Jardine, upon the occasion of his retirement, in recognition
of the many ways he invited all of us to hermeneutics
and
To the Visiting Scholars of the Canadian Hermeneutic Institute:
http://www.chiannual.com/
David Jardine, John Caputo, Richard Kearney, James Olthuis, Gail Weiss,
Nicholas Davey, Jean Grondin
And those yet to come…

TABLE OF CONTENTS

FOREWORD: THE WISDOM
OF HERMENEUTICS

I am pleased and honored to offer a word in advance to *Conducting Hermeneutic Research*. This is a paradoxical invitation for me because in radical hermeneutics everything turns on saying "come" to the coming of what we cannot see coming, of the unforeseeable. So without trying to help the reader see too much in advance, without trying to anticipate everything, let me say that what I find so precious in *Conducting Hermeneutic Research* is that it catches hermeneutics in the act. It brings home in the most vivid way just what hermeneutics really is—in the concrete. Its authors are concretely engaged and hermeneutically enlightened practitioners who are describing the difficult and delicate conditions under which concrete hermeneutical work takes place. How are research and writing conducted in such a way as not to become absorbed in a data-driven and objectifying culture? How to show that more is given than data without having one's work dismissed as random, subjectivistic, and impressionistic? How to show that hermeneutics practices a "rigor" that is not reducible to mathematical "exactness," to invoke a distinction from Edmund Husserl (that is put to work in Chapter Nine)? The task these authors take on is to portray the special place of practice in hermeneutics, to depict the practical wisdom that hermeneutics requires, indeed the practical wisdom that hermeneutics *is*.

As practitioners, the authors understand in their bones what the ancients meant when they said that only individuals exist, while universals are abstractions. In hermeneutics—I offer this as a working definition—it is not a matter of applying universals to cases but instead of applying cases to universals. The only reason that sounds strange is because of the inverted, topsy-turvy nature of the word case. "Case" comes from *cadere, casum*, to fall, as in a casualty, for which we buy insurance. The suggestion is that the individual represents a "fall" from the truth and reality of the universal, a decline into mere particularity. But this is to invert reality. For the individual is what is real. The individual is the first truth, the true being, while universals are abstractions, meaning they are siphoned off (abstract = *ab* + *trahere*) individuals. Universals make handy but relatively empty place-holders, thin, schematic signifiers constituting an efficient shorthand useful for exchanging information. Trading in universals is like passing along linguistic containers which require unpacking to see to what they really contain when we get down to cases. There it is again! We don't get down to cases—we rise to them! We have everything we can do to rise to the occasion of the individual, to ascend to the thick, dense, rich, complexity of the individual situation, instead of lolling lazily amidst the thin transparencies of universals.

In that sense hermeneutics is better served to speak not of the individual case but of the singular situation, not of "cases" but of "singularities," which are always marked by a certain alterity, idiomaticity, idiosyncrasy and conceptual impenetrability. Singularities are not a fall or a defect, but an excess, far too rich ever to be adequately explicated or translated into universals. Just try it for yourself: try to make a list of universals that explicate your feelings for someone you love with a love that surpasses understanding, or that describe an experience that transformed your life, or a work of art that leaves you lost for words. We come up short, but coming up short against singularities is not due to a defect in our language or experience; it is not something to be remedied by building up a still larger stock of universals to draw upon the next time we are confounded by experience. We come up short because of the wealth of the experience. The wisdom of hermeneutics is to have the good sense not to think that reality is a "case" of an abstraction, that the perceptual is a lesser species than the conceptual, that the real is a fall from the ideal, or that "practice" is an imperfect version of the theoretical. Universals are abstracts, extracts, one-sided take outs, a freeze frame, a still which, while serving a purpose, only imperfectly evokes the rush of movement.

In short, in hermeneutics, we proceed from the assumption that the practice is the perfect and the theory is the imperfect. The authors of the present
volume are practitioners, nurses and educators, who alert us to the delicate
art of practice and to the practical wisdom demanded of the practitioner.
They face a dilemma like Kierkegaard's, who wrote books which claimed that
becoming a Christian is nothing to be found in a book, and so tried to write
a book as if he had not written a book. These authors are trying to describe
a method that is not a method except in the deeper etymological sense of
making one's way along (*meta*) the path (*odos*) to truth. To take one of many
examples I could choose here, let me say that there is no theory, no body of
principles, no rulebook, no set of universal norms that would enable us to
"conduct" the interview recorded for us in Chapter Six with parents who have
lost a child to cancer. The situation is steeped in an impenetrable mystery, a
question to which there is no answer—why do children die? But while there
is no answer, there is a fitting response, a response cut to fit—where there are
no mis-fits, just ways of being differently fitted (see the wonderful account
of a camp conducted for children with cancer in Chapter Eight)—which
is compassion. Compassion inscribes a zone of respect around the mystery,
is sensitive to the abyss that stirs beneath the cool clinical words "pediatric
oncology." Compassion provides for the possibility of the impossible, under-
taking to heal an unhealable wound by—in this case—attempting to share
this experience with other parents. The interviewer eases into the delicacy of
a situation of unimaginable pain with "questions" that do not interrogate or
objectify but create a space in which an unbearable suffering, an unspeakable
pain, may find words. The words exchanged are gentle, sometimes hardly
articulate, words that do not propose or defend theses, words from the heart,
from broken hearts. As opposed to the cruelty of introducing a "statistic"
about the divorce rate of parents who undergo this nightmare, a shattering
number which threatens to crush the spirits of these courageous parents. In
this interview we see what the philosophers call the "hermeneutic situation"
in the concrete, glowing white hot and jumping off the pages of the philosophy books.

These authors work on the front line of situations where the only rule is
that each situation is different. Hermeneutics is not a theory about how to
engage in practice. If hermeneutics is a theory at all, it is a theory—which
means a "seeing" (*theorein*, as in a theater)—of what we can't see coming, a
foreseeing of the unforeseeability of what is coming in the singular situation.

Hermeneutics is the theory that practice is not blind but already has its own kind of pre-theoretical seeing—rather the way that it is the fingers of the pianist that "know" where the keys are and how to touch them. It is a theory, if it is a theory, about the limits of theory, what Derrida would call a "quasi-transcendental" theory. Unlike a transcendental theory, which lays out the conditions under which something is possible, hermeneutics is a theory that the most important things are possible only under conditions that make them impossible, like the impossible demands of this interview. It deals with limit cases, situations in which we run up against the most impossible things, where we must go where it is impossible to go. Only when we experience this paralysis may we dare proceed. Its greatest difficulty is that it will get too used to such extremes and begin to take the exceptional as business as usual.

Proceeding with the appropriate fear and trembling, understanding that hermeneutics is not a theory that we apply but a practice, they offer us various principles that are not quite principles. "Principles" are constructions drawn from the past whose predictive power depends upon the future being like the past. Principles unfold on the basis of the past but they fold in the face of what they cannot see coming, of the unexpected. That is why we do not "apply principles to cases." We have the wisdom to know that principles, *principia*, which are sustained by the pretense that they come first (*in principio*), actually come last. Principles come after the fact, after experience has already taken place, and they will be sent scurrying back to the drawing board by the coming of what they do not see coming, by the next unexpected turn of events, by the singularity of something unforeseen—otherwise known as life, where the only preparation is to prepare to be unprepared!

Hermeneutics is wisdom. However postmodern hermeneutics may be, it is also a classical pre-modern wisdom. It goes back to Aristotle who posted himself at the door of ethics and warned all who were about to pass through: if you have come here in search of certainty, look elsewhere. If you come here in search of insurance to keep yourself safe from the "casualties" of concrete ethical life, you've come to the wrong place. Try that place down the street with "mathematics" marked on the door. In mathematics the ideal is the perfect (the perfect triangle is found only in ideal mathematical space) and the real is imperfect (no real triangular thing is ever perfectly triangular). But in ethics, the ideal, say, the definition of courage, is but an imperfect general schema, a finger pointing at the moon, while rising to the demands of the courage called for here and now, in this real and singular situation, is the perfect. Hermeneutics is what Aristotle called the practical wisdom (*phronesis*) which knows that only individuals exist, that individuals are not trimmed down versions of universals but the rich and concretely real, and that our commerce with the reality of singularities cannot be lit in advance by the luminosity of principles.

Hermeneutics is the art of judgment and judgment is the art of the concrete. The person of judgment, Aristotle's *phronimos*, has cultivated the art of discernment, of seeing into the singularity of the situation, into the unexpected demands of the singular, seeing what the situation is calling for, hearing what calls to us in this situation. In exercising a discerning judgment of this sort, we respond to what calls upon us, and we do so in the only responsible way. Hermeneutics is the maximization of responsibility. It recognizes what is called for in the idiosyncratic situation—as opposed to the flight from responsibility, which simply follows the rules. What better way to excuse oneself from assuming responsibility than to say that we are only following the rules? "I wish I could do something for you. I sympathize with your situation. It's nothing personal. But I don't make the rules." What is more irresponsible than that? How much injustice has resulted from that? In hermeneutics we are, beyond being responsible to rules, responsible *for* the rules to which we respond.

The universality of hermeneutics means that such discernment is called for in every branch of life—not only in ethics, but in art where the artist is constantly experimenting with the previously untried, and in science, which reaches its highest pitch in dealing with the scientific anomalies that throw the received theories into turmoil, and in the various vocations—which means "callings" of course—like the physician and the nurse, the teacher, the therapist, the social worker, the pastor, the judge and jurists. Hermeneutics is not a theory of knowledge but the art of life and death, and it ranges over the length and breadth and depth of life. Hermeneutics does not shy away from the difficulty of life but summons the courage to deal with life in all its ambiguity. Hermeneutics takes the risk of embracing the coming of what we cannot see coming.

To see what I mean, in the concrete, I urge you to keep reading.

John D. Caputo
Thomas J. Watson Professor of Religion Emeritus
Syracuse University
David R. Cook Professor Emeritus of Philosophy
Villanova University

· 1 ·

COMING TO HERMENEUTICS

...hermeneutics is a lesson in humility...it has wrestled with the angels of darkness and has not gotten the better of them. It understands the power of the flux to wash away the best-laid schemes of metaphysics. It takes the constructs of metaphysics to be temporary cloud formations which, from a distance, create the appearance of shape and substance but which pass through our fingers upon contact...and no matter how wantonly they are skewed across the skies there are always hermeneuts who claim to detect a shape...a bear here, a man with a long nose there. There are always those who claim they can read the clouds and find a pattern and a meaning. Now, it is not the function of...hermeneutics to put an end to those games, like a cold-blooded, demythologizing scientist who insists that the clouds are but random collections of particles of water...its function is to keep the games in play, to awaken us to the play, to keep us on the alert that we draw forms in the sand, we read clouds in the sky, but we do not capture deep essences...if there is anything that we learn in...hermeneutics it is that we never get the better of the flux. (Caputo, 1987, p. 258)

This is a book about the conduct of hermeneutic research in applied disciplines. To describe this conduct is not an easy endeavor any more than is the actual practice of hermeneutic research. Hermeneutics comes to us as researchers with a long history and ancestry based in philosophy that must first be acknowledged prior to discussing the application of this philosophy to research practice, thus the subtitle of this book – "*From Philosophy to Practice.*" Hans-Georg Gadamer (1960/1989) suggested that we cannot step over our shadows; we are connected in a continuous thread with our past, with traditions, and with our ancestors, living out traditions that have been bequeathed to us by others. The echoes of history are always inadvertently *and deliberately* inviting us into both past and new ways of being in the present and, thus, we live in a world that recedes into the past and extends into the future. Rather than pitting ourselves against history, we therefore we need to *remember, recollect,* and *recall* it.

Hermeneutic or interpretive inquiry is a historical and living tradition of interpretation with a rich legacy of theory, philosophy, and practice. This legacy is being lived out differently in varied versions, understandings, and practices of hermeneutics as a research approach or method.

This book is not intended to be a treatise on the *right* way to conduct hermeneutic research but rather, to reveal fresh possibilities for research by weaving legacies of philosophy into practice. In it, we trace the shadows of hermeneutics, an ancestry that leads us to the philosophical hermeneutics of Hans-Georg Gadamer and more contemporary continental philosophers; this is a scaffolding of philosophy that guides us to articulate one possible way to conduct hermeneutic research in contexts of the applied disciplines.

What Is Hermeneutics?

Hermeneutics is derived from the Greek verb *hermeneuein*, which means to say or interpret; the noun *hermeneia*, which is the utterance or explication of thought; and the name *hermeneus*, which refers to the playful, mischievous, "trickster" Hermes (Caputo, 1987; Grondin, 1994). In bringing the messages of the gods to humans, Hermes entices interpretation. Hermes has the character of complication, multiplicity, lies, jokes, irreverence, indirection, and disdain for rules, however, he is the master of creativity and invention. He has the capacity to see things anew and his power is change, prediction, and the solving of puzzles.

The practice of interpretation known as hermeneutics dates to 17th-century biblical and theological textual interpretation and has followed a changing course from rationalism to romanticism, pragmatism to philosophy, and conservatism to radicalization. The Latin word, *hermeneutica*, was introduced in the 17th century by the theologian Johann Dannhauer, and it has grown into different schools including the realms of the theological, juridical, and philosophical (Grondin, 1994).

Although it defies definition, in a nutshell, hermeneutics could be described as the tradition, philosophy, and practice of interpretation (Moules, 2002). Hermeneutics has been described as the practice and theory of interpretation and understanding in human contexts; the science, art, and philosophy of interpretation; and the "discipline of thought that aims at (the) unsaid life of our discourses" (Grondin, 1995, p. x). It is considered a reflective inquiry concerned with "our entire understanding of the world and thus… all the various forms in which this understanding manifests itself" (Gadamer, 1976, p. 18). Hermeneutics peers behind language; it ventures into the contextual world of a word, considering "what is said, what is uttered, but at the same time what is silenced" (Grondin, 1995, p. x). Gadamer (1960/1989) offered that the venture into the unsaid involves the speculative dimension in language, the mirroring of meanings, and the belief that the said is always in relationship with the unsaid; "we can understand a text only when we've understood the question to which it is an answer" (p. 370).

Hermeneutics involves recognition of sameness, place, and belonging. Hermeneutic interpretation comprehends the recognition that occurs when something rings "true" of what is said; there is familiarity, kinship, resonance, and likeness as well as difference. It is neither replication nor is it justification. It is an acknowledgment that things come from somewhere; they are not simply fabricated. However, along with sameness and recognition, hermeneutics requires a bringing forth and a bringing to language of something new. We work out this newness by working it into a world of relationships that can sustain it. In these relationships, others start to recognize not only something of themselves, but also of the world; they recognize something old and something new.

At the heart of hermeneutics is the idea of *aletheia*, which we will refer to several times throughout this book. Aletheia is a Greek word meaning "the event of concealment and unconcealment" (Caputo, 1987, p. 115). Aletheia occurs when something opens that was once closed, when something reveals itself or is revealed. Aletheia comes from the word *Lethe*, which is a mythical river in Hades, the water of which, when drunk, produces oblivion of the past; thus, it is called the "river of forgetting" (Hoad, 1986). Lethe also is tied to the word lethal. Aletheia works against what was dead bringing it to life; it remembers and unconceals what was forgotten or lost to the business and "work of simply getting by"(Wallace, 1987 p. 12).

In its work of aletheia, hermeneutics is organized around the disruption of the clear narrative, always questioning those things that are taken for granted. In hermeneutics, there is a striking character of attention to the instance and the particular, rather than an effort to generalize. Interpretation is not a move to relieve the instance from its burden, and though things may be raised out of a strict burden of specificity (Smith, 1991). Rather, there is an effort to con-serve the burden and to celebrate the "stubborn particular" (Wallace, 1987). Interpretation moves to represent the particular and to bring it to presence, not essence. Hermeneutics calls forth the ordinary and makes it stand out. In this standing out, however, it does not stand alone, but stands with its history, legacies, and relationships, acknowledging that there are both hidden and apparent traces that constitute and constantly change how something comes to exist. In the end, hermeneutics brings things back home to something that is recognizable and "true."

Paradoxically, hermeneutics is not particularly interested in itself, its own character, or self-definition. Rather, it is more concerned with the "question of human meaning and of how we make sense of our lives in such a way that life can go on…[it] works to rescue the specificities of our lives from the burden of their everydayness…[it] is about finding ourselves, which also, curiously enough, is about losing ourselves" (Smith, 1991, pp. 200–201). Hermeneutics begins with the premise that the world is interpretable.

A Brief Note on "Method" in Hermeneutic Inquiry: How we Pursue a Matter

Hermeneutics pits itself against the notion that human affairs can finally be formalized into explicit rules which can or should function as a decision-procedure…but…such a view does not throw us back into anarchy and chaos-although a little chaos is a good strategy… Our preoccupation with methodology needs to be replaced with a deeper appreciation of methodos, meta-odos, *which is 'the way in which we pursue a matter'…The concern with 'method' so characteristic of modern science…makes science subservient to method, so that method rules instead of serving, constrains instead of liberating, and fails conspicuously to let science be. (Caputo, 1987, p. 213)*

In hermeneutics, we are guided by, and tethered to, the topics we are investi-gating and, because different topics call for different approaches, the research may show as methodologically different for different studies. Hermeneutics, thus, offers a substantive philosophy rather than a strategic method to guide the research. In other words, one might say hermeneutics is substantively driven rather than methodologically given. We pursue a matter according to the matter.

Although hermeneutics does not provide a strict method, it does not ask that we proceed without any guidance at all. This guidance, however, is characterized by different things than other research approaches. Gadamer (1960/1989) suggested that it is not possible to determine a way to proceed without being guided by the topic. At the beginning of interpretive work, there is necessarily a deliberate showing of questionableness, intentionally allowing the topic to guide the direction of the character of the work. This questionableness, however, does not mean that we respond tentatively, but rather that we proceed attentively, recognizing that hermeneutics is a practice of meticulous scholasticism. If we translate the notion of method into something of an inheritance, then method is simply a means of knowing one's way around a particular topography. For even though it is not a pre-determined step-by-step method, one can cultivate hermeneutics and the questionableness becomes answering these kinds of questions: How can I turn my attention to human life and my topic and not require methods which render it to something else? How can I avoid betraying it and not delivering it unto itself? How do I preserve its character without reducing it? More than anything, hermeneutics is concerned with understanding not explanation.

Koch (1996) suggested that we attend less to method and more to methodology, which is "the process by which insights about the world and the human condition are generated, interpreted and communicated" (p. 174). Therefore, to address methodology means to claim a philosophical ground that guides our research and which accurately reflects interpretive practices within its philosophical traditions. Given this groundwork, Koch offered that the soundness or rigor of a particular methodology lies in "excursions into the philosophical literature" (p. 175) that supports it. If we claim a tradition, we must be accountable to knowing it. We live in understanding and interpretation and no amount of measured techniques will save us from the task of interpretation. Hermeneutics has to do with the art of presentation, of drawing people into places where topics live, of making topics compelling, and of "restoring them to their original difficulty" (Caputo, 1987, p. 1; Jardine & Field, 1996). Restoring the difficulty, however, does not mean making it impossible to understand. In Chapter Four, we delve more into this idea of method and what it means to the conduct of hermeneutic research.

This Book

This book is a response to the question we are asked as hermeneutic researchers and teachers: "How do I conduct a hermeneutic study?" We are not left abandoned by philosophy or science in hermeneutic research. There *are* ways to proceed in approaching a research topic hermeneutically and it is our belief that this book will serve as a guide and companion in the conduct of sound, rigorous, and valuable research.

In Chapter Two, we trace some of the historical development of hermeneutics starting with Schleiermacher and working through Dilthey, Husserl, Heidegger, and Gadamer (whose philosophical hermeneutics will be discussed in greater depth in Chapter Three). Throughout, we reference contemporary continental philosophers who have influenced our work including John Caputo, Richard Kearney, Nicholas Davey, and Jean Grondin. There is mention of both the Dutch and the French schools of hermeneutics but our emphasis is on the German schools of hermeneutic philosophy.

Chapter Three is focused on the tenets of Gadamerian philosophical hermeneutics and the implications of these tenets for the conduct of hermeneutic research.

In Chapter Four, we return to the complicated question of method addressing the questionableness and complexity of it in a broader sense and particularly in hermeneutic research. Without being bound to a pre-set unbending method, we offer our ideas of what it means to be methodical and to follow leads that guide us in the research endeavor.

Chapter Five turns to a discussion of research topics and questions. "Hermeneutics begins when something addresses us" (Gadamer, 1960/1989, p. 299). We discuss how a researcher discerns a topic to be studied and, out of that discernment, develops an appropriate research question that will guide how the study will be conducted.

In Chapter Six, we discuss how one might approach recruitment of participants and then engage in the skilled art of conducting strong interviews. The fruitfulness of the analysis in hermeneutic research is highly dependent on the strength of the data collected. Data in this research approach very often arise in the form of unstructured or semi-structured research interviews that are then transcribed to text.

Chapter Seven focuses on the process and conduct of analysis in hermeneutic research, describing ways in which one engages with the data and arrives at interpretations, otherwise known as findings of the study.

Chapter Eight is in response to a frequent question we are asked by beginning hermeneutic researchers: What does good interpretive writing look like? In this chapter, we offer two examples of hermeneutic research. We briefly describe the studies and then include examples of the analysis, which takes the form of interpretive writing. Since this is the heart of hermeneutic research and is a learned and practiced art that is often difficult for beginning hermeneutic researchers, we believe it is useful to provide examples of strong interpretive writing.

In Chapter Nine, we discuss how one conducts hermeneutic research that has integrity and stands up to rigorous appraisal. Issues of validity, veracity, trustworthiness, and ethical conduct are examined.

Chapter Ten addresses the "so what" question of research. We write about the utility, actionability, and implications of applying the findings of a hermeneutic study to practice. We discuss issues of dissemination and knowledge transfer and translation.

We conclude with a final chapter, Chapter Eleven, which leaves the reader with an invitation to proceed with confidence and humility in the conduct of hermeneutic research.

Summary

In the end…hermeneutics does not lead us back to safe shores and terra firma; it leaves us twisting slowly in the wind. It leaves us exposed and without grounds, exposed to the groundlessness of the mystery…this intractable mystery is the final difficulty that hermeneutics is bent on restoring. (Caputo, 1987, p. 267)

Lethe, or the forgetting and concealment of the mystery, is the constant call to hermeneutics. Hermeneutics strives to keep itself open to the mystery and it commits to be true to the movement back and forth that occurs in play. Hermeneutics aims to keep the play in play and to keep itself in the play while simultaneously trying to uncover what is hiding.

On the surface, hermeneutics can appear to have a charming, ebullient, and almost illiterate face, but there is a deep and long-standing tradition of literacy, rigor, and integrity beneath it. When something is not guided by a rigid procedural method or character, its strength and credibility then lies in its history and ancestry, in being citatious, in being literate, accountable to, and able to speak to these things with competence and grace.

In this book, we offer a way to proceed in the conduct of hermeneutic research as guided by Hans-Georg Gadamer's philosophical hermeneutics. We start with philosophy and end with application in practice, in the anticipation that the book will bridge a gap that is always calling us as hermeneutic researchers in applied disciplines: to make a difference to human lives and living.

References

Caputo, J. (1987). *Radical hermeneutics*. Bloomington, IN: Indiana University Press.

Gadamer, H-G. (1960/1989). *Truth and method* (2nd rev.ed.) (J. Weinsheimer & D.G. Marshall, Trans.) New York, NY: Continuum.

Gadamer, H-G. (1976). *Philosophical hermeneutics* (D.E. Lange, Trans.). Berkeley, CA: University of California Press.

Grondin, J. (1994). *Introduction to philosophical hermeneutics* (J. Weinsheimer, Trans.). New Haven, CT: Yale University Press.

Grondin, J. (1995). *Sources of hermeneutics*. Albany, NY: SUNY Press.

Hoad, T.F. (Ed.). (1986). *The concise Oxford dictionary of English etymology*. New York, NY: Harper & Row.

Jardine, D.W., & Field, J. (1996). "Restoring [the] life [of language] to its original difficulty": On hermeneutics, whole language and "authenticity." *Language Arts, 73*, 255–259.

Koch, T. (1996). Implementation of a hermeneutic inquiry in nursing: Philosophy, rigour and representation. *Journal of Advanced Nursing, 24*, 174–184.

Moules, N.J. (2002). Hermeneutic inquiry: Paying heed to history and Hermes. An ancestral, substantive, and methodological tale. *International Journal of Qualitative Methods, 1*(3), 1–21.

Smith, D. (1991). Hermeneutic inquiry: The hermeneutic imagination and the pedagogic text. In E. Short (Ed.), *Forms of curriculum inquiry* (pp. 187–209). New York, NY: SUNY Press.

Wallace, B. (1987). *The stubborn particulars of grace*. Toronto, ON, Canada: McClelland & Stewart.

· 2 ·

A HISTORY OF HERMENEUTICS

For researchers who come from practice disciplines, excursions into German philosophy can seem arcane and remote. Practice, after all, implies practicality, and at times impatience with anything perceived as too abstract. Gadamer (2007), however, saw hermeneutics as a practical philosophy since human life is inseparable from understanding, so that a philosophy of understanding itself has direct relevance to how people negotiate all aspects of their existence. Reaching back into the historical development of hermeneutics prior to Gadamer's work helps to understand his thought by identifying important currents of hermeneutic philosophy. Three such currents over the past two hundred years are language, history, and being. How do human beings achieve an understanding of themselves and other beings through language? How do they make sense of what they encounter in a world that is in constant flux, a world, and hence a self, that is historically constituted? These two questions are also central to hermeneutics-as-research, asking questions about complex human situations that emerge through practical involvement in language and in historical spaces. Hence, it is worth taking a step back to see how language, history, and being have been taken up in different ways by hermeneutic thinkers and to see how contemporary developments are still part of a living tradition of ideas.

Hermeneutics evolved during the 19th and 20th centuries from a discipline concerned primarily with theological texts, then texts more generally, then to the "human sciences" as a whole, and eventually to Heidegger's ontological understanding of being itself as interpretation of our practical involvement in the world. Gadamer subsequently argued for hermeneutics as philosophy concerned with practice, which is where it becomes most obviously available as a source for research in practice disciplines.

In this chapter, we review some of the historical figures involved in the development of hermeneutics such that it has become a philosophy that can guide the conduct of research. We have chosen to follow a line of development leading up to the philosophy of Hans-Georg Gadamer, which is explored in more detail in Chapter Three. Our choice of this approach is admittedly at the expense of other influential figures whose work is explicitly phenomenological and hermeneutic, or has influenced other hermeneutic thinkers. For example, van Manen (1997) is representative of the Dutch school of phenomenology who has described a hermeneutic-phenomenological approach to research. Influenced by Heidegger, French thinkers developed ideas in phenomenology including Merleau-Ponty's working out of embodiment and Sartre's existentialism. Ricoeur is a major hermeneutic philosopher who brought other influences including structuralism and psychoanalysis into his thought. Contemporary hermeneutic philosophers including John Caputo and Richard Kearney have been influenced by French postmodernists, notably Derrida and Levinas, in examining deeply ways in which hermeneutics helps us respond to the voice of the other.

Schleiermacher: Hermeneutics and Understanding

Friedrich Schleiermacher (1768–1834) was a theologian, scholar of languages, and a philosopher. He is "properly regarded as the father of modern hermeneutics as a general study" (Palmer, 1969, p. 97). Schleiermacher believed that, in his time, hermeneutics consisted of a variety of specialized schools of interpretation, in theology or law for example, each of which had its own techniques applicable to a particular type of text. By contrast, he sought to establish a more basic and therefore more universal basis for hermeneutics. "Since the art of speaking and the art of understanding stand in relation to each other, speaking being only the outer side of thinking, hermeneutics is part of the art of thinking, and is therefore philosophical" (Schleiermacher, 1828/1990, p. 74).

Grondin (1994) pointed out that universal theories of interpretation had already been put forward, but marked Schleiermacher's hermeneutics as a new departure by complicating the work of understanding the world in the light of Kant. By separating phenomena as we perceive them from the unknowable "things in themselves," Kant's *Critique of Pure Reason* called into question the "belief in unproblematical, purely rational access to the world" (Grondin, 1994, p. 64) and created new questions about the relationship between subjectivity and objectivity. Schleiermacher wanted to work out a systematic basis for understanding across disciplines that would take into account the subjective workings of expression while also claiming objective value.

It is not difficult to see the relevance of this development to contemporary interpretive research, which, in some quarters, risks summary dismissal as subjective as opposed to the supposed objectivity of quantifiable scientific knowledge. Midgely (2001) made an end-run around this whole question by the simple expedient of pointing out that in everyday human experience (whether that of a bench scientist or a poet), we move quite easily back and forth between the two positions. A nurse asking a patient to score his pain out of ten, for example, is well aware that one does not *feel* pain in numbered increments, and the unforced expression of pain, subjective yet instantly recognizable to others, sounds more like "Ow"! Hermeneutic philosophy includes ways of explaining how it is that people coherently make sense of disparate kinds of knowledge and by deeply exploring meaning-making, it provides a firm basis for sound research.

Schleiermacher identified language as the common denominator behind different applications of hermeneutics. He saw understanding in language as made up of two elements: the expression of a thought by one person, and its reception and comprehension by another. The dialogical relationship is a crucial element for subsequent hermeneutics. It provides one response to the charge of subjectivity, since to be understood, expression has to take place on the ground of a common language and frame of reference. Dialogue also becomes a trope of the research process, whether metaphorically between reader and text, researcher and disciplinary norms, or literally in interviews and often in the relational work that is a frequent topic of interest for interpretive researchers.

There are two kinds of interpretation in Schleiermacher's hermeneutics that work together with each other: the "grammatical" and the "psychological" (called the "technical" in his earlier work) (Palmer, 1969, p. 88).

Psychological interpretation referred to the attempt to reconstruct the thought of a text's author. "By leading the interpreter to transform himself, so to speak, into the author, the divinatory method seeks to gain an immediate comprehension of the author as an individual" (Schleiermacher, 1828/1990, p. 96). Gadamer later cautioned that such an attempt at reconstruction leads to a dead end because, "What is reconstructed, a life brought back from the lost past, is not the original" (1960/2004, p. 159) and can only have interest as spectacle, like a model of a historical figure in a wax museum. Grondin, however, asked, "is it really a mistake to inquire into the subject matter and intended truth that lie behind speech?" (1994, p. 73). The spirit of hermeneutic inquiry is in exploring what lies behind the surface of phenomena, while recognizing that any one source of insight does not stand alone, cut off from other tracks of meaning.

Grammatical interpretation recognizes that the meaning of words is not only a matter of dictionary definitions, but of the context in which they are used. Context includes both the ground of the language to which a word belongs and the whole work in which it is used. Hence:

> A word is never isolated, even when it occurs by itself, for its determination is not derived from itself but its context. We need only to relate this contextual use to this original unity in order to discover the correct meaning in each case. (Schleiermacher, 1828/1990, p. 89)

The grammatical part of interpretation, according to Schleiermacher, depends on the idea of laws governing language that are discoverable. The quotation above reflects such a claim to objectivity in the idea of "correct meaning," even though elsewhere Schleiermacher was much more conscious of the limits to interpretation and argued that hermeneutics started from the prevalence of misunderstanding rather than an assumption that clear understanding is the usual state of affairs.

"There is a more rigorous practice of the art of interpretation that is based on the assumption that misunderstanding occurs as a matter of course, and so understanding must be willed and sought at every point" (Schleiermacher, 1828/1990, p. 82). Schleiermacher's insistence on the primacy of misunderstanding introduces an important theme into hermeneutics of the finitude, or necessarily limited nature of understanding. The inevitability of misunderstanding does not render understanding impossible or meaningless, only that it demands constant practice directed toward understanding better. In choosing topics for interpretive research, discussed in a later chapter, there is often a felt misfit between the taken-for-granted view of a belief or practice and the researcher's own experience. This discomfort, from which good questions often arise, is one manifestation of Schleiermacher's "misunderstanding."

Although he separated the grammatical and psychological for the purposes of explication and analysis, Schleiermacher saw the two kinds of interpretation as an interactive unity, stating "We must always hold the two sides of interpretation together" (1828/1990, p. 86). Dialectics is a recurrent principle in hermeneutic thought that lies behind the combination of interpretive approaches, as well as the importance of dialogue, and the concept of the hermeneutic circle. Dialectic reasoning goes back to formal argumentation in ancient Greek philosophy in order to arrive at the truth of a statement. The basic back-and-forth movement of dialectics is retained in later usage. From the early 19th century onwards, however, dialectics is heavily influenced by Hegel's philosophy. He made use of dialectics as a way of accounting for disparate and conflicting elements of human life in a philosophical system – bringing them together into mutually influential relationships. He also famously gave a dialectical account of change in history as the movement of Spirit taking concrete form in political institutions (Forbes, 1975). Merriam-Webster (2014) gives definitions of "the Hegelian process of change in which a concept or its realization passes over into and is preserved and fulfilled by its opposite" and, more generally, "the dialectical tension or opposition between two interacting forces or elements." The main point is the creative interaction from difference, and although dialectics is sometimes reduced to a mechanistic sequence of thesis-antithesis-synthesis, Forbes offered Hegel's description of the Reichenbach Falls, as a "spectacle of 'free play'" (p. xiv), as a fitting image of dialectical thinking.

Dialectical thinking occurs in various forms in Schleiermacher's work. He even placed it before hermeneutics in relation to dialogue: "Dialectics relies on hermeneutics and rhetoric because the development of all knowledge depends on both speaking and understanding" (1828/1990, p. 74). Grammatical and psychological modes of interpretation rely on each other since individual authors express themselves within the laws of language that makes their work comprehensible in the first instance. Within the psychological mode, Schleiermacher made a further distinction between "a divinatory and a comparative [method]. Since each method refers back to the other, the two should never be separated" (1828/1990, p. 96). Divinatory refers to the interpreter gaining a sense of the author as an individual and the comparative to seeing the author as a representative of a type. Altogether, dialectic for Schleiermacher was "the art of mutual understanding" (Grondin, 1994, p. 73) since the way through misunderstanding lies in sharing ideas with others in order to invite new points of view.

Any discussion of dialectics within hermeneutic philosophy has to include the hermeneutic circle, which is another recurrent concept in the history of hermeneutics from before Schleiermacher onwards and was later taken up by Heidegger and Gadamer. Friedrich Ast (1778–1841), an immediate forerunner of Schleiermacher, saw the hermeneutic circle as a mutual movement between part and whole. For Ast, the whole constituted the unified spirit (*Geist* in German) of a culture in which individual works existed. The spirit as a whole could only be understood by studying it through individual works, and the particular works only came into their full meaning as expressions of the whole (Palmer, 1969). Schleiermacher's contribution was to take the idea of movement between part and whole and to remove the dimension of Ast's grand scheme of unity of spirit. More humbly, in grammatical interpretation, the whole is the genre to which a particular work belongs, and on the psychological side, it is the total life of the author (Grondin, 1994).

Schleiermacher's hermeneutics was innovative in seeking to elucidate the process of understanding itself rather than beginning with texts to be interpreted. His work then focused on the importance of language as the medium of understanding, on dialogue as a way of extending understanding, and the hermeneutic circle as a metaphor for understanding works in relation to the context of their production.

Dilthey: Hermeneutics as Methodology

Later in the 19th century, two more themes became prominent in the development of hermeneutics. One was the question of historicism and the other the problem of method introduced by Wilhelm Dilthey (1833–1911). Both these currents remain significant for hermeneutics and have implications for research.

Historicism is the idea that phenomena have to be understood in relation to their own time. Human values or beliefs institutions are not static, and what is normative in one time and place might make no sense in another. It is not the job of a modern historian to pass moral judgment on the ancient Romans, for example, but to try to understand their world as a culture with its own horizons of social norms, ethics, religious beliefs, economic structures, and so on. For most people, this is now probably an unexceptional idea. It becomes problematic, however, when the logic of historicism is extended to our own time, rendering our own horizons of cultural meaning contingent and relative against the temporal movement of history. Jean Grondin framed the problem as questions: "Doesn't everything dissolve into present-day perspectives and temporal conditionedness?" and "How, if at all, is it possible to escape from the hermeneutic circle of our historicity?" (1994, p. 77).

One solution for thinkers in the 19th century was to look for a unifying principle of reason in history, so that particular events took on a meaning that transcended the context of their own era. In this way, history was seen as a story of human moral progress so that the distinctiveness of different times could be recognized but only in relation to a bigger picture of "humanity's steadily increasing consciousness and awareness of itself" (Grondin, 1994, p. 83). In the 20th century, after two world wars and the rise of totalitarian political systems, the sense of assurance about historical progress was severely thrown into question, and later thinkers such as Gadamer had to approach historicism in more circumspect ways. For now, however, the salient point is that understanding took on an historical dimension that moved beyond Schleiermacher's focus on the author and the text.

Historicism leads in turn to methodological concerns by raising the question of how to place history and, by extension, the other human sciences on a secure foundation of objective knowledge like the natural sciences. The rapid progress of science and technology in the latter half of the 19th century made the relation between the natural sciences and other disciplines a matter of concern for contemporary thinkers. Nietzsche characterized the problem with the image of a double-brain:

> ...a higher culture must give to man a double-brain, as it were two brain ventricles, one for the perceptions of science, the other for those of non-science: lying beside one another, not confused together, separable, capable of being shut off; this is a demand of health. (1882/1986, p. 119)

For Dilthey, the distinction between human and natural sciences lay in the inclusion of inner experience, of thoughts, emotions, and will in the subject matter of the former (Palmer, 1969). Another way of making the distinction was that the natural sciences were about *explaining* phenomena and the human sciences about *understanding*, establishing meanings of manifestations of human life and culture. The former was objective, standing outside phenomena, whereas the latter had to have both objective and subjective aspects.

Dilthey attempted to articulate a methodology of the human sciences around "a procedure based on the systematic relation between life, expression, and understanding" (Dilthey, quoted in Palmer, 1969, p. 107). Hence, it was Dilthey who introduced the expression "lived experience" (Dilthey, c.1900/1990, p. 149) to describe the formation of meaning across time by making connections between disparate events. "Life consists of parts, of lived experiences which are inwardly related to each other. Every particular experience refers to a self of which it is a part; it is structurally interrelated to other parts" (p. 151). There is another movement between parts and whole in this recursive relationship between moments of experience and the continuing self that ascribes meaning to them.

The other terms of Dilthey's system follow from this account of life as experience. "Expression" referred to outward manifestations of experience, not only as works of art but as all kinds of cultural forms including law, language, and institutions. In this sense, the human sciences could lay claim to an objective basis since they have these outward, concrete expressions of life as their objects of study. "Understanding," Dilthey's third term, went beyond the usual sense of cognitive sense-making to encompass a deeper apprehension of life, including the experience of another person (Palmer, 1969) through the medium of expressions.

Dilthey's attention to lived experience and the insight that forms of cultural expression could be a conduit to interrelated meanings are important stages in the development of hermeneutics. What limited his thought, however, was his purpose of trying to establish a methodological foundation for the human sciences. The claim to objectivity came unstuck with his emphasis on the inner aspects of consciousness and of understanding another's lived experience.

The Human Sciences: A Note

"Human sciences" is the English translation most commonly used in hermeneutic literature for the German word *Geisteswissenschaften*. Since human sciences is not a term in common usage in English, it is worth pausing to consider the complexities of the translation, and the applicability of the term to a practice discipline like nursing that historically has no academic standing at all.

Wissenschaft is the German word for science, but it "remains unquestionably broader, as it corresponds to the collective pursuit of knowledge kinds" (Babich, 2009, p. 106). Although science in English has a general meaning, derived from Latin *scientia* meaning knowledge (Barnhart, 1988, p. 968), it has increasingly come to refer primarily to the natural sciences and to scientific method. It is used predominantly in this sense, for example, in public debates in English speaking countries about atheism and religion. *Wissenschaft* to German speakers contains the common root verb *wissen*, to know, and "retains connotations of the 'ways' or conduits of knowing" (Babich, p. 106).

Wissenschaft is at least equivalent to science, if not exactly, but the first part of the compound noun, *Geist*, does not mean human and is normally translated as "spirit." Thanks to Hegel, for whom historical progress was the self-realization of *Geist*, it is a term that pervades German philosophy and confounds English readers. We are probably most familiar with the German word from *Zeitgeist*, which has entered the English lexicon as shorthand for "spirit of the times." *Geist* also has connotations of mind or consciousness so that for Hegel (1975), "Man is active within [spirit]; and whatever he does, the spirit is also active within him" (p. 44). Dilthey (1900/1990) adopted the term from Hegel, stating "how significant the objective mind [*Geist*] is for the possibility of knowledge in the human studies" (p. 155). The editor of the anthology from which this quotation is taken noted, "Dilthey employs Hegel's term *objektiver Geist* to denote the intersubjective products and creations of human culture as constituted by systems of law or economics, political and social institutions or natural languages" (Mueller-Vollmer, 1990, p. 164).

This comes closer to the idea of "human sciences," historically referring to disciplines such as theology, philology, history, and law that are concerned with human cultural phenomena and would overlap with the humanities and social sciences. Contemporary practice disciplines such as nursing, education, and social work, however, do not fit comfortably into these more traditional categories. Nursing entertains a chronic anxiety about its identity, as science, art, or hybrid. Even then, the terms are contested and the discipline invites disparate kinds of knowledge from more definitely scientific or humanities sources. For hermeneutics, ambiguity is not so much a problem of failed definition as the beginning of possibility for understanding. Resistance to categorization is an asset because the reality of being in the world "lies in its inescapable *existence*, deeper than all its specific properties. We are struck by the world, we care about it. We are implicated in it" (Harman, 2007, p. 43).

Husserl: Phenomenology and the Turn to the *Lebenswelt*

Edmund Husserl's (1859–1938) work provides a bridge between developments in hermeneutic philosophy in the 19th and 20th centuries. Although not a philosopher of hermeneutics as such, he is credited with developing the first coherent formulation of phenomenology with "conceptual tools unavailable to Dilthey or Nietzsche" (Carman, 2006; Palmer, 1969, p. 124). Like Dilthey, Husserl formulated a response to the increasingly assertive claims of the natural sciences to hold a monopoly on objective, trustworthy, and valuable access to knowledge about the world.

Husserl's rallying cry was "to the things themselves" (Husserl, 1900, 1901/2001, p. 168; Steeves, 2006) denoting a renewed attention in philosophy to the question of everyday human experience and how to understand it in a rigorous way. It represented Husserl's desire to return the ground of philosophy and inquiry to a direct acquaintance with phenomena, through painstaking attention, careful description, and a rigorous kind of analytic reflection known as *phenomenological reduction* or *epoche*. He asserted the possibility of knowing the world as it is, in which case phenomenological knowledge as he called it, would provide the foundation for other kinds of knowledge, including the scientific. Any experiment, for example, designed to produce new knowledge is predicated upon previous assumptions of knowing what things are, in order to be able to organize them into a systematic process.

The term phenomenology captures his focus on phenomena of human knowing, whether through sense perception, memory, or imagination. Husserl was thus interested in the role of human consciousness in all forms of knowing. Early critics of his work accused him of recycling philosophical idealism, but he was clear that he distinguished between knowing things-in-the-world and knowing products of the mind independent of immediate sensory input. Husserl responded to his critics in his preface to the 1931 English translation of his book *Ideas* (1931/2012), which was first published in German in 1913. "Our phenomenological idealism does not deny the positive existence of the real world and of Nature" (p. xlii) and "the real world indeed exists, but in respect of essence is relative to transcendental subjectivity, and in such a way that it can have its meaning as existing reality only as the intentional meaning-product of transcendental subjectivity" (p. xliii). For Husserl, it made no sense to choose between realism or idealism and his philosophy was dedicated to working out what he meant by "transcendental subjectivity," or what it is for human beings to know the world.

Intentionality

Intentionality is a basic theme of Husserl's phenomenology, "the unique peculiarity of experiences to be 'the consciousness *of* something'" (Husserl, 1931/2012, p. 171). Thus, it follows, depending on the nature of the "something," that "perceiving is the perceiving of something, maybe a thing; judging, the judging of a certain matter; valuation, the valuing of a value; wish, the wish for the content wished, and so on" (p. 171). Intentionality is what binds us, inescapably, to the world and constantly provides meaning. Note, this is not intentional in the conventional sense of making a conscious effort but rather is a meaning-making inherent in all our thoughts and perceptions. Once Husserl established the idea of intentionality to describe the way in which humans are primordially committed to a world of meaning (not necessarily to particular values or rationality – a nihilistic belief that life is meaningless or a state of psychotic mental chaos are still forms of "meaning" as kinds of human experience) he elaborated how it is that we can place knowledge of experience on to a philosophical – and according to Husserl, a scientific – basis.

The Natural Attitude and Phenomenological Method

Husserl distinguished the natural attitude, which is our normal everyday awareness, from the phenomenological attitude, which permits a systematic, deliberate analysis of phenomena. From the natural standpoint:

> I am aware of [a world], that means, first of all, I discover it immediately, intuitively. I experience it. Through sight, touch, hearing, etc., in the different ways of sensory perception, corporeal things somehow spatially distributed are *for me simply there*, in verbal or figurative sense "present," whether or not I pay them special attention by busying myself with them, considering, thinking, feeling, willing. (Husserl, 1931/2012, p. 51)

In order to study the world of phenomena, however, it is not enough simply to go on experiencing things without subjecting them to sustained attention, which requires the phenomenological method. Husserl's phenomenology required a process of reduction, of taking away everything extraneous, by which phenomena could become known in their essence. Rather than constructing and testing hypotheses, formulating cause and effect explanations, or building models and theories, as science is want to do, Husserl thought that, through a careful method of peeling back the layers of appearances, one could get to the true nature of things: stable invariant *essences*, manifested as permanent characteristics and/or structures. This assumption about the way the world is, and Husserl's life-long dream of establishing a singular, unified science, one that would account for all knowledge, locates him squarely in the spirit of Western thinking, a lineage easily traced from Plato through Descartes and Kant (Madison, 1977).

Essence

Eidos is a Greek word meaning essence that Husserl used to denote the essential qualities of an object, the distinguishable characteristics that make a thing recognizably itself and not something else. *"The essence (Eidos) is an object of a new type. Just as the datum of individual or empirical intuition is an individual object, so the datum of essential intuition is a pure essence"* [italics in original] (Husserl, 1931/2012, p. 12). This conception of essence is important to understand, in the first place to follow Husserl's idea of "eidetic reduction" and then to see some of the ways that his students, Heidegger and Gadamer, diverged from his phenomenology.

The essence of a thing (which can be an object of experience, perception, memory or even the imagination), following from the idea of intentionality, is bound up with human consciousness. Husserl gave the example of a tree, which could be reduced to its chemical elements, but that would not reveal the essence of the tree as such since, "the meaning – the meaning of this perception, something that belongs necessarily to its essence – cannot burn away; it has no chemical elements, no forces, no real properties" (Husserl, 1931/2012, p. 187). Although this sounds antithetical to the reductionism of the natural sciences at one level, Husserl was also trying to place phenomenology on a scientific footing. His insistence on the purity of essences required a method of knowing things as separate and stable, which he called the eidetic, or phenomenological, reduction.

Phenomenological Reduction and Bracketing

Reduction was the term Husserl used for the process of consciously setting aside extraneous factors to arrive at the essence of a thing, just as in the culinary sense of the word a cook reduces a sauce by boiling away superfluous liquid. The goal is "the absolutely faithful description of that which really lies before one in phenomenological purity, and in keeping at a distance all interpretations that transcend the given" (Husserl, 1931/2012, p. 188). To move from the "thesis" of the natural attitude, to a phenomenological atti-tude, "the thesis undergoes a modification – whilst remaining in itself what it is, *we set it as it were 'out of action,'* we *'disconnect it,' 'bracket it'* "[italics in original] (p. 57). Thus, presuppositions about experience are put out of play, including the findings of the natural sciences, which still belong to the natural attitude. Bracketing, therefore, implies both a rational agent who is confident in knowing the range and limits of his or her presuppositions, and that objects of whatever kind are sufficiently distinct to stand out once the natural attitude is stripped away.

The following example may help to give some idea of what Husserl was getting at with his phenomenological way of seeing applied to a tree:

> "In" the reduced perception (in the phenomenologically pure experience) we find, as belonging to its essence indissolubly, the perceived as such, and under such titles as "material thing," "plant," "tree," "blossoming," and so forth. The *inverted commas* are clearly significant; they express that change of signature, the corresponding radical modification of the meaning of the words. The *tree plain and simple*, the thing in na-ture, is as different as it can be from this perceived tree as such, which as perceptual meaning belongs to the perception, and that inseparably. [Italics in original] (Husserl, 1931/2012, p. 187)

One observation is that it is probably easier to illustrate phenomenological reduction using an example of a discrete object, like a tree, than an experience-in-the-world, which is more often the object of research.

The Lifeworld

The main principles of Husserl's phenomenology are laid out in his earlier work, but he introduced one further important concept as late as 1936, the "lifeworld" or *Lebenswelt* (Føllesdal, 2005, p. 424). The idea of the lifeworld was a further working out of the idea of the natural attitude, of the world of everyday things and experiences. The lifeworld conveys the sense of unthink-ing immersion in the world, in the way that we pass through a door without stopping to think about the door-ness of the door, its mechanism, its history, or its symbolism. Husserl wrote that, "The lifeworld…is always there, existing in advance for us, the 'ground' of all praxis, whether theoretical or pretheo-retical. The world is pregiven to us…" (cited in Føllesdal, 2005, p. 425). The idea of the lifeworld more clearly delivers a sense of the world as connected experience, of meanings combined into a flow of being and functioning in the world. Husserl also used the lifeworld concept to link back to science, by explaining that scientific knowledge too has to derive meaning from a prior givenness of a world in which knowledge becomes possible at all.

Madison (1988) referred to this contribution by Husserl as "the great archeological-hermeneutic discovery: the *Lebenswelt*" (p. 40)…

> The *lebenswelt* is nothing other than the immediate flow of un-reflective life, the ground out of which arises all scientific thematization and theorizing. It is the world as we actually live it (what Heidegger called "factical life"), a world which therefore precedes the Galilean and modern distinction between subjective and objective…It is the *prescientific* world of lived experience upon which all scientific constructs are based, and which they necessarily presuppose…The "objective" world of science is but an *interpretation* of the world of our immediate experience, the lifeworld, which transcends all objectivistic and subjectivistic categories. (p. 44)

The lifeworld provides hermeneutics with its phenomenological base, more oriented since Heidegger toward *being in the world*.

Phenomenology and Hermeneutics

Phenomenology brings to hermeneutics a philosophically robust way of try-ing to articulate everyday life and experience. In this, it is a product of its time, recognizing a need to find rigorous ways of understanding the human experience of living in the world, which the pure logic of positivism and even the great advances in the natural sciences of the 19th century simply could not address. In one sense, Husserl worked to substantiate Nietzsche's typically terse assertion that, "the great problems are to be encountered in the street" (1881/1982, p. 78). In the introduction to *Ideas*, Husserl wrote, "We shall start from the standpoint of everyday life, from the world as it confronts us…" (1931/2012, p. 3). Perhaps it is the second part of this sentence that betrays the underlying scientific outlook that still affected Husserl's work. The world confronts us, requiring methods of examination that will bring it to under-standing in the unambiguous light of human reason. Palmer (1969), placing Husserl into the context of hermeneutics, pointed out the very different atti-tudes toward science between him and his student, Heidegger, "which seemed to follow logically from the earlier training of the former in mathematics and the latter in theology" (p. 6).

Heidegger: The End of Foundationalism, Beginning of Hermeneutic Phenomenology, and "Unquiet" Relational Notion of Understanding

Martin Heidegger (1889–1976) was a "star" student and apprentice of Husserl, who took phenomenology in a radically different direction and went on to become one of the most influential philosophers of the 20th century, publishing his magnum opus of *Being and Time* in 1927. Heidegger's project was to bring the ontology of the subject into the "exp-erience-of something." Removing the brackets, Heidegger acknowledged that "we are in the matter and not simply enclosed in ourselves" (Gadamer, 1984, p. 59). For Heidegger, experience was already out in the world; experience is not a thing, but a movement in the world. As a result, understanding is deeply entrenched in the profound ontological makeup of *Dasein*: care, existence, temporality, and being (Heidegger, 1927/1996). Heidegger identified *Dasein*, or being in the world, as a thereness of being that is distinguished by the capacity for self-reflection; people are situated in, and constituted by, their worlds.

Gadamer (1984) took up from Heidegger the notion that interpretation is never an isolated human activity, but an experience: "we are always taking something *as* something" (p. 58). Heidegger (1927/1996) maintained that human life is not given to us as a phenomenon which requires our explication, but as a question, an address, as something which is revealing and concealing, coming and going, present absent, a thrownness, – and the work of hermeneutics is entering into the interpretation of these things.

A Departure From Husserl

For Husserl, "to the things themselves" meant to those things that *appear in consciousness*. Husserl accepted, as given, two important Cartesian principles that continue to undergird science today. The first of these is that the world is a world of substances, with stable characteristics or structures that can be mapped and explained with certainty, *given the proper method*. Even though the same things appear differently in the world, a problem first identified by the Greeks as the problem of "the one and the many," underneath these appearances are permanent, fixed properties or essences, and the job of science is to isolate and identify these elements and figure out their causes. The second principle that Husserl followed posits a world of separate, individual things, and this holds true for humans, most importantly, for minds and bodies. Descartes proposed, and Husserl assumed, a world of dualisms, the most fundamental of which for human beings were the severance of mind from world, and mind from body (for more on Descartes' legacy, see Jardine's 2012, *The Descartes Lecture*). Such a move created an inner space that was suspect (constantly changing, "contaminated" with body functions, feelings, and prejudices), and an outer world that was dependable (fixed, pure, value-free, and predictable). The creation of an objective world (a world "out there") and a subjective mind (the world "in here"), however, creates another problem: How is it possible for a separate mind to know anything, with any certainty, about a separate world, given a seemingly unbridgeable gap between them? How can we give any kind of dependable account for that which exists – the "real"? Husserl attempted to circumvent this difficulty by "transforming the very *being* of an object into its meaning for *consciousness*" (Madison, 1977, p. 248). The real for Husserl, was the real "in here," the real of things as they appeared in our minds. It is a foundational science of pure subjectivity that Husserl was after:

> The true being of an object can only be an *idea* in the Kantian sense, that is the idea of the totality of all its appearances. We can have an adequate intuition of an idea, and so if the "real" object is to have meaning, this can only be as an idea. (Madison, 1977, p. 249)

On the other hand, Heidegger did not believe that we can establish direct primitive contact with things "underneath" interpretation, but rather was devoted to a disciplined form of paying attention and to using language carefully to describe the rich, nuanced, layered, and relational character of life as it is lived. This remains a central commitment of hermeneutic work today. Husserl's concept of the "lifeworld" provided Heidegger a hermeneutics with a phenomenological base. Unlike Husserl and Hegel's concern about that which appears in consciousness, Heidegger regarded the lifeworld with a turn toward *being in the world*. His work was committed to staying as close as possible to examining practical life and ascribing to *phronesis*, practical wisdom, as the form of knowledge arising from experience that undergirds hermeneutic-phenomenology.

Heidegger and Metaphysics

Heidegger challenged and deconstructed metaphysics and transcendental knowing, turning metaphysical philosophy on its head. He attempted to reclaim the difficulty that Husserl ignored and to challenge the Cartesian duality that infused much of Husserl's work (Gadamer, 1984). In his working out of the lifeworld in *Being and Time*, he attempted to avoid the fatal metaphysical mistake that he thought Husserl had fallen prey to: that there is a world "out there," and a mind "in here," the split that creates both subjectivity and objectivity as two separate things.

Heidegger thought this way of thinking misunderstood the way the world is, and the way we are in the world. Our relationship with the world, what Heidegger called "our being in the world," comes before, and is underneath both of these entities. In this regard, the human being is "subject," and the world of "things" and "beings" which appear to us are "objects." In Heidegger's view, it is too late to be either purely objective or subjective; we are in the world, fully implicated in an already interpreted way of life, operating in a language full of sedimented (i.e., historical) meanings, and oriented by our relationships toward the world in a particular way. In other words, *subjectivity and objectivity are interpretations*, or the way we can regard ourselves and the world, and our relationship to it, or as Heidegger would say *in* it, but they are secondary to, or derivative of "being there"(*Dasein*). It is our absorption in the world, our being there that provides the fundamental condition for human understanding, for our "sense of being" to occur. Wrathall (2013) characterized Heidegger's use of the term "sense" this way:

> We grasp the sense of something when we know our way around it, we can anticipate what kinds of things can happen with respect to it, we recognize when things belong or are out of place, and so on…Sense is the background way of organizing and fitting things together, which guides and shapes all our anticipations of and interactions with anything we encounter. (p. 2)

It is this sense of things that science presupposes or takes for granted, something Heidegger regarded as both mistaken and dangerous. It is also this sense of things that requires investigation in hermeneutic work, a questioning of the things we take for granted, of our pre-understanding, or *prejudices*, to use Gadamer's term. In this way, the quest for understanding in hermeneutics is also a quest for *self-understanding*. By self-understanding, Heidegger (and Gadamer) did not mean grasping some private, inner self, but rather knowing one's way around in the world, or in a particular subject matter. It involves seeing what is possible in a situation *for me*, what concrete possibilities are available for action, given who I am, given where I am, and given what I am encountering in the particular situation.

In his deconstruction, Heidegger radicalized the Romantic hermeneutics passed on by Schleiermacher and Dilthey, while Kierkegaard, Nietzsche, and Meister Eckhart became guiding influences on him (Caputo, 1987). In *Being and Time*, Heidegger took up the topic of metaphysics, described by Madison (1988) as the art of asking questions, reflecting on difficult notions, and "conferring some semblance of intelligibility on the chaotic reality of our lived experience...by enabling us to have the feeling that we understand the Why, What, and Wherefore of things" (p. 125). Heidegger departed from Kant's view of metaphysics as an apriori sense or knowledge of something beyond experience, to a view of it as an attempt to secure an ambiguous and fragile place in the world within a framework (Grondin, 1995). As Caputo (1987) offered, hermeneutics should not try to make things look easy, but should recapture the difficulty of things present before metaphysics tries to offer a way out of the flux or difficulty. Caputo (1987) wrote of Heidegger: "He thus recommitted phenomenology to the difficulty of life, rooted it in an ontology of care, and so fashioned what has come to be known as 'hermeneutics' in the contemporary, post-Diltheyian sense" (p. 59).

> Metaphysics always makes a show of beginning with questions, but no sooner do things begin to waver a bit and look uncertain than the question is foreclosed... But Heidegger wanted to try something new, something revolutionary...to raise the question of Being as presence and let it hang there and to resist the temptation to cut it down when it starts to look a little blue. (Caputo, 1987, p. 2)

Heidegger, Understanding, and Truth

It should be noted that to further clarify what he meant by understanding, funded by our sense of things, Heidegger distinguished between two kinds of truth. This distinction is important, for it is Heidegger's second kind of truth, truth as disclosure or unconcealment (aletheia) that we are after in hermeneutic work (Davey, 2006). The traditional sense of truth involves the discovery of some fact about the world, and Heidegger did not deny that this kind of truth exists or is not important in our lives (Wrathall, 2011). However without a deep sense of truth, the facts are meaningless.

Hoy (2006) arrived at this with this explication of what Heidegger meant by truth as disclosure:

> The contrasting term (to factual truth) "disclosedness" (*Erschlossenheit*) suggests that the total context is opened up through understanding. Understanding thus does not consist only of making assertions about the world, but also of grasping the entire mode of being-in-the-world. Understanding grasps the world as such, without which the discovery of particular features of the world would not be possible...the isolated, atomistic discovery of one fact after another would not generate an understanding of the world that was significant and intelligible, but only of a disconnected aggregate. An interpretation is precisely not a heap of facts, but an account of how these facts are *possible*. (p. 184)

The world does not exist, as Heidegger pointed out, as a thing or a set of things, but as an event, an event we must participate in to understand through language (Heidegger, 1927/1967; Wrathall, 2013). This is the fundamental difference between Husserl and Heidegger (Wrathall, 2013): this move from the world as a set of things with fixed properties or essences, to the world as a set of interrelated and layered events that happen to us, that in turn, are revealed to us through our practical involvement. It represents Heidegger's radicalization of phenomenology, and the end of foundational notions of being and understanding, as well as Husserlian idealism (Ricoeur, 1981). No longer were things "given in consciousness," as Husserl had posited, but rather existed as *beings in motion*, in a world in motion, beings constantly being made, unmade and remade, in a world undergoing the same kind of ceaseless constitution and reconstitution. The character of our being in the world also gave hermeneutic understanding its "unquiet" nature (Davey, 2006), or as Gadamer would say "doomed" understanding to be constantly caught up in the play of question and answer.

Heidegger set thinking in motion, so to speak, and tied it inseparably to action in the world. At the same time, he tore it loose from Cartesian science and neo-Kantian constructivism:

> ...a concept is not a schema, but rather a possibility of being, of how matters look in the moment, i.e., is constitutive of the moment--a meaning drawn out of something-points to a for-having, i.e., transports us into a fundamental experience-points to a foreconception, i.e., calls for a how of addressing and interrogating. (Heidegger, 1923/1999, p. 12)

Heidegger also placed the ground of hermeneutic inquiry "inside" phenomena themselves, that is, there were no two separate entities, "things to be investigated" and "methods to be applied," but living phenomena that addressed us, revealing in their address, how to inquire, and the path to understanding that opened in their appearance.

> What is revealed in it (the phenomenon) is how the *anticipatory leap forward and running in advance* should be undertaken and can only be undertaken. The anticipatory leap forward: not positing an end, but reckoning with being on the way, giving it free play, holding fast to *being possible*. (Heidegger,1923/1999, p. 12)

To repeat a little differently, because it is tantamount to conducting hermeneutic research:

> ...*phenomenon* means the constant preparation of *the path to be travelled*. This thematic category has the function of a critical, cautionary guidance of seeing...(Heidegger, 1923/1999, p. 60)

Therefore, when we say that hermeneutics is committed to the phenomenon, and not a pre-determined method, we do not mean that anything goes, or as Heidegger (1923/1999) would say, it is not something simply given in advance, nor is it something arbitrary. We are addressed by possibilities for inquiry in the appearance of the phenomenon itself. Again, these exist as possible beginnings, not as givens, as Husserl believed, and not as full-blown procedures, as science believes. Both must be worked out *in practice*, that is, in the practice of understanding, in the ceaseless revealing and concealing of truth, and in the dialectic of question and answer. What is required in the beginning on our part is what Heidegger (1923/1999) called a "radical wakefulness," a holding out for possibility, and a "whiling" or living with a phenomenon in a state of "questionableness" (Heidegger 1923/1999, p. 62).

Heidegger and Hermeneutics, and His Critics

Heidegger had an early appearance of the word "hermeneutic" in his work that appeared in 1919, with his characterization of Husserl's notion of intuition as hermeneutic (Caputo, 1987). *Being and Time*, however, has been critiqued as offering meager remarks on hermeneutics, which makes it "difficult to understand what Heidegger meant, exactly, by hermeneutics...indeed, in *Being and Time*, a mere half-page at the end of Heidegger's otherwise elaborate Section Seven on phenomenology is devoted to situating and systematically defining hermeneutics" (Grondin, 1994, p. 7). Critiquing Husserl's existential phenomenology and, in his later work, even critiquing his own hermeneutics, Heidegger himself dropped the term "hermeneutic phenomenology" and even "hermeneutics" from his vocabulary (Caputo, 1987; Grondin. 1995). Caputo (1987) wrote:

> The later Heidegger became his own most important critic. He submitted...to a searching critique with the result that he no longer described his work as hermeneutic at all...meanwhile, Gadamer (with whom we today most readily associate the word 'hermeneutics')...took over notions which had been brought under fire by the late Heidegger – preunderstanding, the hermeneutic circle...the theory of horizons. (p. 95)

Although Derrida supported the radicalization of hermeneutics, his critique of Heidegger was focused on the way Heidegger questioned metaphysics and the ontological question of Being. This "onto-hermeneutic" project was accused by Derrida (1978) as slipping back into the very metaphysics it was trying to undo. Although Heidegger challenged metaphysics and shifted the focus from meaning in a transcendental sense to the ontological question of "Being," one might think, in his critique of Husserlian transcendental idealism, that he simply shifted the argument and did not abandon metaphysics. Although Heidegger brought back ontology, his work is at risk for being seen as onto-centric (Caputo, 1987). Heidegger was also critiqued by Habermas (1990), who believed that Heidegger's later work exemplified a shift to a philosophy that was void of argumentative rigor and personal responsibility as an effort to justify his involvement with the Nazis. This critique has been disputed by others (Grondin, 1995), but the question of Heidegger's Nazi involvement remains a topic of considerable debate and speculation.

Summary

In this chapter, we have traced the development of hermeneutics as a distinct strand in philosophy, which evolved partly in response to the growth in the power of science during the 19th and 20th centuries. The lineage of thinkers from Schleiermacher to Heidegger brings us to the threshold of Hans-Georg Gadamer's philosophical hermeneutics, which we discuss in greater detail in the following chapter.

References

Babich, B. E. (2009). Nietzsche's "gay" science. In K. Ansell-Pearson (Ed.), *A companion to Nietzsche* (pp. 97–114). Chichester, UK: Wiley-Blackwell.

Barnhart, R. (Ed.). (2006). *Chambers dictionary of etymology.* New York, NY: Chambers

Caputo, J. D. (1987). *Radical hermeneutics: Repetition, deconstruction and the hermeneutic project.* Bloomington, IN: Indiana University Press.

Carman, T. (2006). The principle of phenomenology. In C. Guignon (Ed.), *The Cambridge companion to Heidegger* (pp. 97–119). Cambridge, MA: Cambridge University Press.

Davey, N. (2006). *Unquiet understanding.* New York, NY: SUNY Press.

Derrida, J. (1978). *Spurs: Nietzsche's styles* (B. Harlow, Trans.). Chicago, IL: University of Chicago.

Dilthey, W. (1900/1990). The hermeneutics of the human sciences. In K. Mueller-Vollmer (Ed.). *The hermeneutics reader* (pp. 148–164). New York, NY: Continuum.

Føllesdal, D. (2005). Husserl, Edmund. In E. Craig (Ed.), *The shorter Routledge encyclopedia of philosophy* (pp. 415–427). Abingdon, UK: Routledge.

Forbes, D. (1975). Introduction. In G. W. F. Hegel, *Lectures on the philosophy of world history: Introduction* (pp. vii–xxxv). Cambridge, UK: Cambridge University Press.

Gadamer, H-G. (1984). The hermeneutics of suspicion. In G. Shapiro & A. Sica (Eds.), *Hermeneutics: Questions and prospects* (pp. 177–193). Cambridge, MA: MIT Press.

Gadamer, H-G. (1960/2004). Truth and method (J. Weinsheimer & D.G. Marshall, Trans.). London, UK: Continuum.

Gadamer, H-G. (2007). *The Gadamer reader: A bouquet of later writings.* Evanston, IL: Northwestern University Press.

Grondin, J. (1994). *Introduction to philosophical hermeneutics.* New Haven, CT: Yale University Press.

Grondin, J. (1995). *Sources of hermeneutics.* Albany, NY: SUNY Press.

Habermas, J. (1990). *The philosophical discourse of modernity* (F. G. Lawrence, Trans.). New Haven, CT: Yale University Press.

Harmon, G. (2007). *Heidegger explained: From phenomenon to thing.* Chicago, IL: Open Court Press.

Hegel, G. W. F. (1975). *Lectures on the philosophy of world history: Introduction.* (H. B. Nisbet, Trans.). Cambridge, UK: Cambridge University Press.

Heidegger, M. (1927/1996). *Being and time* (J. Stambaugh, Trans.). Albany, NY: SUNY Press.

Heidegger, M. (1923/1999). *Ontology – The hermeneutics of facticity.* Bloomington: University of Indiana Press.

Hoy, D. (2006). Heidegger and the hermeneutic turn. In C. Guignon (Ed.), *The Cambridge companion to Heidegger* (pp. 177–201). Cambridge, MA: Cambridge University Press.

Husserl, E. (1901/2001). *Logical investigations* (Vol. 2) (D. Moran, Ed., 2nd ed.). London, UK: Routledge. Original work published in 1900/1901.

Husserl, E. (1931/2012). *Ideas: General introduction to a pure phenomenology.* (W. R. Boyce-Gibson, Trans.). London, UK: Routledge. Original work published in 1931.

Jardine, D. W. (2012). The Descartes lecture. *Journal of Applied Hermeneutics*, Article 8. http://hdl.handle.net/10515/sy5pr7n88

Madison, G. B. (1977). Phenomenology and existentialism: Husserl and the end of idealism. In F. Elliston & P. McCormick (Eds.), *Husserl: Expositions and appraisals* (pp. 247–268). Notre Dame, IN: Notre Dame University Press.

Madison, G. B. (1988). The hermeneutics of postmodernity: Figures and themes. Bloomington IN: Indiana University Press.

Merriam-Webster. (2014). Dialectic. Retrieved from http://www.merriam-webster.com/dictionary/dialectic

Midgley, M. (2001). *Science and poetry*. New York, NY: Routledge.

Mueller-Vollmer, K. (Ed.). (1990). *The hermeneutics reader*. New York, NY: Continuum.

Nietzsche, F. (1881/1982). *Daybreak: Thoughts on the prejudices of morality*. (R. J. Hollingdale, Trans.). Cambridge, UK: Cambridge University Press.

Nietzsche, F. (1882/1986). *Human, all too human: A book for free spirits* (R. J. Hollingdale, Trans.). Cambridge, UK: Cambridge University Press.

Palmer, R. E. (1969). *Hermeneutics*. Evanston, IL: Northwestern University Press.

Ricoeur, P. (1981). *Hermeneutics and the human sciences: Essays on language, action and interpretation*. New York, NY: Cambridge University Press.

Schleiermacher, F. D. E. (1828/1990). Foundations: General theory and art of interpretation. In K. Mueller-Vollmer (Ed.), *The hermeneutics reader* (pp. 72–97). New York: Continuum.

Steeves, H. P. (2006). *The things themselves: Phenomenology and the return to the everyday*. Albany, NY: SUNY Press.

van Manen, M. (1997). *Researching lived experience: Human science for an action sensitive pedagogy*. London, ON, Canada: The Althouse Press.

Wrathall, M. A.(2013). *The Cambridge companion to Heidegger's Being and Time*. Cambridge, MA: Cambridge University Press.

· 3 ·

GADAMER'S PHILOSOPHICAL HERMENEUTICS

Hans-Georg Gadamer (1900–2002) was one of the leading hermeneutic phi-losophers of the 20th century, who took up linguistic and ontological themes from Heidegger to work out a thoroughgoing philosophy of how it is that human beings come to understanding. He drew on earlier developments in hermeneutics and on Heidegger's ideas about how human being-in-the-world is itself interpretive to develop a complex philosophical hermeneutics. One of Gadamer's distinctive contributions was his emphasis on dialogue as means of addressing difference. "Stylistically and substantively, the difference between their two modes of thought is the difference between a meditative thinker (Heidegger) and a dialogical one (Gadamer)" (Dostal, 2002, p. 247). Gadam-er's hermeneutics not only incorporates an account of changing understand-ing but also leads us to expect it, which partly explains how it is that his philosophy has been so readily adapted to research in practice disciplines.

Gadamer was born in 1900, the year Nietzsche died and the year Freud first published the *Interpretation of Dreams*. He was born into Imperial Ger-many, saw its collapse in 1918, then the Weimar Republic, the Third Re-ich, communist East Germany, democratic West Germany, and in the last twenty years of his life, German re-unification. He experienced the extraor-dinary technological advances of the 20th century, for example in transport, communications, and medicine, and among the effects of which have to be counted Hiroshima and Treblinka. His work can be seen against this background as a deeply humane project to articulate the very possibility of understanding in the face of ideological and technological threats to individual life and expression in shared social spaces.

Our intent in this chapter is to introduce a number of significant concepts in Gadamer's work that have a bearing on all that follows in later chapters about the conduct of research. By examining a series of concepts in the light of our particular application, we have lost the architecture of his major work, *Truth and Method*. We hope that what we have sacrificed in structural cohesion we have gained in clarity and focus on the purpose of this book. What follow is – it hardly needs saying in this context – our interpretation. There is, of course, no substitute for reading Gadamer's own work, which has been extensively translated into English and first we offer a brief guide to some of the available works.

Guide to Gadamer's Work

Gadamer's major work is *Truth and Method*, which first appeared in German in 1960 when he was 60 years old. He formally retired from the University of Heidelberg in 1968, but lived until 2002 and continued to publish, teach, and attend conferences up until the last couple of years of his long life (Grondin, 2003b). Consequently, he had many years to reflect on his account of hermeneutics, respond to critics, refine his ideas, and communicate them to numerous audiences.

Truth and Method is a long, dense philosophical work but is by no means as difficult to penetrate as Heidegger's *Being and Time*. It is divided into three parts, pursuing the theme of coming to a truth about something in understanding. Part one is concerned with truth "as it emerges in the experience of art" (Gadamer, 1960/2004, p. 1) since art is a locus of social and historical meaning, even though accessed subjectively. Part two takes up truth in the human sciences, including Gadamer's account of his predecessors including Schleiermacher, Dilthey, Husserl, and Heidegger. The third section draws on Heidegger's language ontology to concentrate on language as "the medium of hermeneutic experience" (Gadamer, 1960/2004, p. 384).

Other works translated into English consist mostly of collections of papers and lectures that were written after the appearance of *Truth and Method*.

Gadamer stuck closely to his central project of hermeneutics, so the benefit to the reader of these later works is that they often focus on particular aspects or applications of the ideas in *Truth and Method* (see, for example, Gadamer, 1977, 1981, 1996, 2007). One volume of note to researchers in health-related fields is *The Enigma of Health* (1996), which collects writings about the problems of negotiating technology and humanist concerns in health care. The most recently published major collection is *The Gadamer Reader* (2007), which contains many well-translated pieces organized clearly around themes including language, aesthetics, and hermeneutics as practical philosophy. A good introduction to Gadamer's philosophy is the short book *Gadamer in Conversation* (2001). It is, as it says in the title, a collection of transcribed conversations in which Gadamer responds to questions about his work, often explaining it with refreshing directness.

We note, as well, that although nothing should replace reading Gadamer's original work, there is a decided advantage to reading, too, the work of others who have studied, and in some ways extended, Gadamer's philosophy. In this regard, we refer to the work of Nicholas Davey (2006, 2013), Jean Grondin (1994, 1995, 2003a, 2003b), Georgia Warnke (2002), Richard Palmer (1969), James Risser (1997), Rod Coltman (1998), or Charles Taylor (2002) to name a few.

Concepts of Gadamer's Hermeneutics

We begin this section with three fundamental aspects of Gadamer's philosophy, his assertion of the universality of hermeneutics, and then the intrinsically historical and linguistic aspects of understanding. The third of these includes brief discussions of conversation and questions, two kinds of language that have special bearing on research interviews. The subsequent sections introduce concepts by which Gadamer explained the working out of understanding in human life, among the exigencies of historical and linguistic being.

Universality and Finitude

Gadamer made a bold claim for hermeneutics as universal and also stressed the finitude, or incompleteness of understanding. Clarifying these two terms serves to introduce Gadamer's distinctive hermeneutic philosophy and to position it in relation to the contemporary landscape of research in practice disciplines.

Universality is the focus of the final section of *Truth and Method*, and it refers to the point that understanding happens in language and that this "points to a universal ontological structure" (Gadamer, 1960/2004, p. 470). To live in a world of meaning in the first place is to live in a world that is understood and interpreted through language. For Gadamer, this does not mean that things do not exist until they are put into words but that "[t]he speculative mode of being of language has a universal ontological significance" (p. 470). It is not the verbalization of this or that object of experience that points to universality, but the basic intelligibility of the world for human beings. Understood in this way, universality clearly does not imply special knowledge or lay claim to any particular truth about the world. In fact, the opposite is true, since the interpretability of the world implies that, "the knowledge of experience will be foreign to all dogmatism" (Grondin, 2003a, p. 118).

Understanding-in-language presents a horizon of infinite possibility – not as a system of signs that can be endlessly reorganized but as "an act that is linguistically creative and world-experiencing" (Gadamer, 2007, p. 87). Precisely because language as such is endlessly proliferative, any given word, statement, text, or interpretation is finite within the world of meaning. Finitude provides one of the compositional principles of hermeneutic work. As a researcher, one has to start somewhere and one has to finish somewhere, while the life of the topic – already present before the researcher arrived – continues on beyond each interpretation.

In *Truth and Method* and the 1965 lecture, *The Universality of the Hermeneutical Problem* (in Gadamer, 1977 & 2007), Gadamer addressed what he meant by universality in relation to science and technology. He drew a distinction between the internal logic of science, its adherence to method and striving for objectivity, and the historical fact that science too exists within "the great horizon of the past, out of which our culture and our present live, influenc[ing] us in everything we want, hope for, or fear in our future" (Gadamer, 2007, p. 82). Whilst science and technology will continue to produce new knowledge and have powerful effects on our lives, this is not the same as concluding that scientific method must therefore be the sole recourse to answer questions arising from human life. Rather, the very power of science has a distorting effect because the onrush of scientific progress leaves its own presuppositions "half in the dark" (p. 83). Using the example of statistics, Gadamer observed that, "what is established by statistics seems to be a language of facts, but which questions these facts answer and which facts would begin to speak if other questions are asked are hermeneutical questions" (p. 84). Scientific research, properly conducted, may be objective but the questions it addresses are "always already" implicated in networks of historical and value-laden meaning. Jean Grondin glossed this aspect of Gadamer's thought:

> In stressing the universality of the hermeneutic aspect, Gadamer's fundamental idea is to mark the limits of objectivizing thought, which seeks to gain a hold on the being, for the purpose of domination. So that there is no mistake, this objectification is indispensible in science. But science has acquired an authority and a monopoly so uncontested in our civilization that we have come to think that all knowledge, all relationship to being, resorts to objectification. (Grondin, 2003a, p. 149)

Unlike some postmodern critiques, Gadamerian hermeneutics is not about undermining scientific knowledge in itself, nor relativizing it, but establishing a context of human understanding in which science occupies a significant space, but not the whole space. Prior to – and present with – the method-governed realm of science is the *Lebenswelt*, the human home of being, meaning, and language. The argument from universality thus provides an answer to the questions: why hermeneutic research, and why in practice disciplines that are often heavily dependent on science and technology, yet (so far) continue to be conducted and sustained within networks of human relationships? These relationships, in the hermeneutic reading, "draw for their intelligibility on our ordinary understanding of what it is to be a human agent, live in society, have moral convictions, aspire to happiness, and so forth" (Taylor, 2002, p. 131). Taylor made the point that there is an intellectual divide between those who do find important questions that can only be answered "at this level of cultural difference" (p. 129) and those who believe in the goal – if they think they have not already got there – of securing an account of what it is to be human at a basic, pre-cultural level. Against this dichotomy, hermeneutic researchers often find themselves having to articulate firmly, if not defend, the basis for their work.

History – "Historically Effected Consciousness"

Understanding has a temporal dimension, which is central to Gadamer's hermeneutics. If interpretation can only ever enter into a conversation that is already going on – there has to be something already there to interpret – then good interpretation attends to the history of the topic. Not only that, but we are in the flux of history, under the multifarious influences of our time and place. We can conscientiously do our best to clarify our understanding from within the flux, but what we cannot do is step out of history into a "view from nowhere." Hermeneutics consequently demands a respect for historical awareness, which is again in contrast to the scientific and technological out-look of linear progress whereby old hypotheses can be rendered obsolete, and next year's model is always promised to be better than this year's.

Gadamer's (1960/2004) term for such historical awareness is "historically effected consciousness," which is "primarily consciousness of the hermeneu-tical *situation*" (p. 301, italics in original). Being within our own historical horizon sets another condition of finitude:

> The illumination of this situation – reflection on effective history – can never be completely achieved; yet the fact that it cannot be completed is not due to a defi-ciency in reflection but to the essence of the historical being that we are. (p. 301)

We can never fully catch ourselves as the historically-effected beings that we are because to do so would require a separate point of view. Understanding again is partial in relation to the field of possibility, and also partial because things change in time. Not only do events keep happening, but we (both in the personal sense and as members of larger, cultural units) are also moving and changing so that our position in relation to events is forever becoming, rather than static.

Related to his idea of historically effected consciousness, Gadamer placed great emphasis on tradition – a position that has left him with a lingering, if undeserved, reputation as a conservative thinker. His point was not that tradition ought to be venerated simply because it is tradition, but that we are fooling ourselves if we think we can simply discard tradition and start from a blank slate. It is only when we achieve some awareness of the traditions of which we are already a part that we can begin to evaluate them, and think clearly and critically about where to go next.

> Tradition as conceived by philosophical hermeneutics is not just a stock of inert ideas or values but a manner or style of becoming critically engaged with (and thus continuing if not extending) the influence of a set of questions or subject matters. (Davey, 2006, p. 53)

Approaching a topic of research historically does not therefore mean writing a history of it (though it could), but of establishing a context for the terms of understanding by which the researcher, and readers, can enter into a fresh understanding. McCaffrey, for example, studied therapeutic relationships in mental health nursing. This is by no means a new topic, going back at least to Hildegaard Peplau's work in the 1950s. The persistence of the topic in the literature, with similar themes of advocacy and resistance among nurses, suggested an important interpretive avenue when finding nurses in the research interviews talking about working alongside colleagues with dramatically different approaches to care. Keeping in mind the historical dimension, however, acted as a caution against jumping to any ready conclusions about "fixing the problem" and helped to reframe questioning about what perpetuated an apparent division about therapeutic relationships. For example, there is a thread in the literature of exhortation, of advocating that nurses in acute care should work in a more consciously therapeutic way. Clearly however, the persistence of the theme itself reveals that there have been, and continue to be other forces at work that inhibit or resist the practice of therapeutic relationship. Reading the literature in the light of this historical understanding led to questions about how competing forces play out in both nurses' attitudes and social environments.

Language and Linguistic Being

Language is fundamental to Gadamerian hermeneutics, as discussed above, because it has the universal significance of being the air that understanding breathes. Language, in Grondin's (2003a) phrase, has an "uncanny nearness" (p. 123). Its nearness is its universality and it is uncanny because it remains unstable and carries within it reminders of its limits, of insecurity and possibilities of meaning breaking down. (Uncanny = *unheimlich* in German, a Heideggerian word with the root *Heim*, which means "home" – language has the naturalness of being at home and yet is filled with possibilities of uneasiness and interruption. Think how many horror films revolve around the home that turns out to be full of uncanny events that turn the security of home upside down). There is an important distinction between the projection into the possibility of understanding and the finitude of actual expression and understanding:

> knowledge lives in everybody who speaks when he looks for the *mot juste* – to know the word which can reach the other – but it always knows at the same time that it has not completely found it. The wanting-to-say, the intention, always goes above or slantwise to, what can be truly encircled by a language or in words that go to rejoin the other. (Gadamer, cited in Grondin, 2003a, p. 129)

Language impels toward understanding in the face of its limits, even because of its limits that always leave understanding incomplete. Gadamer recognized that there are parts of human experience that are not immediately linguistic, including sensory experiences such as viewing an artwork or listening to music. He argued, however, against the Kantian view of aesthetic experience as a privileged and separate form of experience. The impact of a painting is primarily visual, of course, and yet it only makes sense as an experience in relation to the dense fabric of meaning that the viewer brings to the experience. One reason why certain artworks persist and take on the mantle of a masterpiece is that they forever run ahead of definition and interpretation – but not for any lack of trying. If we invoke, as an example, the Mona Lisa (by its name, note), readers can instantly bring to mind an impression of the painting, but not without some association of Leonardo da Vinci, or the Renaissance, or perhaps the Louvre, or an opinion of the work. By introducing aesthetics at the start of *Truth and Method*, Gadamer established the idea of interpretation as a mode of being that animates the human world, linguistically and ceaselessly.

Movement is a vital characteristic of language for Gadamer, which leads to a caution against too great an insistence upon conceptual or terminological fixity. Even in philosophy:

> The words that carry its concepts…are not firm markers and signals through which something can be univocally designated, as in the systems of symbols in mathematics and logic and their applications…They originate in the communicative movement of human interpretation of the world, a movement that takes place in language. (Gadamer, 2007, p. 66)

Similarly, technical terms with well-defined applications serve a narrow purpose, but "in the highly artificial form of terminology we encounter only the ossified crust of the living stream of thinking and speaking" (p. 67). The tension between these two approaches to language surfaces in presenting hermeneutics to audiences who are used to, perhaps unquestioningly, expecting language to behave like a mechanical symbolic system. Usually it is incumbent upon the hermeneutic researcher to choose his or her words carefully, explaining what is, after all, methodical, rational, and rigorous about this approach.

Conversation

Perhaps the most distinctive of Gadamer's ideas about language, and the most obviously relevant to research, is the central place he gives to conversation:

"All living together in community is living together in language, and language exists only in conversation" (Gadamer, 2001, p. 56). Conversation is a natural, social form of the open dialectic that lets new understanding appear as each one speaks – and more importantly, listens – to the other. Setting out the structural potential of conversation in this way obviously does not mean to say that all conversations are mutual and productive. Gadamer was laying out the conditions for understanding, not describing a general phenomenon that applies to every actual conversation. He specified that in "every true conversation…each person opens himself up to the other [and] truly accepts his point of view as valid" (Gadamer, 1960/2004, p. 387).

He differentiated genuine mutuality from situations such as a therapeutic interview in which the participants' roles and the pre-given purpose of the exchange prevent the possibility of "genuine" (Gadamer, 1960/2004, p. 385) conversation. This has implications for research interviews in which the researcher is in the position of asking questions of the participant in the name of a previously established topic and goal. Since Gadamer never wrote about hermeneutics with this kind of application in mind, here is a point where we offer our own interpretation. One of the characteristics of genuine conversation is that both participants find themselves subordinated to the flow of the conversation itself, so that it is the subject matter that leads. We discuss this in more detail in Chapter Six, but wish to state here that, in spite of the researcher's intent and guidance, in successful interviews, there is a lively interchange in which the researcher becomes both attentive listener to the other as well as self-conscious questioner. The structure of understanding through conversation is discernible even though the ideal conditions of the genuine conversation are not met. In the text of a 1989 speech to psychiatrists, Gadamer (1996) wrote of "the capacity to attend to another human being" (pp. 166–167), which suggests he was not dogmatic about his own distinction when faced with a concrete form of practice and certainly had no wish to bar particular spheres of activity from interpretive life.

There is something attractive and approachable in the way Gadamer discussed conversation as the everyday occurrence of two people talking. Behind the straightforward image, however, stands his linguistic ontology and historically effected consciousness. Participants in a conversation are not two separate rational agents starting every conversation as if from nothing, but beings who are speaking out of traditions that precede them, using words that are already saturated in cultural meanings. Conversation is "a life process in which a community of life is lived out" (Gadamer, 1960/2004, p. 443). As such, a research interview is not just a question of extracting information from a participant, but a joining with the participant in an exploration of a community, or culture of which they are a part and have expertise to share.

Questions

Interviews or conversations are kept going by asking questions. We go into more detail about asking good questions in research interviews in Chapter Six. Our concern here is with how Gadamer considered questioning as one of the impulses of dialogue and thus of understanding. He noted that a question, when not a rhetorical or trick question, is based on a negative, not knowing. As such, a question is another mark of finitude. Questions bear this mark even though they may not have any hermeneutical intent behind them. They may, for example, be part of everyday conversation, with a superficial desire for knowledge (how are you?), or surrounded by a distinct power imbalance (interrogation). Hermeneutical questioning is informed by a humility toward one's own not knowing, a genuine curiosity toward what the other might have to say, and the goal of shared understanding – not simply taking information for one's own ends. Asking questions of a topic in this way renders the topic questionable: "The significance of questioning consists in revealing the questionability of what is questioned. It has to be brought into this state of indeterminacy" (Gadamer, 1960/2004, p. 357). Thus, the importance of a well-formed research question is that it identifies a topic clearly while also leaving it open.

In the following sections in this chapter, we pursue a number of additional concepts in Gadamer's work that address aspects of how history and language are mobilized in individual encounters with an art object or text, or in the present context, a matter of importance to researchers.

Play

Gadamer took up play as one of the explanatory ideas in his aesthetics, which in turn modeled his interpretive framework. Play appears in the epigraph at the start of *Truth and Method*, in lines from a poem by Rilke about becoming "the catcher of a ball / thrown by an eternal partner" (Gadamer, 1960/2004, p. v). Grondin (2003b, p. 315), in his biography of Gadamer, related his choice of these lines to his love of tennis. For Gadamer, the significance of play is that when one is fully involved in play, it takes one outside of oneself and the game becomes more than a subjective experience. Play at the same time requires seriousness to be properly absorbing but also frees the player into responsiveness to the flow of the game. Play is not random: it has rules, participants, and a field of play but its possible outcome is open (which is why it is such an offence to fix a game – it corrupts its very nature). What anyone will make of a work of art is likewise unknowable in advance and any outcome – if one plays properly – comes out of a period of uncertainty in which impressions, experiences, opinions, viewpoints (literal and metaphorical) are given free play. Play is thus another example of the movement of interpretation, of its vitality and contrast to prescribed formulae. It is important, in addition, to stress Gadamer's (1960/2004) observation that the play goes beyond the players, that "the *primacy of play over the consciousness of the player* is fundamentally acknowledged" (p. 105, italics in original). To be caught up in the play of possible meanings demands more than merely forming a subjective opinion, but letting the artwork – or research topic – stand amidst the cross currents of its presence in the world so that the self is being reinterpreted in the light of the work even while the work is interpreted.

Prejudices

Understanding is always about something that is already there, which means we can never start as if with a blank slate. Thus, Gadamer introduced the notion of prejudices, of those prior understandings that we already bring to the topic (or perhaps more accurately, that bring us to the topic). Prejudice is the most problematic term of Gadamer's because of its primarily pejorative meaning in English usage. All he meant by it is that we never approach a text, experience, or topic as a completely blank slate – we already have a fabric of meaning into which we accommodate, with more or less difficulty, the next new event. Gadamer (1960/2004) believed that prejudice was so important that, "[t]he recognition that all understanding inevitably involves some prejudice gives the hermeneutic problem its real thrust" (p. 272). Interpretation happens in dialogue and it is our prior commitments that give us something to say in dialogue with new experience. So far, this idea of prejudice is neutral in that it is only making the point that we always bring existing understandings to bear on a topic. There are, however, good and bad prejudices, those that leave us open to dialogue and new possibility and those that would close off dialogue, taking new information only as either confirmation or contradiction of an established position. Hence, Gadamer called for "the foregrounding and appropriation of one's own fore-meanings and prejudices, [since] the important thing is to be aware of one's own bias" (p. 271). Given that prejudices are always in play in hermeneutic understanding, it is incumbent upon us to reflect actively on our own angles of concern for a topic and to remain open to the possible surprise of stumbling over our own prejudices or having someone else stumble on them and point them out to us.

The Hermeneutic Circle

The movement of existing understanding, or prejudice, into constructive interchange with another is described by the image of the hermeneutic circle. In the 19th century, as noted in the previous chapter, the hermeneutic circle referred to the dialectic of part and whole in a narrow sense of an actual text. Heidegger gave the circle an existential spin in *Being and Time* by making it about the back and forth of understanding for *Dasein*. Gadamer held on to the implication of the latter sense, that the being of the interpreter is implicated in the process of understanding, and also retrieved the meaning of part-and-whole:

> Fundamentally, understanding is always a movement in this kind of circle, which is why the repeated return from the whole to the parts, and vice versa, is essential. Moreover, this circle is constantly expanding, since the concept of the whole is relative, and being integrated in ever larger contexts always affects the understanding of the individual part. (Gadamer, 1960/2004, p. 189)

The circle is sometimes visualized as a spiral to represent this widening of the "whole" as it is informed and shaped by each partial understanding or viewpoint that lends a new association to the topic and adds to its connectedness in the world. This also means that the whole is not a fixed quantity, a puzzle that only needs all the pieces in the right places to be complete, but more of a complex and living assemblage of meaning.

Experience – *Erlebnis* and *Erfahrung*

Experience, as we discussed in the previous chapter, is one of the routes that phenomenology takes in its attempt to get at the immediacy of what it is to be a human being in the world. In *Truth and Method*, Gadamer used two different German words for experience that expand the sense of the word. He discussed them in the context of aesthetics, but taking the experience of art as exemplary of how events of understanding are not merely subjective. *Erlebnis*, which was used by Dilthey, refers to an intense experience that stands out from the usual run of events as something remarkable that lingers in the memory as an object of reflection and contemplation. The problem with this kind of experience is that it risks being detached from participation in the world. It carries traces of both 19th-century romanticism and love of the sublime and of early 20th-century phenomenology with its hankering after positivist separation and definition. *Erfahrung*, from the verb *fahren*, which means to travel or journey, has the connotation of raw experience taking one more deeply into the world. *Erfarhung* has a "binding quality" (Gadamer, 1960/2004, p. 84) whereby experience happens along with the networks of meaning that are already present. A research participant might, for example, describe a memorable experience of walking into a classroom for the first time as a new teacher. It may have been an intense experience that the teacher has recalled and recounted many times but in itself it has more of the character of *Erlebnis*. When the singular experience is brought into a form of developmental life, through reflection, association, and dialogue – for example, with other teachers, with research literature, with fictional or artistic representations, with similar experiences of other professionals – the experience takes on the character of *Erfahrung*. In the research context, participants will have varying degrees of reflection to offer about their experience, but it is certainly the task of the researcher to locate experiences in ecologies of meaning.

"There is a world already interpreted, already organized in its basic relations, into which experience steps as something new, upsetting what has led our expectations and undergoing reorganization itself in the upheaval" (Gadamer, 2007, p. 87). One implication of Gadamer's emphasis on experience is that there is a dialectical movement between the world as it comes to meet us, and what we are then able to make of it. In this relationship lies another example of the humility in hermeneutics: that we are not all-comprehending masters of the world (nor can become so).

Experience is another example of finitude because, properly understood, it means that one cannot know what is coming. There is a negativity to experience because in order to stand receptive to otherness and the unknown, one has to hold the already familiar as potentially questionable and open to revision. This philosophical principle has clear relevance to research and provides a rationale, for example, for the practice of the semi-structured interview, which needs to be topic-focused but cannot be determined in advance as in a survey.

Bildung

Bildung is another German word that can be translated as "cultivation," which is related to experience. *Bildung* is the kind of cultivation or development that a person achieves who is open to experience in the above sense of continually revealing new possibilities. It implies the continuing formation of the self in the light of experience, beyond the sheer acquisition of experiences. "The result of *Bildung* is not achieved in the manner of a technical construction, but grows out of an inner process of formation and cultivation" (Gadamer, 1960/2004, p. 10) and thus is a process that can never be declared completed.

This helps to articulate how it is that the researcher is changed by doing the research. Experiences – of reading, discovering new sources, interviewing participants and reviewing transcripts, conversations about the work and so on – alter the researcher's own field of understanding as she or he becomes more *gebildet*, cultivated. It is not only a matter of expertise but of a complex relationship with one's own expertise in which unlearning and relearning are part of learning. Davey (2006) wrote that "the process of becoming 'experienced' (*gebildet*) involves the assimilation of a body of ideas, it does not entail the acquisition or the imposition of a *determinate* set of ideas" (p. 49, italics in original).

What we mostly call the "topic" in this book, referring to a worthwhile subject matter for research, can be translated by the German word, *Sache*, which Davey (2006) took up from Gadamer in his elaboration of *Bildung*. Reiterating the point that cultivation takes place within a context, Davey described it as "becoming literate with regard to the *Sachen* that form a given culture" (p. 69). Here is another place where extension of the argument into practice disciplines is justified. Davey was careful to rebut the critique of Gadamer as conservative by separating *Bildung* from its historic associations with a particular idea of what a cultivated person might look like. He argued that, hermeneutically, *Bildung* takes on meaning and value in relation to a particular *Sache*, and not according to a pre-determined standard of social values. Given this flexibility, it makes sense to talk about subject matters as they belong within a social, institutional, or professional culture. The topic of therapeutic relationship, for example, will appear differently according to whether the cultural context is nursing, mental health, education, psychotherapy, or hospitals. In this example, it is more than likely that all the examples are related, but each will have its own literature, its own set of associations and cultural nuances. *Sachen* that are worth investigating have a generative effect because they are not comfortably defined and restricted – looking closely at one part of a topic, associations become apparent, either obviously so or in peripheral vision. "Indeed, for a *Sache* to function, that is, for it to become historically effective, it must shade into meanings different to those associated with its first appearance" (Davey, 2006, p. 72). Hermeneutic research demands the ability to find a culturally lively subject matter to start with, and then to follow where it leads.

Fusion of Horizons

Horizontverschmelzung, the German word for "fusion of horizons," once came up in a hermeneutic research class for graduate students taught by two of the authors. One of the students, who spoke German, said *Verschmelzung* brought up for her the image of melting butter. Melting is one of the meanings of the English "fusion" too, along with blending and bonding together (Fusion, 1993). Fusion of horizons is a frequently cited concept in Gadamer's hermeneutics but it is complicated both by the multivalent meanings of fusion and by his using it in different contexts. At first sight, the phrase can evoke the sense of horizons becoming bonded together into one but it is important to retain the other sense of fluidity.

The first place the phrase occurs in *Truth and Method* is in relation to history, where the horizons in question are those of the past and the present. Our horizon of the present – formed by the values, assumptions, concerns that condition how we look out on the world – is inextricably influenced by horizons of the past. Further, the horizon of the present is always changing in the light of new circumstances and new knowledge. It would be a mistake, however, to conclude from this that progress is all we need to worry about, and to dismiss the past. The past, the other horizon, is always shaping our consciousness of the world and it too changes since we are always interpreting the past from the horizon of the present.

> In fact the horizon of the present is continually in the process of being formed because we are continually having to test all our prejudices. An important part of this testing occurs in encountering the past in understanding the tradition from which we come. Hence the horizon of the present cannot be formed without the past. (Gadamer, 1960/ 2004, p. 305)

There is then a fusion, a coming together of horizons to achieve new understanding (of the present and of the past, depending on the focus of inquiry) but it is always provisional, never finalized. The fusion of horizons, as when a researcher draws conclusions about the history of a concept, is a point of understanding that has validity since it is based upon an informed reading of the past. It can be used to inform present understanding and future decisions. It cannot, however, be declared unchangeable in the light of as yet unknown shifts in horizons.

Further on, Gadamer came back to the fusion of horizons in relation to reading texts, as a more concrete example of where we encounter the horizon of the past. Texts, after all, unlike speech, carry their time of origin with them into the present. A few exceptional texts continue to speak to readers for centuries – bookshops in the English speaking world often have several different translations of Dante's *Divine Comedy* on their shelves, for example – a work from 14th-century Italy that portrays a fundamentally different view of the world and the cosmos from modernity and yet continues to be translated and re-translated and published in popular editions for a contemporary readership. To take a less extreme example from the disciplinary literature of mental health nursing, the pioneering work of Peplau (1952/1988), mentioned above, continues to be cited as a source of understanding of working therapeutically through relationship. There are aspects of her early work, however, that reflect the predominance of psychoanalytic thinking in the mental health care of the 1950s that have to be thought about differently in the changed standards of contemporary psychiatry and mental health care. The continued, if changing, value of a work like Peplau's underlines Gadamer's point that some insights do not wear out easily and continue to generate meaningful and worthwhile understanding even though understanding has to be vigilantly re-examined and renewed in the light of the always-moving horizon of the present.

Gadamer (1960/2004) argued that, to fully engage with the meaning of the text, the reader brings his or her own horizon into play. There is not one ultimate, true meaning hidden in the text but unavoidably one reads from the horizon of the present. As with prejudices, this can be enabling when the horizon is held "more as an opinion and a possibility that one brings into play and puts at risk, and that helps one truly to make one's own what the text says" (p. 390). It is an interesting claim, that one reads and understands the otherness of a text *better* by having an angle of commitment of one's own, but only provided that one can hold that angle as a possibility open to change. Gadamer applied this point also to the play of conversation, "in which something is expressed that is not only mine or my author's, but common" (p. 390).

Fusion of horizons applies then to three of Gadamer's areas of chief concern: history, text, and, by extension, conversation. It is one form in which he discussed the encounter with otherness and how it is possible for understanding to move, expand, and change in the light of encounter with the other. The term neither implies that one side surrenders understanding to the other, nor that the fusion involves complete sublimation of both. In fact, there are many possibilities of combining and blending of prior understandings or holding on to differences – but in a new constellation in relation to each other.

Application and *Phronesis*

One of the appeals of hermeneutic philosophy for researchers in practice disciplines is that, in spite of its complexity, it is rooted in the phenomenological lifeworld, and what is at stake in understanding for everyday human, social activities. It is this rootedness that makes hermeneutics, as we argue throughout this book, naturally movable from the traditional concerns (in *Truth and Method*) of legal, theological, and textual interpretation to problems of classrooms and clinics. Application is one of Gadamer's concepts that serves the purpose of substantiating the extension, and it leads to another idea, that of *phronesis*, or practical wisdom.

Gadamer (1960/2004) used the law as the clearest example of "recognizing application as an integral element of all understanding" (p. 307) since laws live through application that is, at the same time, interpretation. Application, however, does not mean taking an abstract principle and imposing it upon a situation since "means are in general determined by ends, and rules are determined by, or even abstracted from, behavior" (Gadamer, 2007, p. 61). Application, as part of the structure of understanding, has to be conditioned by historically effected consciousness. The intention here is not to restrict application to repetition of what is already known and done, but to seek out possibilities for application that are comprehensible within the horizon of present understandings. Hermeneutical awareness, far from being conservative, encourages a restless questioning of what appears obvious and inevitable through sensitivity to impermanence. Application is situational and flexible since it is interpretation within a concrete situation. Warnke (2002) highlighted an ethical dimension to application: "Our application of the ethical knowledge we possess occurs within a history that is unceasing in its demand that we apply it, however much or little of it we may possess" (p. 84).

Application can be seen as a matter of practice, of reinterpreting principles in the light of circumstances, and reinterpreting circumstances in the light of principles. Practice disciplines like education, social work, or nursing that have at their core personal interrelationships within schemas of technical knowledge and ethical values are clearly sites of hermeneutic application. For application to be done well requires a disposition on the part of the agent – the teacher, social worker, or nurse for example – which Gadamer (1960/2004) referred to as *phronesis*, translated both as "practical knowledge" (p. 19) and "moral knowledge" (p. 312)[1]. Aristotle used the word *phronesis* to distinguish contextualized knowledge from objective knowledge that does not change. One of the features of practical knowledge is that it demands judgment and action within a situation, where "the knower is not standing over against a situation that he merely observes; he is directly confronted with what he sees. It is something that he has to do" (Gadamer, 1960/2004, p. 312). Practical knowledge is different from technical knowledge that can be determined in advance because, however complex, it requires exact and repeatable action. Practical knowledge is also moral knowledge because, as Warnke noted, it functions within the flow of the moment in which values as well as technical skills are operative.

Application and *phronesis* provide a valuable explanatory framework for the complex work of practice disciplines. As such, they may be helpful to researchers in trying to describe phenomena of practice, as well as referring to the conduct of interpretive research itself.

Transformation into Structure

We want to borrow one final term from Gadamer's aesthetics, which we believe illuminates the stage of writing up the finished interpretive findings in hermeneutic research. Gadamer (1960/2004) intended "transformation into structure" (p. 110) to mean the point at which creative play comes to an end through the achievement of the work of art. The artwork is transformative because it takes up the play and in capturing a vision of the world, re-presents the world in new alignments of possibility. The response to an artwork is at the same time the recognition of something known, a self-recognition on the part of the viewer, and "the joy of knowing *more* than is already familiar" (p. 113). Writing a finished version of hermeneutic research similarly brings to an end the play of interpretation, at least for the moment and, in doing so, it reconstitutes the topic in ways that bring to the fore new possibilities for practice. Writing in hermeneutics is, of course, not separable from the writer, so that it is not just that the researcher presents a novel arrangement of the facts, but that the researcher writes from within an altered horizon of the self. "The transformation into structure...allows a subject to see its world differently and to become different to itself" (Davey, 2006, p. 135). As with the image of fusion, however, structure does not mean finality. Davey described transformation into structure "as the disclosure of meaning within a given cycle of events" so that "what was incomplete and fragmentary emerges as a meaningful whole" (p. 136). Structure is necessary as a point in a cycle of interpretation and understanding in which meaning comes together as a unit of articulation and in doing so, the newly articulated meaning becomes available in itself for questioning, reappraisal, deconstruction, and interpretation.

Summary: Hermeneutics as Practice

In his 1972 essay, *Hermeneutics as Practical Philosophy* (Gadamer, 2007, pp. 227–245), Gadamer laid out his view of hermeneutics as a practice. He based this on a foundation of Aristotelian practical philosophy of how citizens ought to live in the community of the *polis*, oriented toward the good. Practice in this broad sense thus takes account of contingency, of the human situation of having to choose with discernment amidst the currents of history and messiness of events. By using the word practice, however, he indicated that humans are not helpless in the face of the world, that we have choice, reason, and knowledge – however finite and mutable – in forming our values and actions.

Hermeneutics as a practice suggests obvious comparisons with practice disciplines such as teaching, social work, counseling, nursing, or medicine. Practice in these contexts too has an underlying moral orientation toward the good of communities. In addition, however, practice disciplines to varying degrees and in different ways make use of science and technology requiring specific technical expertise. Research and management too strive to bring scientific methods and uniformity to the governance and conduct of practitioners. The tension between generalizable scientific knowledge and application in the particular situation thus takes on a particular immediacy for practice disciplines. Practice is constituted in the continual negotiation of "applying this [general] knowledge in the concrete case" (Gadamer, 1996, p. 16). Gadamer discussed this tension in his addresses to medical audiences, and emphasized the importance of keeping open the space of practice as a practice of human responsiveness:

> What we need to do is to learn to build a bridge over the existing divide between the theoretician who knows the general rule and the person involved in practice who wishes to deal with the unique situation of this patient who is in need of care. (p. 94)

In reality, of course, there is no absolute separation between the theoretician and the practitioner, and the negotiation between the two is experienced as an internal as well as social or institutional matter. This only underlines the hermeneutic sense of practice for which the exercise of judgment is primary:

> Being an experienced practitioner does not strictly speaking impose limits on deployable methodical devices or tactics. To the contrary, becoming an experienced practitioner entails sharpening if not acquiring a guiding *sense* for judging which approach to a task is more plausible or appropriate than another. (Davey, 2006, p. 17, italics in original)

This brief introduction to important concepts in Gadamer's philosophy is intended to provide a framework for what follows in the working out of a coherent and effective approach to research, but it can only point toward the practice to come.

Note

1. There are other variant translations of *phronesis*, including Risser's (1997) "practical reasoning," Sachs' (2002) "practical judgment," and Schwarz's (2010) "practical wisdom." For convenience, we have used the versions found in the 2004 translation of *Truth and Method*.

References

Coltman, R. (1998). *The language of hermeneutics: Gadamer and Heidegger in dialogue*. New York, NY: SUNY Press.

Davey, N. (2006). *Unquiet understanding: Gadamer's philosophical hermeneutics*. New York, NY: SUNY Press.

Davey, N. (2013). *Unfinished worlds: Hermeneutics, aesthetics and Gadamer*. Edinburgh, UK: Edinburgh University Press.

Dostal, R. J. (2002). Gadamer's relation to Heidegger and phenomenology. In R. J. Dostal (Ed.), *The Cambridge companion to Gadamer* (pp. 247–266). New York, NY: Cambridge University Press.

Fusion. (1993). In L. Brown (Ed.), *The new shorter Oxford dictionary* (Vol. 1, p. 1047). Oxford, UK: Oxford University Press.

Gadamer, H-G. (1960/2004). *Truth and method* (J. Weinsheimer & D. G. Marshall, Trans.). London, UK: Continuum.

Gadamer, H. G. (1977). *Philosophical hermeneutics* (D. E. Linge, Ed. & Trans.). Berkeley, CA: University of California Press.

Gadamer, H. G. (1981). *Reason in the age of science* (F. G. Lawrence, Trans.). Cambridge, MA: MIT Press.

Gadamer, H. G. (1996). *The enigma of health* (J. Gaiger & N. Walker, Trans.). Stanford, CA: Stanford University Press.

Gadamer, H. G. (2001). *Gadamer in conversation* (R. E. Palmer, Ed. & Trans.). New Haven, CT: Yale University Press.

Gadamer, H. G. (2007). *The Gadamer reader: A bouquet of the later writings* (R. E. Palmer, Ed.). Evanston, IL: Northwestern University Press.

Grondin, J. (1994). *Introduction to philosophical hermeneutics* (J. Weinsheimer, Trans.). New Haven, CT: Yale University Press.

Grondin, J. (1995). *Sources of hermeneutics*. Albany, NY: SUNY Press.

Grondin, J. (2003a). *The philosophy of Gadamer* (K. Plant, Trans.). Montreal, QC, Canada: McGill-Queen's University Press.

Grondin, J. (2003b). *Hans-Georg Gadamer: A biography* (J. Weinsheimer, Trans.). New Haven, CT: Yale University Press.

Palmer, R. E. (1969). *Hermeneutics*. Evanston, IL: Northwestern University Press.

Peplau, H. (1988). *Interpersonal relations in nursing*. Basingstoke, UK: Palgrave Macmillan.

Risser, J. C. (1997). *Hermeneutics and the voice of the other: Re-reading Hans-Georg Gadamer's philosophical hermeneutics*. Albany, NY: SUNY Press.

Sachs, J. (2002). *Aristotle. Nicomachean ethics* (J. Sachs, Trans.). Newburyport, MA: Focus.

Schwarz, B. (2010). *Practical wisdom: The right way to do the right thing*. New York, NY: Riverhead.

Taylor, C. (2002). Gadamer on the human sciences. In R. J. Dostal (Ed.), *The Cambridge companion to Gadamer* (pp. 126–142). New York, NY: Cambridge University Press.

Warnke, G. (2002). Hermeneutics, ethics, and politics. In R. J. Dostal (Ed.), *The Cambridge companion to Gadamer* (pp. 79–101). New York, NY: Cambridge University Press.

· 4 ·

ON BEING METHODICAL
AND FOLLOWING LEADS

The hermeneutics developed here is not, therefore, a methodology of the human sciences…I did not intend to produce an art or a technique of understanding, in the manner of earlier hermeneutics. I did not wish to elaborate a system of rules to describe, let alone direct the methodological procedure of the human sciences…My real concern was and is philosophic; not what we do or what we ought to do, but what happens to us over and above our wanting and doing. Hence the methods of the human science are not at issue here. (Gadamer, 1960/1996, p. xxiii & p. xviii)

There is no such thing as a method of asking questions, of learning to see what is questionable. (Gadamer, 1960/1989, p. 365)

We place these quotes at the front of this chapter to signal the difficulty and risk that confronts anyone attempting to lay out the "how" of hermeneutics, a task made more difficult because of Gadamer's ambivalence toward anything that would qualify as a procedure for doing hermeneutics. It is understandable, then, that a common reading of Gadamerian hermeneutics is that there is no method associated with doing interpretive research, nor should there be and, as authors of this book, we both agree and disagree with this statement. It all comes down to what is meant by the term method. What are the assumptions made by the method? What are its purposes and practices? More importantly, perhaps, what strictures are imposed on the researcher, the participants, the topic, and the outcomes by the method? More to Gadamer's point: What does the method neglect? Ignore? Suppress? Prevent altogether? These are the questions that we need to ask of any method but, in doing so, it does not mean that hermeneutic researchers are against method. In this chapter, then, we attempt to clarify what we are "against" in method and what we are for, if and when we use that term.

Caveats on What Science Has Delivered to Us as Method

The strengths and limitations of method have to be worked through in relation to science and its claim to the progressive accumulation of objective knowledge. In itself, this claim is borne out by the sheer power of the technological consequences of scientific method, which have rapidly transformed the conditions of human experience in the past century and a half. Power alone, however, is no argument: it may account for the tendency among adherents of scientific method to discount or overrule other forms of knowledge by confusing it with rationality as such, but their hubris only makes it all the more imperative to create venues for the practice of well-reasoned hermeneutic reflection.

Davey (2006) argued robustly against what he dubbed "will to method" (p. 20), implying a distinction between scientific method as a tool with its own range of suitable purposes and the overreach of anticipating a final explanation of "the complexities of human experience" (p. 20). The philosophy of science since Kuhn in the early 1960s has long since incorporated various self-interpretive stances and yet without positive forms of affirmation of human experience in its turbulent pluralism and of expressions of cultural life and meaning such as artworks and literature, then science always threatens to impose an impoverished version of the human world.

One of the effects of will to method is the devaluing of experientially acquired wisdom (*paidea*), such that people's testimony as to their experience is simply regarded as "soft data," as opposed to the "hard evidence" generated by scientific procedure. Will to method is not about method as such, but is a manifestation of a deep, taken for granted historical *prejudice* (Gadamer, 1969/1989) against other ways of knowing and understanding. If method obliges a researcher to act as if she or he is a neutral, disinterested spectator to an objectified world of objects with fixed essences, then will to method overspills the contingent point of the experiment to insist that human life *ought to be like that* – the expedient utility of the method becomes a deep, irreparable form of alienation, what Davey (2006) called a "dehumanized form of conscious-ness" (p. 22) that functions as an illusion about the world we live in, and the nature of being in that world. Following this, if method comes to mean the manipulation of people as objects, and circumstances as static factors, as if the world were simply at our disposal, there for us as an instrument completely under our willful control, then we see this, not as a desirable way to proceed, but rather as a "will to power" (Nietzsche, 1968) that exhibits a "colonizing tendency" (Davey, 2006, p. 21), and that "betrays an imperious insensitivity to other voices and reduces the complex variety of human experience to its own terms"(Davey, 2006, p. 21). If method is followed blindly, along strict, algorithmic procedures, decided entirely in advance, and pursued relentlessly, irrespective of what one encounters in the field of action, in *spite of others* (the hermeneutic pun is intentional), then we do not regard that as method, but rather as an "obsessive concern for purity and a corresponding desire to ex-orcise all the messier (e.g., bodily, emotional) dimensions of experience from science" (Bordo, 1975, p. 4).

Toward a Practice of Being Methodical

So where does this leave us? It certainly does not leave us "method-less," with-out any sense and direction to accomplish insightful and dependable work. Gadamer himself explained that his work "is phenomenological in its meth-od" (Gadamer, 1960/1989. p. xxxvii), and later in his life, reinforced what is important: "One does not always have to insist that what one was doing was phenomenology, but what one ought to work phenomenologically, that is descriptively, creatively-intuitively, and in a concretizing manner"(Gadamer, 2001, p. 113).

A first gloss of these statements might seem to be quite confusing, for Gadamer appears to both eschew method and to call upon it at the same time. Perhaps this reveals his own deep ambivalence toward method, but we think he is not speaking to method in general, but rather particular kinds of method, as is revealed in this assertion by Dostal (2002):

> By referring to his method, Gadamer means, not a procedural set of rules, but rather the *discipline of attending to things* (my emphasis). By calling his method phenomenological, he does not thereby subscribe to Husserl's method of phenomenology, but rather

indicates that the task of the enterprise is descriptive, in this case descriptive of the human experience of understanding, i.e., of hermeneutical experience. (p. 251)

A further clue to this was given by Gadamer (1960/1989) himself, in the closing statement of *Truth and Method*, as if he knew what lay ahead for those wishing to take up the work of hermeneutics: "what the tool of method cannot achieve must-and really can-be achieved by a discipline of questioning and inquiring" (p. 491). What Gadamer's words refer to here is human action in the world and, in particular, coming to an understanding of human action in the world, which is more a kind of *praxis* (*practice*), than it is a method, a much larger, more encompassing form of human endeavor. As Gadamer (2001) noted:

> The word praxis points to the totality of our practical life. All our human action and behavior, the self-adaptation of the human being as a whole in this world...Our praxis, in short, is our form of life. (p. 78)

Further, there are three important differences here that need to be pointed out. As a practice, hermeneutics is not a neutral enterprise; we do not simply select a method and aim it at the world to accomplish something we want to do. Rather, it is action called upon for the achievement of some moral good. There is an ethical obligation-in health care, in education, and in other practice disciplines that its practitioners be guided by an ethic of care. Gadamer stated this succinctly when he characterized hermeneutic work as "the art of strengthening." It is a call that addresses us in the first person: What can I do for this child or this patient, in this situation, at this particular time to help them flourish? What can I learn from this patient or child that will help me strengthen my own practice? What can I add to the larger conversation, in the discipline, that might help us see, think about, act differently toward the phenomenon?

Second, and in relation to the first point, practice is dominated by what Gadamer has phrased as "deliberation and decision-making." No one can escape from the task of choosing well, to paraphrase Aristotle – to do the right thing, at the right time, in the right way, and for the right amount, and for the right reason. All those "rights" have to be worked out in the course of an inquiry. One can never say, for example, that "ethnography or grounded theory made me do it." There is no way to shift the burden and responsibility for acting from the shoulders of the researcher and assign it to a predetermined script. This is why Madison (1988) has called hermeneutics "a method for choosing appropriately" (p. 176).

This brings us to a central point that has profound implications for methodology. Unlike method, which requires a degree of abstraction and de-contextualization, a practice is necessarily a collective enterprise, aimed at achieving a common good. In hermeneutics, we must engage with others in coming to an understanding of a phenomenon, which also involves coming to an understanding of self. This is not to deny the collective and social practices of scientists, but their functioning in the lifeworld is not required by scientific method as such and is, ironically, better and more easily understood hermeneutically. Neither is practice a form of mystical quietism—one cannot withdraw from the world to work out his or her understanding of it in splendid isolation.

> …the practice of hermeneutics pursues dialog and dialectic encounter with the other. It seeks a disciplined openness to the strange and foreign. It encourages a creative tension between the assumptions of our own horizons and those that are different. (Davey, 2006, p. 4.)

Such a commitment reveals the importance of *character* and *wisdom* in hermeneutic practice. The ability to encounter the other, in dialogue, requires *modesty* and *humility*, in that we know that our knowledge is limited and in need of revision. It requires *courtesy*, in that we acknowledge our indebtedness to others, and welcome their capacity to teach us something new. Most importantly perhaps, it requires *tact*, what Gadamer (1960/1989) described as "a special sensitivity and sensitiveness to situations and how to behave in them, for which knowledge from general principles does not suffice" (p. 16). Tact involves both sense and feeling, but also a kind of knowledge-knowing how to orient ourselves in a situation, knowing which resources to draw upon to make sense of what we encounter, knowing which questions to ask next, knowing when to probe, and when to let the silence speak for itself. "But to pass over something does not mean to avert one's gaze from it, but to keep an eye on it in such a way that rather than knock into it, one slips by it" (Gadamer, 1960/1989, p. 16). It is not simply "a natural capacity for feeling," as Weinsheimer (1985) suggested, but "closely allied to a sense of the beautiful and to the historical sense that knows what is appropriate in interpreting a past age because it can distance itself from itself in order to sense the difference of the past from the present" (p. 72). Method, on the other hand, in its strictest sense is "tact-less" since the procedures are universally applicable and one need not be concerned with whether they apply for they always apply, everywhere. Tact cannot be acquired in the abstract, because it does not have to do with abstract rules. It can only be learned in and through experience, that is, by being practiced, from encounter to encounter, from case to case, to learn, as Caputo (1987) has said, from a series of "intentionally frustrated expectations" (p. 58). From this, we can see that hermeneutics hopes to generate something more than theory, knowledge, or efficient technique. It hopes that, in coming to an understanding through our practice, we become cultivated human beings. What hermeneutic researchers are drawn toward is a larger ideal, both in their research, but beyond that, in their lifeworlds: "cultivating the kind of dialogical communities in which *phronesis*, judgment and practical discourse become concretely embodied in our everyday practices" (Bernstein, 1983, p. 224).

We return to the methodological implications of this below, but first it is worth noting that hermeneutic method, being dialogic, and essentially unfinished, does not involve induction, that is, the "upward" generation of theory and general principles from data, as does grounded theory. As mentioned, induction leads to general principles, and in doing so, tends to come to rest in theory and leave the particular behind. When this happens, the generative power that would help us see things as existing differently disappears in a set of affirmed principles. Worse perhaps, hermeneutic experience gets extinguished. Gone are the differences and disappointments. What is lost is the process for overturning what one expects, what is already known and taken for granted, and what is predictable. How is it that we guard against simply finding out what we expect to find, if the process is essentially one of affirmation?

If hermeneutics does not involve induction, it is equally true that it does not involve deduction either – the "downward" logic of deriving practice from theory, or subsuming the particular under the general. Rather, hermeneutic analysis requires an interaction between the general and the particular that renders simultaneously a nuanced understanding of the concrete situation, and a set of questions and possibilities for seeing, thinking, and acting in the future. Generating an array of possibilities for future concrete action is very different from generating theory inductively or a set of "best practices" deductively. One might say that the *next practice is the best practice* in hermeneutic work. Thus, hermeneutics is "horizontal," that is, temporal or historical in its movement. It involves utilizing the resources of past, what is known, to interpret the present, what is encountered in the moment, to enrich our understanding of what is possible in the future. It enacts "historically effected consciousness" (Gadamer, 1983), and produces, not "a view from everywhere," as does science, but rather what Gadamer (1999) called "mutual co-perception"(p. 251). The view provided is not either up or down, but forward, "not positing an end, but reckoning with being on the way, giving *it* free play, disclosing it, holding fast to *being possible*" (Heidegger, 1923/1999, p. 13).

Guidelines for a Hermeneutic Research Praxis (Practice)

The term "guidelines" was chosen carefully to signal an older meaning of the term, that is, "that which serves to steady the motion of a thing or journey" (OED, p. 491). Guidelines are not methodological imperatives. They are in the service of steady, dependable motion. They are not meant to displace good judgment or extinguish experience. They will not, indeed cannot, tell a researcher how to respond to an encounter, interpret a particular case, make a good case for an interpretation, take a particular course of action, or clarify how understanding occurs. Guidelines are there to simply orient the researcher, to help them make responsible, reliable, and defensible decisions. They operate much like stars do for navigation. One does not sail toward the stars; they do not tell when to sail, or how, and certainly not where to sail. In other words, stars do not cause someone to sail. All of that careful practice of sailing depends upon locally determined, mutually interacting conditions, which need constant consideration and re-consideration: the nature of the vessel, the destination, the cargo, the weather conditions, the traffic encountered, the skill and character of the navigators, to name but a few. Many different ways can be made from the stars; they allow for a diversity of sailing. However, the stars do serve to properly "steady" the sailing, to provide an answer to the questions: Where are we now? – and, from this, to help the navigators decide, steadily, methodically, the answer to: Where do we head next?

It is the same with the guidelines below; they are offered as being in service of practice and in hermeneutics this also means being in service of the phenomenon. They are also offered with the knowledge that they are human constructions, and therefore, are incomplete and fallible. There are always more guidelines to be specified. In the spirit of hermeneutic work, we offer the list to the reader to be interpreted anew.

1. The way of hermeneutic practice is determined by the phenomenon, not the method

Hermeneutic practice is a lot like detective work in that one proceeds on the basis of attuned perception, concrete discovery, and the imagining and re-imaging of possible meanings and courses of action. This does not mean that anything goes in detective work—warranted courses of action, chains of evidence, and persuasive arguments have to be established in the course of the investigation, and all of this has to stand up to careful scrutiny and through going critique. "Cases for" have to be made and subjected to rigorous argumentation. Clear, retrospective "accounting for" is required, as it is in hermeneutic work. So, upon the discovery of a body, for example, the detectives do not immediately choose "the Raymond Chandler method" for detective work, and launch themselves into the field of action. They do attend carefully. They walk around the phenomenon, seeing it from different angles. They may take pictures, or make drawings, or detailed notes. They consult with others. Slow patient shifting with regard for contextual strata is required. They engage in the creative construction of possibilities, all based on the concrete particulars they experience.

In hermeneutic work, being called by a phenomenon does not immediately license one to rush into the world armed with a method, but rather, calls for the careful probing and questioning of what appears. One must learn from the phenomenon, both about what it is a case of, but also about what this one case requires to deepen understanding of both the instance and its context. This careful consideration with what appears before us is a learning process, as Gadamer (1983) has stated above, focused on "learning how to ask questions" (p. 365) that will drive the investigation. What is this thing that appears before us– does it appear to be a homicide? A suicide? An accident? Why does it appear like this? What are we assuming? An interpretation, both of possibilities for being, and for possible lines of action, is required, and every interpretation or "seeing as" yields a different way to proceed. Homicides are not treated the same way as suicides, or accidental deaths. It is the same in hermeneutic work. The requirement of "learning how to ask questions" is never extinguished in a single round of asking questions; every encounter with the phenomenon requires close scrutiny; every experience of learning from the phenomenon requires a new set of questions to be generated, because if the encounter "works," it produces new understanding, and hence a different course of action. In this way, practice is not so much driven by procedure as it is by substance (*die Sache*), by the subject that matters. Action follows the logic of making one's way in the world, of being responsive to what appears in the lifeworld, of taking all the (unpredictable) twists and turns required to stay with the phenomenon. This process Gadamer thought of as the logic of experience, of "seeing what is questionable," and not the formal logic of abstracted rational thought. "Though the insights of the practitioner—'knowing' how to find one's way about within an endeavor—are a consequence of 'experience,' they fall outside the strictures of 'method'"(Davey, 2006, p. 6). Learning from experience, the way of hermeneutic practice, is a wider, more complex, and thickly variegated dimensions of living one's life than is method.

2. Hermeneutic practice requires a disciplined (phenomenological) focus on the particular

Because of its commitment to studying the lifeworld and, in particular, situated human action, hermeneutics has been called the "science of examples" (van Manen, 1990, p. 121). That phrase probably simplifies the practice too much, as it is as much an art as it is a science. Examples need to be read hermeneutically. They need to engage our imaginations and become evocative. The phrase, however, does give us a glimpse into how important concrete examples (and particular people) are for hermeneutic inquiry. That is because hermeneutics is concerned with the facticity of life (Heidegger, 1923/1999). As Harmon (2007) wrote:

> Human life is not something visible from the outside, but must be seen in the very act, performance or execution of its own reality, which always exceeds any of the properties that we can list about it...The facticity of life simply means that life cannot be adequately described in theoretical terms. Human life is always immersed in a specific situation, involved with its surroundings in a very particular way. (p. 25)

When something addresses us in the particular, it does so as a case of something that is already significant, as Heidegger insisted. We are thinking of "case" beyond its modern professional connotations, avoiding the construal of case as a professionalized object and regarding it in its older meaning of something that has befallen one. Hermeneutic understanding is always tied to a concrete situation; it is always applied, consciously or otherwise, to a particular case—*this* student, *this* patient, *this* event, in *this* context. Application in hermeneutics is, in Risser's (1997) words, "seeing what's at stake" in the case. In hermeneutics, however, application "happens" to us the other way as well: the case applies to our understanding, conditioning it. So it is not simply that a case gets subsumed under our current understanding when we see something, but also that the act of seeing has an effect on us. Quite simply, good cases teach us to see differently. This dialogic application characterizes the back and forth motion of interpretation. It is the detailed familiarity of the cases that strikes us; it is the detailed strangeness of the case that surprises us; it is the unfathomable mystery of the case that intrigues us. Cases both catch us (we recognize), and catch us out (are unrecognizable). They produce bewilderment and raise questions that cry out for answers: What does the case mean? What is it a case of? (see for e.g., Moules, Jardine, McCaffrey, & Brown, 2013).

There is another dimension to cases that makes them sticky: they enlist our care and concern. We are not simply curious about cases; we are also stuck by the moral implications they have for our lives. We can learn about the "oughts" and "shoulds" of the practices in which we engage, about the kind of world we wish to live in, about who we are. Good cases should provoke us to talk about what we ought to do and who we ought to be. They should orient the conversation to what it means to be good, to be worthwhile.

Much of data collection in hermeneutics could be seen as the seeking out and selection of good cases. This is as far as the "data reduction" should go in hermeneutic research—the case as it lives in a particular setting. Context, both social and historical, matters in hermeneutics. Cases have no meaning as isolated entities, the social conditions of the case contribute to their meaning, as do the historical "conditioners." Although they have an immediate presence, cases come from somewhere, as something. This arrival as something already needs careful investigation. Unlike Husserlian phenomenology, in hermeneutics that which appears to our consciousness is never given. A part of the interpretation of cases involves reading cases back into their histories, from different vantage points. For example, what happens when we regard children as deficient adults? How did they appear to us? How did we "treat" them on the basis of their appearance? What did they become "a case of" when we treated them this way? More importantly, what did we prevent them from becoming?

Cases also require reading back into our lives, as "what ifs": what if we saw children as capable, would that make a difference to how they appeared, to how we treated them, to what they might become? What if we saw chimpanzees as first cousins, as sentient beings, would we continue to mutilate, dismember, and murder them for the sake of "scientific understanding"? What if we saw history from the perspective of the vanquished instead of the conquistadors, might we see a different case and a different case history?

Reading cases into the past, into our lives, and into the future is also required because it produces the necessary distance to see the phenomenon properly, as it manifests itself differently. It develops a fundamental skill in interpretive work, "the skill of being critically distant, while being involved, caring and attentive" (Davey, 2006, p. xvi).

3. Hermeneutic practice requires that we be vigilant and open in our encounters with the lifeworld

Martin Heidegger, in his careful, life-long devotion to the notion of *beginning*, as in the *necessity of constantly beginning anew* in our understanding, contended that "(e)verything depends upon our understanding being guided onto the right path of looking" (Heidegger, 1923/1999, p. 62). If our understanding was not on the right path, then we would take "a covering up of the subject matter for the subject matter itself" (p. 59). For Heidegger, getting on the right path involved practicing what he called "radical wakefulness," and it involved a kind of dismantling of the traditions we operated within by questioning them, so as to interrupt the projection of meaning into the lifeworld – "lettings things be" so that they would reveal something that was previously hidden. Gadamer thought about this as putting what we know at risk, to make our pre-understanding part of the phenomenon of study by seeking out what was strange and foreign to us, such that, confronted by difference, our understanding is broken open, refigured so a new world could open in front of our prefiguration. Irrespective of whether it is that our histories have to be dismantled for us to wake up to the world, or we have to allow our experience to be over-turned by the world, we need to practice a disciplined kind of vigilance, to develop a practice of being open to the world, so that new worlds can appear and the effects of appearing are not lost on us.

4. Reading in the hermeneutic tradition involves a practice of learning to read self and world differently

Reading in the hermeneutic tradition is a matter both of what to read and how to read. The "original texts" are dense and layered in their complexity, some would even say obtuse. In many cases, they reach back into traditions, Greek and otherwise, that are relatively obscure, and many use language that

sends us scrambling for philosophical and etymological dictionaries. They resist being read. This can and does cause people wanting to work hermeneutically to avoid reading people like Gadamer and Heidegger, to set them aside,
or dismiss them as impenetrable. Heidegger for example, has been accused,
even by academics like Adorno, of writing texts that only people like Heidegger could understand (Harman, 2007).

When we read hermeneutically, we are required to read against the way
we have learned to read – not to look for the literal meaning in the text, not
to search for the author's intentions behind the text, but to read for the possibilities that open in front of the text, the possibilities that the text opens
up in our "fields of action" (Ricoeur, 1991). We have to let our actions transform what we see, and what we see with. Action in the world refigures both
our perceptions, and the elements that condition our perceptions and our
pre-understanding. Thus it is that we may find ourselves transformed by reading, emerging into a different self, and our actions too are transformed, in the
dynamic transaction between text, self, and world.

This makes hermeneutic reading difficult, but not impossible. We do admit that patience and tolerance of uncertainty are required in developing the
kinds of skills necessary for reading difficult texts. Tolerance of uncertainty is
required to push on when the interpretation is constantly stumbling, when we
are constantly living with our own inadequacy as readers, and the text easily
outdistances us. Tolerance of uncertainty is required to live on the scraps of
understanding that come from difficult reads, and most importantly, it is required to let the reading change what we know and what we do to become es-
tranged from ourselves. Patience is required for the skills to develop; learning
to read, and reading to learn at the same time is a slow process. Forgiveness
is required for our failure to "get it" instantly when we read, even though
we have been schooled all of our lives to think that understanding ought to
come quickly. Forgiveness must be practiced for the authors also, struggling
with coming to an understanding of the complexity of human understanding.
Gratitude must be practiced for their trail-blazing efforts to understand. They
are becoming readers along with us.

What is learned from engaging over time with hermeneutic scholars is
that slow, methodical reading is exactly what is required. Commenting on the
meticulous reading habits of both Nietzsche and Foucault, Payne (1997) wrote
"there is nothing hasty or haphazard about this kind of reading. It requires patient shifting and a careful regard for contextual strata...reading amounts to

sustained contact with the gritty texture of thought" (p. 14). It also requires gritty contact with the lifeworld, and with self.

There is no substitute for the hard work of reading and learning to read, but we need not, indeed should not, think that we can do it alone. Reading and re-reading in the company of others experiencing the same transformations yields both communion and understanding. When we are thwarted by dense hermeneutic texts, we must seek other writers, whose life-long devotion to hermeneutics yields dependable and accessible translations. Our gratitude for scholars like Nicholas Davey, John Caputo, Richard Kearney, and Jean Grondin shows in our writing. We learn from them that there are many ways to read Heidegger and Gadamer, for example, and "reading around them," and reading against them even – their critics – is a useful way to deepen our understanding of the work from the point of view of the progenitor, the advocate, and the critic.

In all of this kind of reading, it becomes possible to turn Gadamer's work this way and that, to engage in the patient shifting Payne (1997) talked about, to experience hermeneutic texts from our own and others' viewpoints, and even to read Gadamer against Gadamer, to test what he says carefully. We believe Gadamer would not want it any other way. Hermeneutics is an unsettled discipline and necessarily an unsettling discipline. Every assertion about what hermeneutics is anticipates a critical response from the world of action and other readers of that world (Davey, 2006). No one who practices hermeneutics is excused from this kind of exchange. Developing defensible hermeneutic practice is part and parcel of "knowing one's way around" the subject matter, but also imagining a different way around in a different field of action. Being disciplined by the world, and from the trials and tribulations of reading, serves to "steady the motion" (and commotion) of hermeneutic practice.

5. The nature of hermeneutic practice is dialogical

In the two previous points, we have attempted to demonstrate the nature of the dialogue that constitutes our relation with the world, with others, and with self. It is not the case that dialogue is simply a tool, a technique for hermeneutics, but fundamental to our existence. Like understanding, it is who we are. Our interpretive relationships in the world are dialogic: the world speaks to us, and most importantly, we listen to its address. The nature of hermeneutic experience is dialogical, in that it enters into a relationship with the unusual and the strange and is transformed by it. Hermeneutics is dialogical in its orientation because it takes the view that the other might be right. Hermeneutics is dialogical in its intent because it seeks, not to have the last word, but to keep the conversation going. Hermeneutics is dialogical in its method in that it is driven by the interplay of question and answer.

Summary

In this chapter, we have attempted to examine Davey's (2006) notion of the "will to method," understanding that the received definition of method, the "natural attitude" we have inherited, is a historical construction. If this is true, then we need to remember that method can be constructed other-wise.

Second, we have made a case for treating hermeneutics as a practice driven not by formal logic, but by the way revealed by carefully examining the phenomenon, by a practice driven by substance and not procedure. We have also argued that hermeneutics be guided by practical wisdom, by decision making and deliberation with others, oriented toward right action, and not by the formal logic of scientific method. It is not method that we are against, but the fact that we are committed to the recovery of its phenomenological and hermeneutic dimensions.

Third, we have made a case for cases, for staying close to the lifeworld, "to work phenomenologically" as Gadamer would say. Life can only be understood from the inside, in witnessing its performance, or how it unfolds in action. Hermeneutics depends on finding good cases of "life unfolding in action" for us to build good cases for our interpretations. Hermeneutics also depends on the power of good cases for us to learn from and deepen our experience.

Fourth, we have argued that being open to our encounters in the world requires vigilance to develop "the discipline of attending to things" (Dostal, 2001, p. 251). This is so that we can be disciplined by the contingencies of life, "to be hard-hearted and work 'from below' " (Caputo, 1987, p. 3).

Fifth, we have insisted that hermeneutic practice be disciplined and methodical, to establish its validity in intelligent, "in-formed" (formed from within) action. This so that our understanding yields new, significant, and reliable insights into the subject matters of the world (Davey, 2006) – the subjects that influence who we are and how we act.

Sixth, we have made a plea for learning to read hermeneutically so that we can be literate in our practice. We have argued that being literate in our practice is in the service of becoming disciplined and methodical in our actions.

Last, we have pointed to a fundamental way of being in the world, the way of dialogical encounter, to bring to light "the method that we are," and to bring to attention to the ceaseless motion of our understanding that sits under all our methods.

References

Bernstein, R. (1983). *Beyond objectivism and relativism: Science, hermeneutics and praxis.* Philadelphia, PA: University of Pennsylvania Press.

Bordo, S. (1987)75. *The flight to objectivity: Essays on Cartesianism and culture.* Albany, NY: SUNY Press.

Caputo, J. (1987). *Radical hermeneutics.* Bloomington, IN: Indiana University Press.

Davey, N. (2006). *Unquiet understanding.* Albany, NY: SUNY Press.

Dostal, R. (2002). Gadamer's relation to Heidegger and phenomenology. In C. Guignon (Ed.), *The Cambridge companion to Gadamer* (pp. 247–266). New York, NY: Cambridge University Press.

Gadamer, H-G. (1983). *Reason in the age of science* (F.G. Lawrence, Trans.). Cambridge, MA: MIT Press.

Gadamer, H-G. (1960/1989) *Truth and method* (2nd rev. ed.) (J. Weinsheimer & D. G. Marshall, Trans.). New York, NY: Seabury Press.

Gadamer, H-G. (1999). *Hermeneutics, religion and ethics.* New Haven, CT: Yale University Press.

Gadamer, H-G. (2001). *Gadamer in conversation: Reflections and commentary* (R. Palmer, Ed.). New Haven, CT: Yale University Press.

Harmon, G. (2007). *Heidegger explained.* Chicago, IL: Open Court.

Heidegger, M. (1923/1999). Ontology: The hermeneutics of facticity. Indiana, IA: Indiana University Press.

Madison, G. (1988). *The hermeneutics of postmodernity.* Bloomington: Indiana University Press.

Moules, N. J., Jardine, D. W., McCaffrey, G., & Brown, C. B. (2013). "Isn't all of oncology hermeneutic?" *Journal of Applied Hermeneutics,* Article 3.

Nietzsche, F. (1968). *The will to power* (W. Kaufmann & R. J. Hollingdale, Trans.). New York, NY: Random House.

Payne, M. (1997). *Reading knowledge.* Malden, MA: Blackwell Publishers.

Ricoeur, P. (1991). *From text to action* (K. Blamey & J. Thompson, Trans). Evanston, IL: Northwestern University Press.

Risser, J. (1997). *Hermeneutics and the voice of the other.* Albany, NY: SUNY Press.

van Manen, M. (1990). *Researching lived experience.* London, ON, Canada: Althouse Press.

Weinsheimer, J. (1985). *Gadamer's hermeneutics: A reading of Truth and Method.* New Haven, CT: Yale University Press.

· 5 ·

THE ADDRESS OF THE TOPIC[1]

"Understanding begins when something addresses us" (Gadamer, 1960/1989, p. 299). The conduct of a research study guided by the tenets of Gadamerian philosophical hermeneutics rarely has a definitive starting point or endpoint, but if one had to delineate a place where inquiry begins, it is often around the experience of being addressed personally about something at work in one's life or practice. An address is the feeling of being caught in some aspect of the world's regard, of being called or summoned. In this chapter, we speak to the experience and importance of the address of a topic in the working out of a hermeneutic inquiry.

What Is an Address?

Addresses catch us off guard and break through our regular routines. They cause us to pause and take note, ask not that we speak or do something immediately, but rather that we stop and listen. It is through this process of listening, or what Bruns (1992) called "reading with our ears" (p. 157), that the topic of inquiry often arrives. To listen when we are addressed means that we are vulnerable and open, that we are prepared to be guided by a topic and its own form of address, rather than assumed versions of it, or by a pre-determined method. As stated previously in this book, it is not the case that there is not a method in hermeneutics, but rather, that *method serves the topic and is informed by the topic.* The question becomes one of how we serve the topic in a disciplined way. How are we to be disciplined by the topic? In other words, the topic asks for rigor from us, an attentiveness, and a discipline to stay with it and stay true to it.

An address functions to interrupt or unsettle our everyday taken-for-grantedness of things. This is why it arrives typically in the form of a question or set of questions. As Dunne (1993) explained: "There is often a *suddenness* about it that makes us say that a question 'comes' to us, that it 'arises', or 'presents itself'"(p. 135). There is a case though that an address might not always be sudden; instead, it may have lingered for years and nagged in maybe not quite noticeable ways. However, there is a process of actually "waking up" to this or starting to pay attention to it and to begin to question. Bergum (1991) explained what it is that generates questions, and the effects they have:

> Questioning indicates the existence of an unsettled issue, a difficult matter, an un-certainty, a matter for discussion. It also invites a reply, a dialogue, a searching out of opportunities and similarities. It opens possibilities and leads, in some sense, to uncertainty, for it throws what may have been thought secure into dis-equilibrium or imbalance. (p. 57)

The address that occurs is a substantive one. We are hailed by subject matter, or better stated perhaps, *a subject that matters* so that, when we are addressed, we are obligated to respond, not in "any old fashion," but to respond to the best of our abilities, to do the right thing, in the right way, as Gadamer would say.

When a topic shows itself, *it haunts us*, because it also "hides" itself. It is, as Bergum has alluded to, shrouded in mystery. As a result, we are called to the mystery of the topic, to do justice to the questions that it can raise in us, to approach it care-fully, with both curiosity and suspicion, suspense and intent, discipline and free play. In hermeneutics, tenants with proper names inhabit topics; they are things of human concern, and also, things that have concern for us, that is, living things that literally make a difference in our lives.

Address, as experienced, can be a breathtaking and breath-sustaining gift. When it arrives, it asks that the researcher suffer the mysteries of the topic — and this means to put what they believe at risk, to be open to learning from risking what matters, and most importantly, to speak of this in human terms, to do well by "the tenants" that greet you at the portal. Thus, the servitude demanded by a topic is not primarily methodical, but rather ethical in nature (Caputo, 1993); it is a call of our conscience, that comes with an obligation to respond to the call of *what should be done*, and not simply, as can occur in the natural sciences, *what can be done*.

> Obligation is the event of someone; of something personal in the midst of this inarticulate hum…Events happen anonymously, like the roar of the surf, while obligation is like the cry of a small child who has lost his way on the beach calling for help. (Caputo, 1993, p. 246)

The obligation to respond to the call of the topic is not simply a question of "how do I broach my topic?" but rather, "how do I cultivate what is already there?" — existing, speaking, opinionated, teasing, and teeming with mystery. In responding to this address, there is a sense of an opening, or as Heidegger might have suggested, a clearing, and the promise of being transformed by a living, provocative conversation that was already underway. Conversational topics, then, have entrails; they are historically located, and we must listen carefully to pick up on the entrails. In this way, the topics are not new; they are already at play. Hermeneutic inquiry demands that, as late arrivers to a conversation, we both let what is at play move us forward, and that we join in moving it forward.

This demands attention. Davey (2013) suggested that "being attentive… implies that one knows one is being addressed and that one's self understanding is caught up in the entailments of that address" (p. 80). He further offered that attentiveness has aspects of passivity and activity in the vulnerability to the topic and the responsiveness of addressing it with "patience and focus" (p. 80). Akin to the notion of obligation, Davey claimed that "attending is also profoundly ethical: it is a practice through which the one who attends changes" (p. 83).

The Substance of a Topic

What constitutes a topic? In practice professions, such as nursing, social work, psychology, and education, topics are often grounded in the field of practice. They have a place, a geographical territory, so to speak, in which they dwell. For example, a psychologist might be struck by the notion of shame in eating disorders, a nurse by the experiences of having nursed children who sometimes die, an educator by the coding and naming of "slow learners," or a social worker by the issue of child abuse. Practitioners *suffer these things in their practice*.

Within each practice, there are as many topics as there are questions, but not all topics are experienced as a form of address. Even the ones that do address us are partially hidden from us because of our *prejudices*, as Gadamer (1969/1989) would say, or to paraphrase Heidegger (1927/1962), by our practical involvement with the things themselves. To use Heidegger's example, one cannot properly notice or understand running for the bus when one is running for the bus. One starts to notice a topic when one is "pulled up short" (Gadamer, 1969/1989), when we miss the bus, so to speak, and are left breathless in its disappearing exhaust. In the same way, one is not often aware of health except in its absence (Gadamer, 1996). Unless something like this happens to us – *and* we do not *will* it to happen – we often continue in our practices in unquestioning ways, assuming taken-for-granted discourses and ways of being around what we do in everyday practice. It is, however, the disruption of success in our everyday practices that allows a topic to emerge, in completely familiar, but also strange and disrupting ways.

For example, one of the authors (Moules, 2002, 2003, 2009a, 2009b) was involved in family therapy work and practiced using therapeutic letters as a routine part of the clinical work. It continued to amaze her to witness the power of the written communication in a practice that had its tradition in the power of talk, and yet the written communication seemed to have a different and sometimes even stronger influence. She was struck with how even family members who might not immediately been seen as particularly "literary," were captivated by the letters and moved to extremes of keeping them in bedside drawers or, in one case, framing them. This disruption of the familiar and the kind of amazement that goes with it, a puzzlement, wondering, and passion for understanding, represents the call of topics.

As we have said, discerning what constitutes a topic requires that we first listen to its call, and then to work out how we might best answer. At times, the topics are too immense and unanswerable; these do not lend themselves to a hermeneutic study. If the topic is, for example, "why do children die?" one can imagine that this is not a question that any amount of hermeneutic research (or any other kind of research) could offer an answer. However, inside of this existential and unanswerable question lies other topics and questions that can be addressed, such as "How might we understand oncology nurses' experiences of working with children who sometimes die?" or "What is it like for the parents of children who die, or the grandparents of children who die?" Each of these topics is different, but the same in this way: each requires the "voice of the other" (Risser, 1997). For us to understand, each requires that we engage with those who have lived through the experience so that we might learn from them. Davey (2006) suggested that this also involves speculative thought and speculative thought involves being "caught up in the motion of ideas, and...arrested by them" (p. 113).

Topics involve a phenomenon or sometimes many phenomena, yet hermeneutic research is not the same as pure phenomenological research in that the goal is not to essentialize, define, or even simply describe the topic. The goal is not to carve away at all the extremities of the phenomenon of interest to reach an essence or core, to achieve an uncontaminated description of it stripped of its context. Rather, the desire is to conserve the topic in all of its complexity, in the words of Caputo, " to restore it to its original difficulty" (1987, p. 1). As stated, very often our practices go unnoticed and unexamined, lost to discourse, assumption, and involvement; often they remain in the state of being taken-for-granted. When the address of a topic arrives, it troubles something and problematizes it. When this happens, the work becomes about "exoticizing the domestic" (White, 1993, p. 35), taking what is assumed and unquestioned and looking at it as something new and exotic. This involves looking at it from fresh perspectives, trying to understand it differently, while still preserving the topic's integrity, the whole of it, as it lives in the world.

In looking to a topic, to understand a topic while conserving its complexity, we are not searching for an essence; rather this is an act of truth-seeking – of looking for what might be true in and of the topic. This does not mean to imply that there is one "Truth" to be known about topics but rather that we stay true to the work of aletheia in unconcealing topics in all of their messiness and richness.

The Hermeneutic Notion of Truth

We admit, up front, that any discussion of truth is difficult and tricky, partly because truth in research, and this holds for a lot of inquiry that would be called "qualitative," is often thought of *only* as correspondence between thought and world, between an "inner" and "outer" representation of the thing itself. There is no inner and outer in hermeneutic research, in the sense of an unbridgeable chasm between self and world. We are, as Heidegger (1927/1962) maintained, always in the world, and hermeneutic research is always about understanding, about what it means to be in the world in a particular way.

This is to say that, as practitioners, we are deeply involved in our practices, and it is only through our practical, everyday involvement that the truth, that is, *the meaning of something*, becomes available at all (Heidegger, 1927/1962; Wrathall, 2013).

Truth, at least the truth about being human and human practice, is also tricky because it is located in time and place. It can and does change (and stay the same) over time and between places. Hermeneutic truth is plural, not singular, in this way: *There is not one right way* to help all patients recover from cancer, for example, or a single method for helping every child learn to read. At the same time, *not every way is right*. We *can* get it wrong; we can make people sicker in trying to help them heal. We can make learning to read impossible; while trying to teach, we can deceive ourselves thoroughly and fall into untruth (Wrathall, 2013) in the very pursuit of truth. The history of nursing and education is littered with such examples. Finally (here at least), truth is tricky in hermeneutic work because it disappears as it appears. We never get "the whole truth and nothing but the truth," because *truth is both revealed to us and concealed from us at once*. This is why Gadamer, following his teacher Heidegger, appropriated the notion of truth as *aletheia* for hermeneutic work.

Hermeneutic work is more about conservation than preservation. To preserve something is to hold it in all its sameness, to protect and save it from spoiling, and changing, *to kill it*, whereas to conserve something means *to keep it alive*, to keep it from being damaged, lost, or wasted (Websters online). In our efforts to conserve a topic, to not allow it to be lost or forgotten as something simply accepted, the unconcealment and enlivening that comes with truth necessarily comes into play. As mentioned earlier, hermeneutics is the practice of *aletheia*, the event of unconcealment and unhiddenness (Caputo, 1987, p. 115; Coltman, 1998). Aletheia first occurs when we are addressed, when something opens which was once closed, when we become aware of something that was not there as being there. Aletheia can be represented by the metaphor of opening the lid of a well, of flipping the lid open and letting it rest so one can look into what lies beneath it. In this opening of one side, another side is closed, for with every opening there is closure and some things are necessarily left behind. The opposite of Lethe and lethal, aletheia works against what is dead or forgotten; it enlivens and remembers. Aletheia is the clearing of things into the mystery beneath; it is the "ongoing, historical, epochal process by which things emerge from concealment into unconcealment" (Caputo, 1987, p. 177). The three meanings then of aletheia are a portal or opening, an enlivening, and a remembering. When topics address us, they open something, they call on us to remember why it is that certain things matter, and they ask us to bring these things alive in the here and now of our lives.

The Centrality of the Notion of Phronesis to Hermeneutic Work

Gadamer was committed to staying close to concrete, factual life. His approach focused on *understanding life as it is lived* and, for Gadamer, that meant achieving an understanding of how to act well in concrete, particular circumstances. This is why he based his notion of understanding on the form of knowledge the Greeks called *phronesis*, because it provided him with a notion of practical knowledge, knowledge in action, that remains *experiential* through and through (Davey, 2006). Dunne (1993) elaborated:

> ...phronesis is a habit of *attentivenesss* that makes the resources of one's past experience flexibly available to one, and at the same time allows the present situation to 'unconceal' its own particular significance—which it may do comfortably within the terms of one's experience or else only by evincing as insight, which while it could not occur without one's past experience, still transcends, and so enriches it. (pp. 305–306)

So while it is true that we can be struck by something, addressed in a way that opens a topic for us, it is only through a "habit of attentiveness" that we can keep the topic open, that we can follow the direction implied in the questions that arise, and learn from the event of being addressed. The role of deliberation in this process is key, and holds an important position in Gadamer's (1960/1989) description of phronesis. In the following, we offer examples of the work of phronesis in its experiential understanding of "life as it is lived" in everyday practices.

Examples of Topics and How They Arrived

The hermeneutic experience of being addressed, of grasping that there is clearly something true about what is being said, involves, first: recognizing something that one was already acquainted with but had not fully grasped, and second: in reappropriating what had not been initially grasped, coming to realize its significance for the first time. (Davey, 2006, p. 117)

Example A

Doubled and Silenced: Grandparents' Experiences of Childhood Cancer (Moules, Laing, McCaffrey, Tapp, & Strother, 2012; Moules, McCaffrey, Laing, Tapp, & Strother, 2012).

Working in pediatric oncology, both Laing and Moules knew firsthand how cancer is a family affair. Childhood cancer affects not only a cell, but a body, a life, relationships, and communities. There has been much research done on the experiences of siblings of children with cancer and parents, but very little attention to the extended family, in this case, the grandparents. A part of the address of this topic was that, a few years ago, Moules had the experience of having her only child in the Intensive Care Unit due to an acute cardiac crisis. He is also the only grandchild of her parents and she became aware of how her parents were not only suffering and worrying for their grandson, but also their own daughter and her fears and concerns. They, however, did not want to burden her with their worries so this doubled concern was suffered silently and alone. Grandparents of children with cancer live this duality and the study invited voice to an experience that had been, to some extent, silenced.

Example B

"It's not just camp": Understanding the Meaning of Children's Cancer Camps for Children and Families (Laing, 2012; Laing, 2013; Laing & Moules, 2013; Laing & Moules, 2014; Laing & Moules (2014); Laing & Moules (in press)).

Laing credits a short film about cancer camp, shown in the second year of her undergraduate nursing degree, as the impetus to get into the field of pediatric oncology. It was a simple film showing children with cancer attending camp, supplemented by interviews with several children, and nurses who were attending as camp counselors. While the details are forgettable, she never forgot that moment in time when, as she described, "pediatric oncology chose me." As she traversed through her clinical career in pediatric oncology, Laing was struck by how important camp was for kids with cancer and their families. She never understood why camp was so important, why the kids started talking about summer camp shortly after Christmas trying to gauge the likelihood they could go the same week as their friends, or that they would not be too sick to go for one of the weeks. While she did not understand why, the fact that camp seemed such a profound experience for most kids and families always stuck with her. After deciding to pursue doctoral studies, and struggling at first to identify a topic for research, Laing eventually came back to the idea of camp. She wanted to understand what it was that made camp so special, so important for these families, and why it mattered. It was camp, after all, that had claimed her in the first place.

Example C

The Case of the Disappearing/Appearing "Slow Learner": An Interpretive Mystery (Williamson, 2012; 2015; Williamson & Field, 2014a, 2014b; Williamson & Paul, 2012a, 2012b).

As someone who, as a student, struggled academically in ways that would align with Alberta's current definitions of educational disability, as a parent of a child with a Down Syndrome, and as a teacher/coordinator of disability services at a large urban high school, Williamson had been experiencing disability for most of his life. His impetus for entering doctoral studies was to interpret the assumptions and practices involved in working with slow learners, a particular category of students who are predicted by way of intelligence testing to struggle in school but for whom the Albertan special education system has granted no formal support. Williamson had been teaching in an instructional tier aimed at these students for many years and had come to see how this category on the border of disability exposes the frequent rigidity of educational thinking about disability and intellectual potential. Tools meant to address student diversity and disability categories can, ironically, become unwieldy, imposing further restraint on a system that is already too inflexible for all students. Despite this, Williamson has also been privileged to bear witness to the transcendent moments when generous teaching practices meet engaged learners, and disability categories, at least in their deficit framings, disappear. It is the appearing and disappearing of categories that finally called out to Williamson, who is also a life-long fan of detective fiction, as way of framing the complexities of this topic. He chose to present his research in this area as a "hard-boiled" detective story: "*The Case of the Disappearing/Appearing Slow Learner.*"

Example D

Understanding Nurse-Patient Relationships on Acute Mental Health Units, Buddhist Perspectives (McCaffrey, 2012; McCaffrey, Raffin Bouchal, & Moules, 2012).

While working in an interdisciplinary position on a mental health unit, McCaffrey was struck by contrasting perceptions of how nurses did their work. Nurses saw themselves as having good therapeutic relationships with patients, while team members including occupational therapists, social workers, and psychiatrists often felt frustrated that nurses seemed under-informed about patients, and their work with them was undirected. After starting to explore more deeply the question of how nurses work with patients on mental health units, McCaffrey became aware of how much his nursing practice was informed by an earlier experience of working in a therapeutic community, in which relationship was the medium of care and change was paramount. The topic was, at the same time, formed by a study of Zen Buddhist traditions of thought and practice, which offered new ways of looking at nursing. Obvious affinities between Buddhism and nursing, such as practicing with suffering and compassion, became a starting point for deeper and more complex exploration.

Example E

"Do You Think the Angels Will Speak Spanish?": Nurses' Experiences of Death in *Pediatric Oncology* (Morck, 2014).

Morck's (2009) previous work, which will be described in the following section in this chapter, was looking at the emotional marks that happen to psychiatric nurses after hearing stories of trauma and suffering. As her clinical work shifted to the area of oncology rather than mental health, she became addressed by the impact on pediatric oncology nurses when children die as they can do in this population. The work of Rashotte (2005) in *Dwelling With the Stories That Haunt Us* spoke to her about the ways that loss haunts and marks, not just the family of children with cancer, but also those professionals who care for them.

Speaking for the Address

How do you write about address? Topics start somewhere and most often they start with an instance. This instance needs to be described in the work as a way of locating and populating the topic with a living example that shows it for all its power. An example of this is the paper published in the *Journal of Applied Hermeneutics*, "Isn't All Oncology Hermeneutic?" (Moules, Jardine, McCaffrey, & Brown, 2013). Although the paper does not reflect a research study, it is a response to the critique that has been made about the relatively small numbers of participants that often appear in hermeneutic research, and an argument about the fit of hermeneutics as a research method that attempts to understand practice and phenomena that arise within practice. The authors of this work start by describing an instance that gave rise to the discussion – an arrival of the topic. In this case, the topic was about hermeneutics, numbers, power, and verification through numbers in contrast to the "fecundity of the individual case" (Jardine, 1992). Throughout the paper then, the discussion of theory and philosophy had to also be instantiated and Moules et al. did so through two very powerful descriptions of the experience of an oncologist and his patients.

In the introduction of topics in hermeneutic research, most often there is a story around the arrival of the topic, a narrative of dialectic with the topic and a reason as to why the topic matters to the researcher, and an instantiation of the meaningfulness and call of the topic. In a master's thesis hermeneutic study by Morck (2009) entitled *"Right There, in the Midst of it with Them": Impacts of the Therapeutic Relationship on Nurses*, she was attempting to understand the topic of the impact on mental health nurses of hearing stories of pain, suffering, and trauma. In the thesis, she recounted being a young, new nurse and starting her work in a hospital inpatient mental health unit. Very early in her career, she recalled encountering one of the patients she was working with cowering in the corner of her room. As she approached and engaged in conversation with the patient, she was to hear a terrible story of abuse where the patient claimed that the rain outside the window smelled of urine. Following this seemingly incomprehensible statement, Morck gently knelt down with the patient and asked her more about how the rain smelled like urine. The patient proceeded to tell her an event she remembered: she was five years old, just raped by her father and his friend, thrown down the steps, urinated on, and then they left out the door. It was raining outside. Morck discussed how this instance was one of many that had a profound impact on her as a new and young nurse hearing of such suffering. Hearing stories like this one and countless others was then the address that called her to her research, a topic full of complexity and obligation to do well with it.

Topics cannot just matter to the researcher alone; they must be something relevant in the world. They are not selfish indulgences, trying to work out something individually for individual curiosity, gain, or even therapy, but rather a working out that is meaningful in relation to the phenomena that surround it. It is not just Morck who experienced the weight of hearing and bearing stories of pain and suffering but other psychiatric nurses who hear and bear the same responsibility – and it is not just psychiatric nurses. Social workers bear witness to stories of violence and abuse. Teachers hear stories of children's child abuse, stories of torture and escape from war torn counties. No one profession owns what has been referred to as "vicarious trauma" (see for e.g., Figley, 1995; Mathieu, 2011).

Asking Questions of the Address: Developing Research Questions

Out of topics, one needs to narrow and focus a research question. In hermeneutics, there is a particular kind of flavor to the question. One would not necessarily seek an ontological question such as "What is something," as hermeneutics is not in search of phenomenological essences. It is not intended to shave off extremities to narrow something down to a definition of what it is or is not. Rather than definition or explanation, it is in search of understanding and interpretation, looking for possible and good ways to understand a particular topic.

More hermeneutic in intent than a "what is" question are questions that imply interpretation. A question such as "how might we understand the meaning of children's cancer camps for children and families?" would be a question that aims for meaning, interpretation, and understanding rather than assessment or measurement of impact.

In a similar way, hermeneutics does not set out to develop theories or templates so a research topic that might be described as, for example, "Developing a Theory of New Social Workers Learning" would not be consistent with the way we have taken up hermeneutic research. The title of the study and the guiding research question then must show integrity with the philosophy that informs it. This is an important point of congruency. If one develops a question that is unanswerable from a hermeneutic perspective, such as "Why do children die?," the credibility of the work is compromised and incomprehensible.

The process of determining one definitive research question is often one that is under the gaze and demand of funding bodies and granting bodies, but in many ways, it is counterintuitive to hermeneutics. Questions beget questions and the answer to a question is only one response. We are reminded that Gadamer (1960/1989) suggested that hermeneutics is the answer to a question that could have been answered differently. The research question that began the research is sometimes forced to change, given the shifts in thinking that arise as the researcher engages with the data. Research questions are only intended to guide the research and serve the topic and, often as the study progresses, the question becomes clearer.

Speaking to the Address: What Constitutes Data in Hermeneutic Research?

Understanding *begins* with an address but it only begins there. Understanding about a topic has to be cultivated. Everything is potential data if it helps to further the interpretation of the questionability of the topic. Data may come in the form of photographs, art, poetry, textbooks, policy, newspaper articles, scholarly literature, philosophical texts, literary texts, conversations, or any other medium. Address spreads outwards as the interconnections of the topic become apparent. It is another mark of the relevance of effective hermeneutic work when a topic is seen to live in worlds of shared cultures.

One can conduct a hermeneutic study without the traditional qualitative method of interviewing participants, but there has to be a good demonstration that researchers have gone beyond only their own perception and reflections of the topic. Very often, however, this kind of research strives toward involving conversation, the Latin of which is "conversa," which means to turn around together. Gadamer (1960/1989) took up the notion of dialogue as central to hermeneutics. Hermeneutics is dialectic, a "fusion of horizons" that cannot happen alone. For example, to understand a topic such as grandparents' experiences of childhood cancer, there are many portals of understanding but the most obvious is by engaging in research conversations with grandparents directly.

Once a topic has emerged, it opens up to a process of inquiry that attempts to conserve it in all its complexity and pursues it through its associations and connections to the world – with the conscientious intention to remain rooted in the original human situation and to bring back to those involved some new and sustaining ways of understanding themselves. Address signals the complexity that lies beneath the surface of everyday activity. Borrowing from the lexicon of grounded theory, where data "saturation" indicates an end to data collection, by contrast, hermeneutic inquiry begins in saturation, with a topic that is already overloaded.

As mentioned, often in hermeneutic research, data are collected through interviews. Understanding only begins with an address; the address then summons the researcher to move into the conduct of the study in order to obtain answers to the questions that arise. In the next chapter, we discuss the selection of participants, and the nature, skill, and focus of interviews to collect rich data fertile for interpretive analysis and very necessary in the conduct of this kind of research.

Summary

In the bigger picture of the conduct of hermeneutic inquiry, we start here with the experience of "address" – the ways one is called by topics, invited into positions of curiosity and wonder, tethered by what is known, and untethered by the possibilities of what remains to be discovered. Address is the call to dis- and un-covery as well as the call to recovery of what was forgotten. It is the beacon that summons and lures us to topics, but also the quiet warning and reminder that we are obligated to do well by them.

Note

1. It should be noted that a version of this chapter has been previously published in the Journal of Applied Hermeneutics and is reprinted with permission.

References

Bergum, V. (1991). Being a phenomenological researcher. In J. Morse (Ed.), *Qualitative nursing research* (pp. 43–57). Newbury Park, CA: Sage.

Bruns, G. L. (1992). *Hermeneutics ancient and modern*. London, UK: Yale University Press.

Caputo, J. D. (1987). *Radical hermeneutics: Repetition, deconstruction and the hermeneutic project*. Bloomington, IN: Indiana University Press.

Caputo, J. D. (1993). *Against ethics: Contributions to a poetics of obligation with constant reference to deconstruction*. Bloomington, IN: Indiana University Press.

Coltman, R. (1998). *The language of hermeneutics: Gadamer and Heidegger in dialogue*. Albany, NY: SUNY Press.

Conserve. (n.d.). In Merriam-Webster's online dictionary. Retrieved from http://www.merriam-webster.com/dictionary/conserve

Davey, N. (2006). *Unquiet understanding: Gadamer's philosophical hermeneutics*. Albany, NY: SUNY Press.

Davey, N. (2013). *Unfinished worlds: Hermeneutics, aesthetics and Gadamer*. Edinburgh, Scotland: Edinburgh University Press.

Dunne, J. (1993). *Back to the rough ground: Practical judgment and the lure of technique*. Notre Dame, IA: University of Notre Dame Press.

Figley, C. R. (1995). *Compassion fatigue: Coping with secondary traumatic stress disorder in those who treat the traumatized*. New York, NY: Routledge, Taylor & Francis Group.

Gadamer, H-G. (1960/1989). *Truth and method* (2nd rev. ed.) (J. Weinsheimer & D. G. Marshall, Trans.). New York, NY: Continuum.

Gadamer, H-G. (1996). *The enigma of health: The art of healing in a scientific age*. Stanford, CA: Stanford University Press.

Heidegger, M. (1927/1962). *Being and time* (J. M. E. Robinson, Trans.). New York, NY: Harper and Row.

Hoad, T. F (Ed.). (1986). *The concise Oxford dictionary of English etymology*. New York, NY: Oxford University Press.

Jardine, D. W. (1992). The fecundity of the individual case: Considerations of the pedagogic heart of interpretive work. *Journal of Philosophy of Education, 26*(1), 51–61.

Laing, C. M. (2012). In play, at play. *Journal of Applied Hermeneutics*, Article 6, http://hdl.handle.net/10515/sy5474766

Laing, C. M. (2013). *"It's not just camp": Understanding the meaning of children's cancer camps for children and families*. Unpublished doctoral research, University of Calgary, Calgary, AB, Canada.

Laing, C. M., & Moules, N. J. (2013). The island of misfit toys. *Journal of Applied Hermeneutics*, Article 8, http://hdl.handle.net/10515/sy5js9hq4

Laing, C. M., & Moules, N. J. (2014). Children's cancer camps: A sense of community, a sense of family. *Journal of Family Nursing, 20*(2), 185–203.

Laing, C. M., & Moules, N. J. (2014). Stories from cancer camp: Tales of glitter and gratitude. *Journal of Applied Hermeneutics*, Article 3, http://hdl.handle.net/10515/sy5qf8k16

Laing, C. M., & Moules, N. J. (in press). Children's cancer camps: A way to understand grief differently. *Omega: Journal of Death and Dying*.

Mathieu, F. (2011). *The compassion fatigue workbook: Creative tools for transforming compassion fatigue and vicarious traumatization*. New York, NY: Routledge, Taylor & Francis Group.

McCaffrey, G. P. (2012). *Nurse patient relationship and Buddhist thought*. Unpublished doctoral thesis, University of Calgary, Calgary, AB, Canada.

McCaffrey, G. P., Raffin Bouchal, S., & Moules, N. J. (2012). Buddhist thought and nursing A hermeneutic exploration. *Nursing Philosophy, 13*, 87–97.

Morck, A. (2009). *"Right There, in the Midst of It with Them": Impacts of the Therapeutic Relationship on Nurses*. Unpublished master's thesis, University of Calgary, Calgary, AB, Canada.

Morck, A. (2014). *"Do You Think the Angels Will Speak Spanish?": Nurses' Experiences of Death in Pediatric Oncology*. Unpublished doctoral thesis, University of Calgary, Calgary, AB, Canada.

Moules, N. J. (2002). Nursing on paper: Therapeutic letters in nursing practice. *Nursing Inquiry, 9*(2), 104–113.

Moules, N. J. (2003). Therapy on paper: Therapeutic letters and the tone of relationship. *Journal of Systemic Therapies, 22*(1), 33–49.

Moules, N. J. (2009a). Therapeutic letters in nursing: Examining the character and influence of the written word in clinical work with families experiencing illness. *Journal of Family Nursing, 15*(1), 31–49.

Moules, N. J. (2009b). The past and future of therapeutic letters: Family suffering and healing words. *Journal of Family Nursing, 15*(1), 102–111.

Moules, N. J., Jardine, D. W., McCaffrey, G. P., & Brown, C. (2013). "Isn't all oncology hermeneutic?" *Journal of Applied Hermeneutics.* Article 3. http://hdl.handle.net/10515/sy5w95141

Moules, N. J., Laing, C. M., McCaffrey, G., Tapp, D. M., & Strother, D. (2012). Grandparents' experiences of childhood cancer, Part one: Doubled and silenced. *Journal of Pediatric Oncology Nursing, 29*(3), 119–132.

Moules, N. J., McCaffrey, G., Laing, C. M., Tapp, D. M., & Strother, D. (2012). Grandparents' experiences of childhood cancer, Part two: The need for support. *Journal of Pediatric Oncology Nursing, 29*(3), 133–141.

Preserve. (n.d.). In Merriam-Webster's online dictionary. Retrieved from http://www.merriam-webster.com/dictionary/preserve

Rashotte, J. (2005). Dwelling with the stories that haunt us: Building a meaningful nursing practice. *Nursing Inquiry, 12*(1), 34–42.

Risser, J. (1997). *Hermeneutics and the voice of the other.* Albany, NY: SUNY Press.

White, M. (1993). Deconstruction and therapy. In S. Gilligan & R. Price (Eds.), *Therapeutic conversations* (pp. 22–61). New York, NY: W. W. Norton.

Williamson, W. J. (2012). Codes. *Canadian Journal of Disability Studies, North America, 1,* May. http://cjds.uwaterloo.ca/index.php/cjds/article/view/47/50

Williamson, W. J. (2015). *The case of the disappearing/appearing slow learner: An interpretive mystery.* Unpublished doctoral thesis, University of Calgary, Calgary, AB, Canada.

Williamson, W. J., & Field, J. C. (2014b). The case of the disappearing/appearing slow learner: An interpretive mystery. *Journal of Applied Hermeneutics,* Article 4. http://hdl.handle.net/10515/sy53b5wq7

Williamson, W. J., & Paul, W. J. (2012a). The level playing field: Unconcealing diploma exam accommodation policy. *Journal of Applied Hermeneutics,* Article 13. http://hdl.handle.net/10515/sy5f766p2

Williamson, J., & Paul, J. (2012b). The "slow learner" as a mediated construct. *Canadian Journal of Disability Studies, 1*(3), August. http://cjds.uwaterloo.ca/index.php/cjds/article/view/59

Wrathall, M. A. (Ed.). (2013). *The Cambridge companion to Heidegger's Being and Time.* New York: Cambridge University Press.

· 6 ·

CONDUCTING INTERVIEWS
IN HERMENEUTIC RESEARCH

Data in hermeneutic studies are often (though not exclusively) gathered through interviews and cultivated in interpretive analysis. In this chapter, we discuss the conduct, complexity, and nuances of interviewing. Despite claims made by some that there is such a thing as a "hermeneutic interview" (Geanellos, 1999; Vandermause, 2011), we maintain that there is *not* a distinctively unique entity called a hermeneutic interview. Alternately, we claim that there are *good* interviews that generate *good* data, interviews that are conducted thoughtfully, openly, and deliberately to create space for understanding of the topic under inquiry. Conducting interviews in hermeneutic research is a skillful and practiced art, what Kvale and Brinkmann (2009) termed a "craft" that involves "intellectual craftsmanship." By this, they described craftsmanship as a "mastery of a form of production, which requires practical skills and personal insight acquired through training and extensive practice" (p. 86).

Interviews take on particular significance for hermeneutic research, based on the importance of language and conversation in the philosophical background. Heidegger regarded language as a house of being, a house that is big enough to hold many worlds, not just a house that includes some and excludes others. In this regard, we see data for human research as arising from a gathering and harvesting of experience. Heidegger (1975) further suggested that language or *legein* is connected to the German word *legen*, which means to lay down and lay before:

> In *legen*, a "bringing together" prevails: the Latin *legere* understood as *lesen*, in the sense of collecting and bringing together. *Legein* properly means the laying-down and laying-before which gathers itself and others. (p. 60)

> To lay is to gather (*lesen*)…But gathering is more than mere amassing. To gathering belongs a collecting which brings shelter. Accommodation governs the sheltering; accommodation is in turn governed by safekeeping…*legein*…means just this, that whatever lies before us involves us and therefore concerns us. (pp. 61–62)

Gadamer emphasized the dialogic model of conversation and his description of a genuine conversation is often conflated with the description of interviews in hermeneutic work with this widely cited quote:

> We say we 'conduct' a conversation, but the more genuine a conversation is, the less its conduct lies within the will of either partner. Thus a genuine conversation is never the one we wanted to conduct. Rather it is more generally correct to say that we fall into conversation, or even that we become involved in it. The way one word follows another, with the conversation taking its own twists and reaching its own conclusion, may well be conducted in some way, but the partners conversing are far less the leaders of it than the led. No one knows in advance what will 'come out' of a conversation. Understanding or its failure is like an event that happens to us. Thus we can say that something was a good conversation or that it was ill fated. All this shows that a conversation has a spirit of its own, and that language in which it is conducted bears its own truth with it – i.e., that it allows something to 'emerge' which henceforth exists. (Gadamer, 1960/1989, p. 383)

Here, Gadamer was talking about the nature of genuine conversation; he was not describing a therapeutic conversation, which has its own intention, nor was he describing a research interview, which has its own purpose and focus as well. Therefore, we emphatically state that his quote about the conduct of a genuine conversation does not hold fully true for good research interviews. "The research interview is not a conversation between equal partners, because the researcher defines and controls the situation" (Kvale & Brinkmann, 2009, p. 3). Good research interviews *are* conducted and conducted well, even though there *is* an aspect of conversation involved that we discuss.

The Conversational Nature of Interviews

The word conversation comes from the Latin *conversa*, which means "turning around together" and the Latin *conversari* meaning "to dwell with; to keep company with, to wander together with" (Online Etymology Dictionary). Research interviews are not of the same casual nature as that of phatic or social conversations. They have a structure of sorts, and more importantly a purpose. This is not to imply that the interviewer enters with an immutable list of questions, but that the structure is defined by the topic and the interviewer attempts to keep the topic central in the conversation, while "turning around" with the participant. In this turning around, careful and mindful listening and skilled questioning are required.

In the more general qualitative research literature, Morse (1991) called these kinds of interviews "interactive" where the direction of conversation is reciprocal. There is an aspect, at times, of the participants having already interpreted what they are relating, but the researcher can help them move into a deeper interpretation. Kvale and Brinkmann (2009) identified 10 qualities of good interviewers: knowledgeable, structuring, clear, gentle, sensitive, open, steering, critical, remembering, and interpreting (pp. 166–167). To obtain good data, the research is highly dependent on the practiced skill of the interviewer, for the interviewer in this kind of work is the key research instrument. It requires a discernment and instinct around choices of which direction to take the conversation, which leads to follow and which to divert, which statements to probe further, when to engage the participants in interpreting, and ultimately keeping the topic as the focus while respecting the participants, needs to tell their narratives of experience. Letting participants direct the interview is not always in the best service of the topic. It is not *just* about them telling their stories and recreating them or preserving them to explain human experience such as some phenomenological work does, but rather what in their stories and experience has something to say to, and about, the topic. "Yet, this restates Gadamer's problem: how to reconcile participation and critical distance" (Davey, 2013, p. 83). The act of participating while maintaining a distance is a crafted skill that is highly contingent on each circumstance.

The character of these kinds of interviews includes intense listening, finding a balance between allowing the person to finish and bringing attention to what seems most meaningful, avoiding invitations to counsel or teach, recognizing critical junctures, following leads, and curiosity as a means to remain engaged. Participation and conduct, engagement and distance, focus and flexibility are at constant play in the navigation of a good interview.

Gathering Participants

Hermeneutics seeks the best participants on purpose, while remembering that the topic is not the participants, nor should the writing be a portrait of them (Moules, 2002). "Hermeneutic research is not validated by numbers, but by the completeness of examining the topic under study and the fullness and depth to which the interpretation extends understanding" (Moules, 2002, p. 14). "An adequate sample size in qualitative work is one that...results in...a new and richly textured understanding of experience" (Sandelowski, 1995, p. 182). In search of exemplar "cases" or the best participants, we are also faced with the realities and pragmatics of the research process. Ethical approval is often based on the provision that participants will volunteer, not be invited directly, or coerced in any conceivable way. As a result of this, those who volunteer are not necessarily those sought or chosen and do not always offer the "best" data. It has to be considered, however, that those who volunteer do so for a reason and when one listens deeply enough, there is a truth that needs to be heard. This idea will be further discussed in a section included in this chapter.

The Pragmatics of the Interview

Unstructured interviews with guiding questions or areas of curiosity are generally employed in this kind of research. The questions generated before the interview do not have to be asked in all interviews if the direction of the conversation is led elsewhere, but they do help to orient the interviewer to the topic and the research team's curiosities and wonderings related to it. Though "unstructured" in content, the interview is structured in format with careful attention to context, settings, explanations, consents, audiotaping, engagement, process checking, and closure.

Context

The context and focus of the interview must be considered in any hermeneutic work. In fact, hermeneutics is about context and the recognition that phenomena cannot exist uncontextualized. For example, if one were studying children's cancer camps, one would need to attend them, to know them in some way, to have experience of what happens at them, to appreciate the atmosphere, process, and interactions. This is not the same as in ethnography where participant-observation or observation-only is an essential part of the research; it is more of an awareness of the topography of the topic, the *topos*. If one is interested in examining issues of mental health nurses, school principals, or disabilities in schools, one must become "schooled" about the topic. Unlike some other qualitative methods, then, the researcher immerses him or herself in the topic through extensive literature reviews, documents, lyric, novels, media, and anything else that has something to add to the context.

Setting

Typically, it is written in proposals and ethic applications, that the interview will occur at a place and time of the participant's choosing. This indeed is a very generous and open intent, however, not always pragmatically possible. The time and location has to be carefully negotiated to fit both schedules and be in a place that is conducive to the interview. Considerations of privacy, quality of audio recording (public places do not work well because of ambient noise), and convenience for the participants (finding an office at a university campus and parking costs can be deterrent) must be well thought out and negotiated.

Consents and Explanations

Consent forms are legal documents intended to provide full information to the participant regarding the nature of the study, risks and benefits, compensation, confidentiality, and rights of withdrawal. Prior to audio taping, the interviewer must be assured that the participants fully understand the nature of the study and any implications of their involvement in it. Offering an explanation, in addition to clarifying aspects of the consent, helps to focus the participants and the interviewer on the topic and offers a tether to which the interviewer can return throughout the interview process.

Audio Taping

Audio taping of interviews is a standard practice in hermeneutic research, as the interview content is the data and needs to be transcribed verbatim to capture the language of the research conversation, both verbal and non-verbal as much as possible. Hermeneutics is not concerned with a linguistic discourse analysis but there are linguistic and non-verbal aspects that are important to consider such as silences. In the transcription of the oral conversation to text, one attempts to capture these nuances as they may well factor into the interpretation. This will be discussed further in the next chapter.

Engagement

One of the first tasks of the interviewer is to engage the participants and create an atmosphere of comfort and trust where the participants feel safe to articulate their experiences. Some aspects of engagement are simply social courtesies: checking about the time constraints, thanking in advance the participants for taking part in the interview, ensuring that people have immediate needs taken care of such as refreshments or parking, and inquiring about any questions they may have regarding the study or their participation in it. Engagement might also take the form of crafting a genogram (family tree), or ecomap (a graphic representation of a person's or family's relationship with its environment). These tools offer a way to engage in meaningful conversation while eliciting important information about the participant's experience in a non-threatening way (Wright & Bell, 2009).

Process Checks and Unexpected Events

Engagement is an ongoing process that does not simply exist at the beginning of the interview. The interviewer must be conscious of maintaining engagement throughout, allowing for possible interruptions (phone calls, door bells, children), and then re-engaging after such events. Process checks are done periodically throughout the interview, asking the participants if the time allotment is still fine, if the line of questioning is comfortable for them, and how their energy levels are. Depending on the focus of the study, some interviews can be very emotional and the interviewer must have the skill to acknowledge strong emotion and be personally comfortable with it. An interviewer also needs to recognize that silences are important and to be able to sit through them without a pressured need to interject. Upon occasion, the interviewer might note incongruence between words and affect (outward manifestation of feelings), and make a decision about whether to comment on it openly and ask about it, or just to keep a record of it to add to the transcription as a side note. It is important to remember that the *point* of the interview is not therapeutic, but rather is research. This can be a difficult balance to maintain, yet important to keep in mind as a guiding approach to the interview. Where interviews are conducted with more than one person, for example two parents, there are further potential issues that might arise. Where there is disagreement or tension, it requires sophistication on the part of the interviewer to hold it without closing down the conversation.

Closing the Interview

Interviews of this nature typically take between an hour to an hour and a half. At some point, either through time constraint or what appears to be a dwindling of any new information, the interviewer would start to "wind up" the conversation. This is often done by statements such as: "I just have one other thing I want to ask you about but before I do, is there anything you were hoping I would ask that I have not, or anything else you can think of that might be helpful to me?" In the end, the interviewer can also conclude by thanking the participants and assuring them that they have been very helpful. If there is something in particular that has stood out as a new learning for the interviewer, this can also be stated to the participants as evidence that they have contributed and that the interviewer has learned from them. In our experience, participants are often quite concerned whether or not they have said anything of value and are grateful when they hear that they have made a contribution.

Deep Listening, Openness, and Truth

Although we make a distinction between the "genuine conversation" and the research interview, there is an aspect of Gadamer's notion of the genuine conversation that *does* apply to research interviewing. Gadamer maintained that "the possibility that the other person might be right is the soul of hermeneutics" (Gadamer, July 9, 1989, Heidelberg Colloquium, as cited in Grondin, 1994, p. 124). In the famous 1981 encounter between Gadamer and Derrida (Michelfelder & Palmer, 1989), which has been described by many as an "improbable debate," the debate never moved into the realm of conversation. Gadamer's genuine conversation is driven by attention to allowing the subject matter to conduct it, rather than to have either of the conversation partners conduct it. It is aimed at unraveling a truth in regard to a particular subject. This may not involve consensus or agreement but involves a commitment on the part of the conversation partners to remain in the conversation with the aim of gaining insight, not simply to confirm what either already holds to be true. This does apply to research interviews as well, as the interviewer listens to what the participants hold to be true, whether the interviewer agrees or not.

In a similar way but from a very different discipline, Humberto Maturana, a Chilean neurobiologist, suggested that there are two ways we can listen to another. We can listen to see if the other person agrees with what we already know or we can listen to find a truth in what the other person is saying. In the first instance, we are really only listening to ourselves; in the second, we are listening to the other (Maturana, 1988). "Anyone who listens is fundamentally open. Without openness, there is no genuine human relationship and no responsiveness to an...address" (Davey, 2013, p. 84).

Listening well is a fundamental skill for the hermeneutic researcher, and one that is often done poorly. Fiumara (1990) offered that we live in a culture that knows how to speak, but not to listen, and urges us to find balance by attending to the other side of language – listening. However, just as we have stressed the distinction between a therapeutic conversation and research interview, so too does there exist a distinction in the way one listens in a hermeneutic interview. It is not listening the way one might listen to a friend, or to a someone engaged in therapy; it is more purposeful or, said differently, it is with different intent. It is not done to empathize or sympathize (although that might happen anyway); it is done to explore, question further, and understand. When one listens deeply, there is a sense that the person is what one of the authors (Moules) has named being "right behind their eyes" – a presence of attentiveness that is apparent to the other in the conversation. Listening right behind your eyes requires watchfulness, openness, and searching to find a truth in what the other is saying.

Asking Good Questions

Heidegger (1996) suggested that posing a question is disclosure and provides the context of meaning in which a particular inquiry will move. Kvale and Brinkmann (2009) offered two contrasting metaphors for interviewing: the first metaphor is seeing the interviewer as a miner who seeks to uncover buried knowledge without contamination; the second is the interviewer as a traveller who wanders with the participants in conversation on a journey that leads to a tale to be created together and then told upon the traveller's return home. It is the second metaphor that fits most closely with interviews in hermeneutic research, however, we would offer that the traveller is not simply "wandering" but striding very purposefully with the participants in an open conversation that is very much influenced by the posing of good questions.

The art of asking good questions has to be honed and practiced because it is fundamentally important and leads to distinct qualitative differences in richness of the data obtained in the interview. Good questions are carefully crafted, timed well, and are ones that hold the most potential to invite the participants into deep reflection. Good questions cannot always be answered in the moment as they are invitations to reflection and silence is less the sign of a bad question than indication of a phenomenological nod or pause – an experience of being caught in an immediate and often reflective experience of something.

Questioning Possibilities

Questions are tools used by researchers to invite data that is useful and directly related to the focus of understanding the topic being investigated. As stated, the art of knowing how to ask good questions is very much a skill, or as Kvale and Brinkmann (2009) suggested, a craft that can be learned, honed, and developed over time and through practice. There are several different types or categories of questions that are often employed in interviews.

Opening questions. These are questions that lead to descriptions of experience or of the phenomenon under investigation. They generally are open ended and invitational, designed in part to make the participant comfortable and also to move into the focus of the interview. Examples include: "Can you tell me about a time…?"; "Can you recall an occasion when…?"; or "Could you describe in as much detail as you can a situation when…?" Other opening questions might be the invitation for the participants to recount their experiences, as in the example interview later in this chapter, where the parents are asked to tell the story of their daughter Molly's diagnosis and treatment of cancer.

Follow-up and probing questions. As a way of "turning around together" in conversation, the responses given by the participants invite a response from the interviewer. It is here where curiosity motivates the interviewer to "go deeper." Sometimes when we think we know, curiosity shuts down and questions and inquiry end so, therefore, remaining curious is the way to stay open to the newness that comes to meet us. These questions can be of a direct nature such as "That is really interesting. Can you tell me more about that?," or an indirect nature through non-verbals, such as nodding, saying "yes," or "hmmm" or even just saying "and?" to invite the participant to continue. An example of a probing question might be: "You mentioned that you were glad when the Public Health Nurse came to do a home visit, even when you did not expect to see her. What did that say to you that she continued to come? What did you say to yourself about why she did that?"

Interpretive questions. These questions are used to invite the participant into some of their own interpretations of the story/event/experience they are describing. How the participant understands or makes sense of what is being told is often very useful in developing the interviewer and the research team's understanding. It is not about looking for explanations but understandings. Such a question may sound like this: "That is a really useful situation with the school principal that you have just told me about. How do you make sense that you were able to form such a good relationship with her when you didn't with the last principal you worked with?"

Interjections of structure. Though not necessarily a question, these are decisive moves that the interviewer makes that are intended to interrupt and to refocus the interview onto the topic of the inquiry, or to shift to another line of inquiry. It involves a transparency, which makes the interruptions less intrusive and is respectful of the participant. An example might be: "I'm just going to do a little shift here if that's okay with you as there is another area I'm really interested in hearing about. Are you okay with that?" Another example might be to acknowledge the importance of something an interviewee has said and being transparent about setting priorities: "That sounds very important, and I would like to come back to that, but for now, could you say more about…"

Reflexive questions. In 1988, family therapist Karl Tomm, under the influence of the Milan family therapy group, devised and named a cluster of questions that he then termed as interventive questions (Tomm, 1988). Wright and Leahey (1990, 1994, 2000, 2005, 2009, 2013) then incorporated these questions, identifying them as circular questions in family nursing literature. Though intended to be therapeutic in nature, we have learned that the structure of such questions has utility in bringing out important distinctions and a depth of response that is richer than what another style of questioning may elicit. These reflexive questions are unique in their ability to make distinctions, invite reflection, offer or speculate about the perspective of another, and make the connection between the effects of one person's behavior on others. The kinds of questions first offered by Tomm and refined by Wright and Leahey include: *difference questions, behavioral effect questions, observer perspective questions,* and *hypothetical or future oriented questions.*

Difference questions pursue differences in beliefs, relationships, people, time, or behaviors and are useful for drawing distinctions. An example of a difference question might be: "Who of the two of you was most worried about the status of your relationship during that time?" The use of the word "most" is an invitation to reflection that takes the responder deeper than simply asking "Were either of you worried?" *Behavioral effect questions* inquire into the effect of one's behavior on another: "When your daughter would not share with you the news about the latest lab results, what effect did that have on you? What did you say to yourself about her choice to not do so?" An *observer perspective question* is aimed at trying to elicit a person's speculation about what another person might feel, experience, or think. "If your father were to be here right now and I could ask him what he needed from you at the time, what do you think he'd tell me?" Finally, *hypothetical or future oriented questions*, allow the participant a chance to suspend beliefs and entertain other possibilities, inviting an insight into things that may not have previously been available to them. Wright, Watson, and Bell (1996) and Wright and Bell (2009) offered the example of a hypothetical belief question that is particularly useful in this endeavor. Such a question might be of the nature of: "If you were to believe that it was your mothering that gave your daughter the strength to go through her child's cancer experience in the way she has, and that her silence about the lab results is an effort to protect you in some ways, would you be able to understand the silence differently?" A future oriented question might be: "If you look ahead five years, what would you see that would indicate that things were going well for you?" While these questions may well have a therapeutic value for the participants, they are not used or intended for that purpose in research interviews but rather to increase the reflection necessary to offer deep, rich, and useful responses that bring understanding to the topic.

Crossing Boundaries

Hermes had the ability to cross boundaries.

> Like language...he can travel between realms freely – what he wants, he goes after. And it is in his playfulness, irreverence, and disdain for the rules, that his capacities

for seeing things new, for invention, also reside...The power of Hermes is that of change. (Hirshfield, 1997, p. 186)

Interviewing in this kind of inquiry necessarily means stepping over the boundaries and conventions of social conversation. This is not, however, an easy maneuver and it must be done with delicacy and tact. Kvale and Brink-mann (2009) wrote of the ethical nature of these kinds of interviews, which depends on the ability of the interviewer to create a condition where the par-ticipants are safe to talk of personal things and yet aware that what they are saying will be in some form made public. They referred to the work of Sennett (2004), who wrote

> In-depth interviewing is a distinctive, often frustrating craft...the in-depth inter-viewer wants to probe the responses people give. To probe, the interviewer cannot be stonily impersonal; he or she has to give something of himself or herself in order to merit an open response. Yet the conversation lists in one direction; the point is not to talk the way friends do...The craft consists in calibrating social distances without making the subject feel like an insect under the microscope. (pp. 37–38)

Conventions of social conversation in some ways apply to research interviews, such as engagement, listening, and manners, but other rules and boundaries necessarily are broken. An example of this is interrupting to re-focus the in-terview on the topic at hand. Another is asking questions of a personal nature. This is often one of the most challenging skills that new interviewers have to develop, as there is a tendency to fall into practices of polite social conversa-tion and, as a result, opportunities for a depth of data may be missed by the interviewer not being willing to re-focus, interrupt, or to ask about areas that in another context would be seen as intrusive.

Reflexivity of Interviews

As mentioned, interviews in hermeneutic research are unpredictable, gen-erative, and often very powerful experiences for the participants and the in-terviewer alike. The interviewer brings something to the interview, as does the participant, and it is unlikely that either will depart from the interview unchanged as a result. When the topic deals with human concerns and ex-periences, there is often emotion at play. There is also the factor that partic-ipants volunteer for reasons – for wanting to make a contribution, tell their stories, be heard, make changes, or to work things out for themselves – the reasons are varied and individual and therefore the effect of the interview cannot be known in advance or often even during it, as the reflective potential of questions linger. In this regard, ethics boards are rightfully careful and cautious about the sensitivity of such interviews, biding their obligation to protect vulnerable populations and human rights. We would argue along with Corbin and Morse (2003), however, that people who volunteer for such studies do not suffer but rather stand to benefit from the sensitive interview. Years ago, one of the authors (Moules) was asked by an ethics board member around a study about grief: "Do you think it is ethical to make people revisit and talk about their grief?" Her response was "I think it's unethical not to." After all, people who volunteer to talk about their grief already know their own grief. Corbin and Morse wrote that "qualitative research using unstructured interviews poses no greater risk than everyday life and expedited reviews are sufficient" (p. 335).

An Interview Example

Here, we offer excerpts from a blinded transcription of an interview. The topic of this study was to understand the possible ways in which childhood cancer can affect the relationship between the parents of the child with cancer. The interviewer is an experienced researcher as well as having a background in family counseling. The interview transcript is in italics, interspersed with comments in regular font to explain the thinking behind particular questions or statements offered by the interviewer.

The interviewer starts by engaging the participants, in this case, a mother and father of a child who died of cancer. Interviewer = I. Mother = M. Father = F. Deceased daughter = Molly (M).

I: *First I want to start by thanking you very much for contacting me and for being willing to speak of your experience. I believe that takes a lot of courage and it is a generous thing to do.*

F: *We want to do what we can to make her life worth something, to give back, you know.*

I: *To give back to other parents?*

F: *Yah (looks at wife who nods). We have talked about this a lot. If there is anything we can do to help other parents get through this experience, we are willing to tell them what we went through...are going through.*

I: *That is very generous and certainly a commemoration of Molly's life and I'm grateful to you as I believe other parents will be. I do need to mention here that I will keep your names out of the report and remove any identifying information but I cannot guarantee, given how small the community of childhood cancer is, that someone might recognize you in the findings and the publications, so I can't promise that you will be anonymous.*

M: *That's okay. You can even use our names. We are okay with that.*

I: *Do you prefer I use your real names?*

M: *It doesn't matter. I just mean if someone figures out it's us, that's ok.*

I: *I appreciate your openness. If, however, you say something that you think later, you'd rather not have shared, I can take that out of the official transcript. I can't promise, of course, that I won't be influenced by it having heard it.*

F: *No problem.*

I: *Okay, we'll get started here. As you know, the recorder has been on and all of this will be transcribed to text and used as information for the study along with the other interviews I have done. We signed the consent prior to turning on the recorder but I just wanted to be sure that we were all clear on the issue of confidentiality. Are you still okay for the next hour or so to talk? Do you have any other commitments after this that I can honor by staying on time?*

The interviewer up to this point has been ensuring that the participants are fully informed and aware that, though confidentiality is attempted, complete anonymity cannot be guaranteed. This is explicit in the written consent but needs to be revisited in the face-to-face conversation. The interviewer then starts by trying to map out the direction of the interview by revisiting the purpose of the study.

I: *What I've found is most helpful to me is if we kind of walk through, you tell me a little bit about your cancer journey if you will or your narrative of what you've gone through with Molly right from beginning to end and then, cause I need to get sort of the context of where I want to ask you questions around your relationship. I need to try to hear and understand what you have gone through. And then we'll go back to it, but we'll do it through the lens of your relationship and ask you some of the questions that I'm interested in for this particular study. The premise of the study is that the experience of cancer in a family, and having a child diagnosed with cancer, treated with cancer and in your case, having lost your child can have huge effects on the family, we know of, it's a family with cancer, not just a child, right?*

(Both parents mumble yes).

I: *And it can have some effects on the parental relationship, sometimes good effects, sometimes not so good, sometimes just confusing, and so what we're trying to understand, at the end of the day, is for you to help me understand, how you, as a parent, as a couple, handled this and what we can we do to be more helpful to other parents. That's kind of what our biggest goal is. So we'll get to that in a second, but do you mind talking a bit about Molly and that experience that you had with her having cancer?*

M: *Not at all. (To husband). Since you're so good with memory, do you want to go through and if you miss anything, I'll tell you. If I remember it differently from you?*

F: *I was gonna say the reverse. Why don't you start and I'll chime in if I think you miss something?*

M: Okay. So, I just have to think about this. Molly was showing symptoms for a long time, we can now see in hindsight. I knew something wasn't right but our doctor just couldn't figure out why she was so tired all the time...

Molly's mother proceeded to recap the medical narrative with her husband adding details or correcting inconsistencies. They walked through the diagnosis, treatment, and eventual death and aftermath of continuing grief. During this telling of the "story" of Molly's cancer experience, the interviewer injected only rarely, and that was to ask for more specifics around timing and clarity about the events that were punctuated in the recall. The interviewer's choice at the time, as mentioned, was that she needed context for their experience and also recognized that these kinds of stories are stories that need to be told and retold over time as a way for people to make sense and meaning of what they have undergone (Moules, 1998, 2009; Moules, Simonson, Prins, Angus, & Bell, 2004; Moules, Simonson, Fleiszer, & Glasgow, 2007; Wright & Bell, 2009).

There were many moments where things were said that could have been portals for inquiry, trails that the interviewer may have chosen to pursue, and discernment and choice about what leads to follow were made, always guided by this question: "If I follow this line of inquiry, will it offer me a road to an understanding about the TOPIC at hand, or will it derail us and take us further from the topic?" After a very tender discussion about Molly's death, the interviewer made a decisive shift in the conversation but only after carefully navigating the sensitivity of the conversation.

I: So when you said that she'd basically died in your arms, was that in taking her to the hospital? I'm sorry, (noticing his tears) I know this, it's hard to re-visit this huh? Yeah.
F: Yeah (whisper). (Deep breath).
    (Silence of 10 seconds).
I: How many years has that been now? That was 2004 you said?
F: (Tearfully) nine years yep.
I: Nine years. It's always...
F: (Sigh).
I: ...in the work that I've done...because in my clinical work prior to when I was a professor, I was a bereavement counselor.

The interviewer made a choice here to disclose something of herself. "To probe, the interviewer cannot be stonily impersonal; he or she has to give something of himself or herself in order to merit an open response" (Sennet, 2004, pp. 37–38). This was very intentional as a way to offer that she knows something about the topic and to some extent appreciates and understands their reaction.

F: Oh, okay.
I: It always strikes me that it doesn't matter if it's one year or nine years, or twenty years, that it's just as real as if it were today.
M: (Sniffling).
F: Yeah, when you talk about it right?
I: Yeah.

F: *I mean you can certainly do your daily life, because we don't talk (emphasized) about it anymore. We don't talk this in-depth about...*

I: *Yeah, is that a deliberate choice or are you...?*

F: *I think it's because life continues on and you can't talk about it everyday right?*

I: *Yeah. Yeah. So maybe, thank you for telling me that. And as much as I've done a lot of, I've had a lot of conversations and had a lot of work, I've never had that experience of holding my child and having them die and so I, my heart goes out to you.*

Even though the death of a child is not the topic of this research, such a conversation and the depth of the emotion cannot go unacknowledged or unrecognized. In order to move on, it has to be acknowledged.

F: *Yeah, thanks (tearfully).*

M: *(Sniffling).*

(Silence of 5 seconds)

The interviewer has delicately let the conversation rest temporarily on the grief that lives with this couple, the difficulty, messiness, pain, and angst that are handmaidens that accompany grief (Moules & Amundson, 1997). One could argue that this lingering on the pain of grief did not directly serve the topic but the interviewer made a studied choice that, out of respect and honoring, out of an ethical imperative, the grief of having a child die had to be heard and acknowledged before the interview could move on. It is also about the context of the experience. This is a couple whose child did not live and that outcome should be considered in examining the effects of childhood cancer on this family. The interviewer then makes a deliberate interruptive turn after the silence.

I: *I wonder if we can kind of look back during that period of time and try as I had mentioned before, the focus of this study is on...*

M: *(Blows nose).*

I: *...maybe what kind of effect this might have had on the two of you and your relationship, both during the time that Molly was diagnosed and sick, and treated and then since you've lost her as well. If you can, because I think relationships, marriages aren't easy at the best of times, and that sometimes when you go through something, this would be the worst thing you could go through, I'm guessing, that did you notice anything between the two of you during any of this time?*

M: *Like when, after she was diagnosed, before she passed away? Is that the period?*

I: *Yeah well in the whole period, because I would consider this still part of the period so... So maybe at any points along the way, did the two of you struggle or did you feel really in sync around what you were facing?*

M: *Well I think just generally speaking there's a...*

F: *(Sniffling).*

M: *...(sigh) I don't know, sort of a, it's not a worry sort of mentality, but a mental approach that you'll have to do whatever is necessary to beat this.*

I: *Can you say more about that?*

M: *And what happens a lot (emphasized) is a lot of it's quite technical and clinical right?*

I: *Mmmhmm.*

F: In terms of you have to be there at this time; this is what's going to be done; this is some of the repercussions; this is sort of the rescue approach you know when you're, if you have bowel problems or you're throwing up. All those sort of tactical things or things that you just sort of execute almost on auto pilot...

I: Yeah.

F: ...after a while right? You get quite used to that. So I think what happens a little bit is you, not that you suppress your emotions, but you only let them out at certain times. And I mean that could be difficult because you're, as the married couple, you're not necessarily in sync as to when those are right? And so if one of them is sort of "batten down the hatches" and, "we'll ride through the storm" and the other one wants to sort of talk about it and go through the mushy parts, I mean both parties have to be in sync for that conversation to really happen or have any value. And I know that that (sniffling) that's just at least the way I felt anyway, that was sometimes hard to get that synchronization of ideas and thoughts and willingness to do it I guess too.

I: Yeah. It, that's so true, because I've actually had a lot of parents say that to me that I'm beginning to believe that you can't ever be in sync with that.

F: Well, it's kind of what I was thinking is if you're, well sometimes it happens...

I: Yeah.

F: ...you are in sync with it.

I: But not all the time.

F: But...

M: Mmm pretty rarely actually.

F: Yeah...

M: I think (chuckles).

F: ...but and I think part of that is what keeps you going right? Because if you were both in that all the time you're totally, emotions run everything and emotions, if you're running in emotions all the time I don't think you're thinking clearly and you're not as productive and so...

I: But if you were of the belief that you had to be always in sync all the time, could that have caused trouble between you? And did the two of you accept that you were just when one was up, one was down and or did you find that...

M: Well, I think we're inherently that way (laughing).

I: Oh, is that right?

M: I mean the two of us before we were married, albeit it wasn't a long time between the time we met and the time Eric arrived but there, it is a bit of a challenge to be in sync with kids and jobs and whatever else. I mean it's just...

F: (Sniffling).

M: ...as you say it's, at the best of times marriage is a generally peaceful even keel, but there are little peaks and valleys that happen.

I: Sure, yeah.

M: So.

I: How long have you been married?

M&F: (in unison): 16 years.

F: Essentially.

I: And how long together?

M: Seven years before?

F: Almost 17.

M: 17 years.

F: 18 years I guess. It'll be 18 years in March.

M: 90...(laughing)

I: 18 years that you've been together?

F: Yep.

M: Since 96.

I: Yeah. And so what you're saying is that there, two people can never always be in sync right in terms of...

At this point, the interviewer is following a line of inquiry that is fueled by a core curiosity and a beginning interpretive conjecture in this study: being in sync – what that means to people and how it plays out in this context of being parents of a child experiencing cancer.

M: Well, I don't know it you'd want to be (laughing).

I: (Chucking).

M: Really I mean. Yeah.

F: I mean I think for the hard decisions, we were in sync, which I think was important.

I: Yeah.

F: Taking her off treatment and what you do, the big decisions we would come together we didn't have, wouldn't have blow out fights about...

I: Mmmhmm.

F: ...when we were in treatment there was a family there that was, I don't know if you'd, the Jehovah witness family the mom didn't want to do blood transfusions and the dad did...

I: Mmmhmm.

F: ...for their daughter and they ended up in a great big legal custody. So I think that for the big decisions we were there...

I: Yeah.

F: ...and for the tough decisions we came together whether it was emotionally like to tell Eric that, "your sister's..." he was six right?

I: Mmmhmm.

F: So how do you tell a six year old that your sister is dying? (tearful).

I: Even when the concept of death isn't quite formalized in their mind yet.

F: He didn't really get it.

I: Yeah.

M: And he's shut down emotionally I would think pretty much (sniffling). And I'm not a big, I don't share a lot.

I: Mmm.

M: And probably through a lot of this we kept from him, he didn't see us cry a lot while Molly was sick. We tried to keep our house, in my mind we kept it, this is normal and I, Molly didn't remember life before cancer, so it was normal for her, going to the hospital was normal for Eric, he was always happy to go, he was always happy to go.

I: Mmmhmm.
      An area that the interviewer could have chosen to pursue is the idea of nor-
      malcy and "new normalcy" in the context of childhood cancer. This inter-
      viewer did not follow this line of inquiry, juggling the decision to pursue it
      with the other option of seeing where the participants were going to go in the
      interview.

M: *We, it was just a part of our life. And we're going to go to the hospital or we're going
      to go to clinic and can we have friends there? She had friends there. So I think in those
      kinds of decisions we were together.*

I: Mmmhmm.

M: *I think probably where we, what he is sort of referring to is that I'm, I don't go there as
      often probably as he would have liked me to. I think…*

I: *Emotionally?*

F: *To the mushy part, yeah.*

I: *Okay. When you say the mushy part you mean when you talk about the emotions
      yeah.*

M: *Well I think the emotional, yeah. I'm, and I still run my life pretty much the same way,
      I don't go to the emotional as much. I'm more about, I'm a doer right? So I'm let's okay
      let's get the kids up, out the door, gotta make lunches…*

I: *So more pragmatic?*

M: *Yeah.*
      At this point, the interviewer is going to bring her prejudices and knowledge
      into play – offering an idea, not with the intention of teaching or therapy but
      with the openness to the possibility that this way of talking about the difference
      in styles of grieving might further reflection and comment from the participants.

I: *And that's an interesting thing too around even some of the research that's been done
      around grieving is that they used to think there was a male and female way of grieving,
      but they don't think so anymore, they actually think now that there's different grieving
      styles…*

F: *Right.*

I: *…and one of them is what they call more instrumental, which is to do things as a way
      to work through grief.*

I: *And the others the people that tend more to grieve intuitively, which is more emotion-
      ally…*

M: *Mmm.*

I: *And neither one's right or wrong, or healthy or not healthy, but it's when sometimes
      when a couple have different styles of grieving that they almost perceive that the other
      person isn't grieving enough, or is grieving too much. And that they run into some
      conflict around that.*

M: *Mmm.*

I: *Was that your experience at all? When you think about even after you lost Molly?*

F: *I would, I mean (sighing) (tearfully) I took, I don't know, six weeks off work or some-
      thing after Molly died…*

I: Mmmhmm.

F: ...and we went away. And I think we were both just raw (emphasized) at that point during that time (crying and sniffling).

I: Yeah.

F: So, and then one day we sort of looked at our house and looked at our son and he was doing everything in his little power to make us laugh or be happy...

I: Mmmhmm.

M: ...and it sort of at that point that I think that, you know I don't know if it's changing a grieving style but at first we were both just devastated and (sighing) but about that point, and we both sort of came to it I think about the same time and maybe it was because he was going back to work shortly, but sometime in September (clears throat) we sort of had a discussion that we need to pull it together. We can't be crying all the time because life still goes on right?

I: Mmmhmm.

M: So as devastated as we are, we have to do something because, poor Eric, our son was, and he didn't cry. He didn't cry, I didn't see him cry about Molly. I'm sure he did, but just that we didn't see until my, when he was in grade nine, he just said he was having some issues sleeping (sniffling) and didn't want to talk to me about it, and I said, "well do you want to go to a counsellor?" I didn't know what the issues were...

I: Mmmhmm.

F: I still don't really know. But so he went and saw somebody and, sorry he did go to hospice sibling support group.

I: He did? Okay.

F: She was his sort of counsellor...

I: Mmmhmm.

F: ...at that point in time and I don't know if they had tears or not. I didn't, that was again a private session with him.

I: Mmmhmm.

F: Anyways, so Eric didn't cry about Molly until, that I know of, until he was like 13 or 14 years old or so.

I: Do you think, was there any chance that you said that he was doing everything in his power to get you folks to laugh, was he, do you think he was protecting you from his tears?

      To the interviewer, at this point, the complexity and reflexivity of the research interview becomes apparent. This hypothetical question is quite sophisticated and holds the potential of being therapeutic, even though it was not intended as a therapeutic intervention.

F: (Sigh) could be and maybe he was just doing that so he didn't cry.

I: Mmm.

M: He was whatever. But, so I think, we had a discussion about it because it was just sitting here and it was like death (emphasized) was just hanging in the room. And we needed to bring some life back to our...

I: So how did you do that?

M: I don't know, I mean we just started doing things with him that we like playing cards or...

I: Mmmhmm.

F: ...going swimming again or doing things that were fun. We had a friend that gave us painting classes for Eric, so he had something because we just weren't even thinking about signing him up for anything and he still paints to this day, he doesn't sort of know, or maybe he does know that Kathy gave him those lessons as I think a place for him to have a bit of an outlet.

I: Mmmhmm.

M: So, sorry I sort of side tracked there a little bit but I would think that at that point in time we were grieving the same right?

I: Mmmhmm.

F: We were very much, and then probably but we agreed that we needed to sort of change our strategy a little bit. And we had brought some happiness back into the home because I would say that it wasn't a happy place for a long time. You know a long time we were sad right?

I: Yeah, of course.

M: But and then probably structure came back. He went back to work, we made a decision about that time, maybe even sooner that we would have another child.

I: I wondered if that was a deliberate decision that you, or was it something you struggled over? Did you both agree that you wanted to have another child? Because I know that some couples after they've had a child die that they, they're afraid to sometimes because they also know what they could lose, right?

F: Yeah, well I mean we did talk about it. I don't think we were, one of us had to talk the other one into it from what I remember.

M: Well and I think we had never really ruled out, we had never, we hadn't gotten to the point of saying, "we're not having any more kids."

I: Oh, I see.

M: Yeah. Even when Molly got sick we said sometimes sort of talked about, "well maybe we should have a third," I guess before she got sick. We'd sort of I think we hadn't actually said, "ok we're not having three children."

F: Right.

M: ...this is it.

F: Then she got sick and then...

M: And then that takes it out of the equation.

F: ...all, yeah.

I: Yeah.

M: I did have friends that even when their son was on, or child was on treatment they went ahead and got pregnant and had another child during that process or but to me I didn't want to be, I didn't want to be pregnant and dealing with, and feel like I couldn't deal with her because, "oh I can't go into the room while you're having this because I'm pregnant."

Different boundaries exist in these interviews and questions around territories that might be considered very private and personal may occur – but again only in the service of the topic. Questions cannot be based on an intrusive curiosity but rather a mindful and respectful curiosity that is driven by not "already knowing the answer." In this study, these might be questions about financial concerns or sexual and emotional intimacy, which are known to be relevant to a couple's relationship. The questions, though bold, must be offered sensitively and with an effort to normalize them as in the example below.

M: *And then I went on long-term disability for a year. And then Molly had been off treatment three or four months, things were good, they said, "do you want to come back to work now?" and I said, "no," so I quit (emphasized), basically on, end of March 2003. And then they said to me, "well you know we have this little part-time gig if you're looking for something at home."*

I: *Mmm.*

M: *And I said, "that would be great." So then I started, I did some pre-work but officially I took that contract on July, so essentially I didn't work for two years.*

I: *Was that a hardship financially for you?*

F: *Well, yeah when you have less money but I don't think it really curtailed…*

M: *Well essentially I was…*

F: *…our activities a lot.*

M: *…essentially I was making the same amount of money for the six months…*

I: *Mmm.*

M: *…short term disability was full pay and then long-term disability was 70% a year pay and…*

I: *The reason that I ask that is we actually know through some research that financial stresses on a marriage are really not easy to deal with either…*

F: *Yeah.*

I: *…and I just wondered if that factored in at all.*

F: *Well I never felt that we changed our spending habits or saving habits…(incomprehensible) (laughing)…anyway.*

M: *Mmm, yeah. We pretty much have had the same style…*

I: *Okay.*

M: *…I would say ever since we've been together right? That's sort of just been.*

I: *And did in terms of going back to your relationship too then, was during the time when Molly was sick and then after she died was your intimacy as a couple affected at all? And I don't mean intimacy as only sexual but emotional intimacy and affection and all those things. Did you see any changes in that area of your lives?*

M: *I would say probably didn't start because of Molly being sick it probably started with having children.*

I: *(Chuckling).*

This chuckle was a recognition of being a new mother and the interviewer knew it.

M: *Right?*

I: *No, I think you're, every single couple has said this to me…*

M: *Yeah, just…*

I: *…that things change once you have kids.*

M: *You don't have, you're not, if you're sitting around on the couch or whatever, you've got a baby in your arms.*

I: *Yeah.*

M: *And we had Eric and Molly only 19 months apart so...*

I: *Mmmhmm. You were pretty busy.*

M: *Yeah, so essentially you had two, somebody said to me in the park one day, a little boy, he was like five, Molly was like brand new and Eric was basically just walking, well 19 months or whatever, and the little girl said to me, "wow you have two babies!" And I thought yes, what was I thinking? (Laughing) I have two babies.*

I: *(Laughing).*

M: *So I think that changes your intimacy.*

The couple then moved into a discussion that revealed their beliefs about different needs in relationships. For the most part, the interviewer deliberately allows them to talk without interjection. This choice was based on flow, rhythm, tone, and cadence of their conversation, a discernment in the moment to let it evolve without interruption.

M: *...some people need physical touch so it doesn't have to be sex or whatever it just needs, they just need to be...*

I: *Hugged or...*

M: *...hugged or whatever. Doing things together, quality time is one. So it doesn't matter like whether someone is going skate shopping or...*

F: *(Laughing). She looks at me!*

F: *She wanted to come with me to shop for skates and I was sort of...*

M: *He's like, "really? So you want to come with me?" I said, "yeah, just doing things with you, doesn't matter right?"*

F: *(Laughing).*

M: *And he's, so for me doing things together is important.*

I: *Mmmhmm.*

M: *For him, physical touch is important.*

I: *Mmmhmm.*

M: *So we recognize that about each other, but it's hard to, and I'm not a physical touch person.*

F: *Well you don't recoil when I touch you!*

M: *Well I don't recoil...no!*

I: *(Laughing).*

F: *But...*

M: *But it's not my way...*

I: *And yours would be more the quality time?*

M: *Yeah doing things together or having people do things for me.*

F: *So acts of service...*

I: *Were there ever any times that you thought your marriage was in jeopardy?*

F: *Yeah, last Tuesday (laughing).*

M: *(Laughing).*

F: *Nah, well, I mean overall I would say no. I think the reality is that as you started off with, marriage is an entity, the process itself is fraught with all kinds of challenges obviously and Molly getting sick was probably the biggest one we'll ever have. And I'm only speaking for myself, I mean sometimes you think is this what I want? Is this, not that I don't want it but…*

F: *…does this make sense? (Clears throat) we heard, I don't think read (emphasized), although maybe we did, that quite often couples who've got kids that have to go through cancer struggle from a marriage standpoint and I think I remember somebody saying the divorce rate is much higher than for the normal population.*

M: *Someone told us that at the hospital…pissed me off. Told us that 87% of marriages end in divorce right and I was like, "so on top of it…" I remember very, I was really……pissed off. I walked out of that room and I said to him (husband), I said, "oh great, not only is our child going to struggle, we're probably going to end up divorced."*

I: *So and can…I just say here that's actually not true anyways.*

M: *I know that after the fact right?*

I: *You didn't find that comment useful?*

M: *No it was devastating (emphasized)…because you're not only are you thinking, "oh God my child's going to die…now I'm going to be divorced, a single mom, a single dad.*

M: *…it was a total waste of time.*

I: *Say that that had been said to you in a different way. Like I'm just saying, say that you weren't offered a number, but say she had said that this can be quite stressful on a relationship so…*

M: *Well then I would have said…*

I: *…try to keep communication open. Try to talk to each other. Would that have been a useful comment to have been made?*

M: *Well I think that it was self-evident to us that this wasn't going to be an easy battle. Regardless.*

I: *You didn't need someone to say that…*

M: *No.*

I: *Because did anybody ever ask you, other than that comment, did anybody ever ask how things were going between the two of you? And well this is a two-part question, did any health care professional ever ask that and if so, if, would it have been helpful if they would have or would you have found that intrusive?*

M: *We basically went through that whole program and it wasn't until the end I joined the Parent Advisory Committee the last year Molly was alive and I met a social worker in the department…*

M: *And then, just discussions with her, because she became like a friend…*

I: *Mmmhmm.*

M: *…that might have been, and I don't necessarily recall, and that would have been somebody that I opened up to.*

I: *Did she help you?*

M: *Yeah.*

I: Yeah. So it sounds like as though it would have been fine for someone to inquire but it would depend on who that person was and what was the nature of the relationship with them?

M: Yeah.

I: Is that fair to say?

M: Yep. I think so.

F: Well, I mean, I suppose. I mean they're sort of checking in with you to see if you're aware of some of these issues. Your child's sick and (deep breath) the odds may or may not be in your favour but that the odds aren't really, you don't get two thirds of a kid, you get one or you get zero. So, I don't know, I mean it's, I'm not sure what the value would be of any kind of advice or question that way.

I: Mmm. Okay.

F: Maybe there would be some, but I don't know.

I: I mean it's an interesting thing because, like I kind of agree with you, you don't get one third of a kid, like those stats have, when I worked in Hawaii, that's when I worked in paediatric oncology we had an oncologist who when the families would say, "well what are the chances?" he'd say, "I can give you numbers but there's only two numbers that matter to you, and it's zero or a hundred...and we're working with the hundred." That made such sense to me.

F: Yeah.

M: But as a parent you still need to know that number because you need to know realistically...

I: To prepare?

M: Yeah. I mean I think we went into it with "Molly's going to survive." But we also knew, like we also knew when we were sitting next to, or maybe I did I don't know, the leukaemia patient and Molly...you know what, chances are your, in three years time you're done and your child's going off, chances are...

I: Mmm.

M: You know?

I: Yeah.

M: So, I think you need to know that.

F: And with the Internet being so...now prevalent, well even when Molly was diagnosed.

I: Everything's accessible.

M: There's not too much that's sort of secret anymore. Right?

I: Yeah.

M: So, unfortunately we knew because we knew of someone else going through the same thing before.

F: Yeah.

M: And was horrified with that situation that they were facing. And then little did we know that within just a limited amount of time we'd had the same scenario.

I: Did your friend lose her child?

F: No.

I: Oh. That would be hard for you too.

F: Yeah.

I: I mean...

I: Have you stayed, well Eric's involved with the kids cancer camp, so have you folks stayed involved with the camp community at all?

F: We go to some of their events, they had a memorial event in September...

M: They do an ornament sort of tree ceremony at the hospital.

I: Is that through the grief group?

M: Yeah that's a different group. Yeah.

I: I'm trying to think if there's anything else, how's our time? I don't want to keep you too long. Is there anything that you were thinking that would be helpful to me in this study that we haven't talked about?

F: I don't think so.

I: Any advice that you'd offer other couples facing the same thing?

M: I guess what I saw with family relations and family dynamics of all of our friends and the people that we knew that went through the cancer world, we're all together still right?

I: Mmmhmm.

M: So, I think personally, if you are struggling when your child got cancer, you might not make it right? But if you're doing good when your child gets cancer, you'll probably come out of it okay.

I: Yeah.

M: So I mean that's not something you want to tell people right? Because if they're looking at their husband thinking, "I'm thinking about leaving ya," well chances are having a child have cancer is not going to make that change right?

I: It's interesting though, I did interview one person who said that they were struggling prior to and the cancer experience actually brought them...

F: United?

I: ...it brought them together, but then when their child died, that was the end of the relationship.

M: Yeah. So maybe they were a unified front for that period...

I: Yeah.

M: ...but then when that (emphasized) goes away all the stuff that was problems before...

I: Yeah. And that...

M: ...are still there.

I: That's really fascinating to me that you say that because when I actually first conceptualized this study, that was a hypothesis in my mind is that maybe we're going to find that it's more the state of the relationship prior to that is a determinant.

F: Yeah.

I: Yeah.

F: And I think that that's the case. In my experience.

I: If you were to frame that in, like you say you can't really say that to someone to be useful, but what kinds of things could you tell another couple that, like if you were to give your best advice, say I was given 10,000 dollars and I could hire you to write an advice manual for parents going through what you went through, what would you advise?

M: *I mean I think that we were in a lot of ways in a fortunate situation that I could quit my job...and I could be the full-time caregiver. Some families didn't have that option right? So there you'd see the grandma there and the mom was working and the dad you know like...*

I: *Mmmhmm.*

M: *...or the daughter, or the child was older, some of it depends on your child's age too right? Maybe you don't need to quit, but when you have a two year old, I, we felt that I needed, and we were in agreement on that.*

F: *The idea of both of us continuing to work and just leave Molly, because I think 30 or 40 years ago, people might have done that. You just put your child in the hospital...and the parents weren't as involved right?*

I: *Yeah. And sometimes, well probably a bit longer than that but there was even just visiting hours. The parents were only allowed to come from two to four.*

M: *Yeah. So times have changed and I think part of the expectation was, I mean not that I was ever told that I had to be there 24/7 but I think the expectation was that I would be there 24/7. So we were in a situation where we didn't see each other the first, well five weeks I don't think we slept in the same bed. Because either one of us was at the hospital with her.*

I: *You were tag teaming then?*

F: *Yeah. Tag teaming. So we would see each other...*

M: *Well I can remember when your mom was here and we had a little rendezvous because, I don't know exactly when that was but...*

I: *Did you think having the rendezvous was important to your relationship?*

F: *Not really. We just kept thinking about Molly and that we should be with her and not out having a holiday. I think the thing I'd tell other parents is that your relationship is gonna be put on hold during this time and it should be. All that should matter is your child. You just have to learn to tag team and trust that you'll get back together when it's all over. That's what is important.*

M: *He's right.*

Further discussion continued but even in this moment of the interview, the interviewer knew that something important had just been said in the service of the topic. This comment from the father would eventually develop into an interpretation of "relationships on hold tethered by trust."

I: *I'm aware that we have gone beyond the time we booked for this and I apologize for that.*

F: *No problem; it's been good.*

M: *Yeah.*

I: *I'm just wondering if there is anything else that you would like to add or actually, let me ask you this: When you were thinking about me coming today was there one thing you were most hoping I would or would not ask you about?*

M&F: *(laughing at the last part of the question)*

M: *I don't think so. I think it was kind of what we expected.*

F: *Nothing for me but I will be interested in seeing the report.*

I: *Of course. And I'm wondering if there is something that comes up for you when you think about our conversation or something that comes up for me, is it okay if we stay in touch by email?*

M: *Of course. For sure.*

F: *Ya.*

I: *Well, I'd like to end here by thanking you so much for your time, honesty, openness, and trusting me with your tears. You have made a real contribution to this study and I believe what you have taught me WILL make a difference to the lives of other parents going through what you have and are still facing. So, I'm most grateful and I thank you.*

M: *You're welcome. And thank YOU for doing this.*

F: *Ya, it's really important.*

This portion of the interview does not reflect the entire experience or the fullness of the many things offered and discussed but it does represent the powerful nature of these intense conversations of human experiences. In this case, the interviewer, having a wealth of interviewing experience from both research perspectives and therapy perspectives, did not enter into it with any set guiding questions but rather with a clear focus on the topic, an unbridled curiosity, and immense respect for the strength and wisdom of the participants.

Chapter Summary

Participation is a strange word…participation is not taking parts, but in a way taking the whole. Everyone who participates in something does not take something away, so that others cannot have it. The opposite is true: by sharing, by our participating in the thing in which we are participating, we enrich them, they do not become smaller, but larger. (Gadamer, 1984, p. 64)

Participation in research interviews is not about taking something away but about creating something that adds to understanding, enriches our knowledge, and offers portals to interpretation. An act of aletheia, a good interviewer seeks to enliven, awaken, remember, and open up understanding about the topic at hand. These interviews cannot be prescriptively described, but need to be learned through experience and practice so that, in time, the interviewer has a honed dexterity with language and relationship, tact, discretion, courage, and timing, enough that every condition is set for the arrival of good data.

In this chapter, we have discussed the character and conduct of research interviews in hermeneutic inquiry. We turn now to the heart of this work – interpretation as analysis in hermeneutic research.

References

Corbin, J., & Morse, J. M. (2003). The unstructured interactive interview: Issues of reciprocity and risks when dealing with sensitive topics. *Qualitative Inquiry* 9(3), 335–351. doi 10.1177/1077800403009003001

Davey, N. (2013). *Unfinished worlds: Hermeneutics, aesthetics and Gadamer.* Edinburgh, Scotland: Edinburgh University Press.

Fiumara, G. C. (1990). *The other side of language.* New York, NY: Routledge. *Hermeneutics, Aesthetics and Gadamer.* Edinburgh, Scotland: Edinburgh University Press.

Gadamer, H-G. (1960/1989). *Truth and method* (2nd rev. ed.) (J. Weinsheimer & D. G. Marshall, Trans.). New York, NY: Continuum.

Gadamer, H-G. (1984). The hermeneutics of suspicion. In G. Shapiro & A. Sica (Eds.), *Hermeneutics: Questions and prospects* (pp. 54–65). Amherst, MA: University of Massachusetts Press.

Geanellos, R. (1999). Hermeneutic interviewing: An example of its development and use as research method. *Contemporary Nurse,* 8(2), 39–45.

Grondin, J. (1994). *Introduction to philosophical hermeneutics* (J. Weinsheimer, Trans.). New Haven, CT: Yale University Press.

Heidegger, M. (1975). *Early Greek thinking* (D. Farrell Krell & F. A. Capuzzi, Trans.). New York, NY: Harper & Row.

Heidegger, M. (1927/1996). *Being and time* (J. Stambaugh, Trans.). Albany, NY: SUNY Press.

Hirshfield, J. (1996). *Nine gates: Entering the mind of poetry.* New York, NY: HarperCollins.

Kvale, S., & Brinkmann, S. (2009). *InterViews: Learning the craft of qualitative research interviewing* (2nd ed.). Thousand Oaks, CA: SAGE.

Maturana, H. R. (1988). Reality: The search for objectivity or the quest for a compelling argument. *The Irish Journal of Psychology,* 9(1), 25–82.

Michelfelder, D. P., & Palmer, R. E. (1989). *Dialogue and deconstruction: The Gadamer-Derrida encounter.* Albany, NY: SUNY Press.

Morse, J. M. (1991). Qualitative nursing research: A free-for-all? In J. M. Morse (Ed.), *Qualitative nursing research: A contemporary dialogue* (2nd ed.) (pp. 14–22). Newbury Park, CA: Sage.

Moules, N. J. (1998). Legitimizing grief: Challenging beliefs that constrain. *Journal of Family Nursing,* 4(2), 142–166.

Moules, N. J. (2002). Hermeneutic Inquiry: Paying heed to history and Hermes. An ancestral, substantive, and methodological tale. *International Journal of Qualitative Studies,* 1(3), 1–21.

Moules, N. J. (2009). A parent's worst nightmare: Grief, families and the death of a child. *Relational Child and Youth Care Practice,* 21(4), 63–70.

Moules, N. J., & Amundson, J. K. (1997). Grief – An invitation to inertia: A narrative approach to working with grief. *Journal of Family Nursing,* 3(4), 378–393.

Moules, N. J., Simonson, K., Fleiszer, A. R., Prins, M., & Glasgow, B. (2007). The soul of sorrow work: Grief and therapeutic interventions with families. *Journal of Family Nursing, 13*(1), 117–141.

Moules, N. J., Simonson, K., Prins, M., Angus, P., & Bell, J. M. (2004). Making room for grief: Walking backwards and living forward. *Nursing Inquiry, 11*(2), 99–107.

Sandelowski, M. (1995). Focus on qualitative methods: Sample size in qualitative research. *Research in Nursing and Health, 18,* 179–183.

Sennett, R. (2004). *Respect.* London, UK: Penguin.

Tomm, K. (1988). Interventive interviewing: Part III. Intending to ask lineal, circular, strategic, or reflexive questions? *Family Process, 26*(6), 167–183.

Vandermause, R. K., & Fleming, S. E. (2011). Philosophical hermeneutic interviewing. *International Journal of Qualitative Methods, 10*(4), 367–377.

Wright, L. M., & Bell, J. M. (2009). *Beliefs and illness: A model for healing.* Calgary, AB, Canada: 4th Floor Press.

Wright, L.M., & Leahey, M. (1990, 1994, 2000, 2005, 2009, 2013). *Nurses and families: A guide to family assessment and intervention.* Philadelphia, PA: F. A. Davis.

Wright, L. M., Watson, W. L., & Bell, J. M. (1996). *Beliefs: The heart of healing in families and illness.* New York: NY: Basic Books.

· 7 ·

INTERPRETATION AS ANALYSIS

...though philosophical hermeneutics does not constitute a system or method its critical procedure has a clear style and a discernible signature. (Davey, 2006, p. 18)

Data analysis is another term that ought to carry a hermeneutic health warning, although it is no bad thing once more to draw attention to the tension between the generally given structures of research and the far more fluid interconnections of a hermeneutic study. (McCaffrey, Raffin Bouchal, & Moules, 2012, p. 221)

Hermeneutic research has a focus on a particular topic in relation to how it is lived out in the world of practice, how it has evolved over time, how it relates to the surrounding culture, and what it means to the practitioners involved. Analysis requires a comportment toward the data on the part of the researcher which makes room for complexity and "the development of a practice, of a preparedness or skill in changing mental perspectives" (Davey, 2006, p. 37). Data analysis in hermeneutic research differs from other research approaches because it is divergent rather than convergent: it involves carefully opening up associations that strengthen understanding of the topic rather than focusing in on a single governing theme. Thus, for hermeneutics, analysis is synonymous with interpretation; analysis *is* interpretation. Interpretation occurs throughout the multifaceted engagement with a topic via literature and research interviews, transcribing the interviews to text and reading and re-reading them, developing interpretive conjectures and writing about them. It also requires, as Gadamer (2007) has stated, that there be "some kind of methodological consciousness at work. The interpreter not only possesses the art of exegesis (*Auslegung*), he or she knows how to justify his or her exegesis theoretically" (p. 45).

This approach to analysis contrasts with quantitative research, where analysis involves the adherence to a strict method and often the application of rigorous measurement tools. In some qualitative methods too, there is a clearly delineated method in approaching the data, such as in grounded theory and the use of procedures of category coding, or thematic analysis and line-by-line coding. In some forms of hermeneutic phenomenological inquiry, authors have offered procedural steps in approaching the data (see for e.g., Colaizzi, 1978; Fleming, Gladys, & Robb, 2003; Giorgi, 1985; van Manen, 1984). In this chapter, we offer a less defined procedural approach to data analysis but rather describe the philosophical underpinnings that guide the intent and, therefore, focus the conduct of analysis. This is itself an interpretive enterprise, offering one way of applying aspects of Gadamer's philosophical hermeneutics to research in practice disciplines.

Interpretive analysis can be thought of as movement through the landscape of the topic, such that perspectives change with the varied points of view of interview participants and are informed by reference to disciplinary and other pertinent literature. Crucially, it is the researcher who finally commits to an interpretation of the material. Interpretation requires shaping and articulation so that insights are developed and honed and finally written up in a research report. At the early stage of analysis, the search for interpretive elements is a search for those aspects that catch our attention and call for a deconstruction of their meanings. Analysis involves careful reading, re-reading, and writing around significant interpretations that arise from the data. When working with a team, the initial individual interpretations of researchers are then raised to another level of interpretive analysis in the research team's conversations through in-depth, rigorous, reflexive, and communal attention to the data.

Identifying "significance" in this context is a matter of judgment that always depends on a plausible connection to the topic. Teamwork is one way of supplying rigor by testing out the worth of an emerging interpretation in dialogue with others. Madison (1988) described criteria of good interpretive work that can be taken as guides in research. He identified context, agreement, coherence, comprehensiveness, potential, and penetration as aspects of sound interpretation. We take up these criteria of rigor more fully in Chapter Nine, but for now they can be treated as characteristics of analysis that usefully elaborate on the topic without losing touch with the topic.

Hoy (1998) reminded us of another essential feature:

> one central aspect of what makes an interpretation better will be whether it understands, not only its object and subject matter, but also itself. Interpretations that are methodologically more self-aware are therefore better if they bring to light unnoticed features, not only of the object of interpretation, but also of the conditions and procedures of interpretation…An interpretation presupposes a self-understanding, and bringing features of this implicit self-understanding to light will make the interpretation insightful. (p. 193)

In other words, good interpretive work should disclose something about the meaningful existence of the interpreter and the world.

Unlike some other qualitative methods, the practice of hermeneutics is not aimed at inducing themes, semantic codes, constructs, or theories, but rather seeks to deepen understanding of a topic in such a way that it can be seen differently and, ultimately, can be practiced differently. Although the goal is not to end up with themes, it can be helpful to identify themes in transcript data in order to organize the material and relate statements from participants to emerging interpretations. The art of interpretation, that is often only learned through experience and is difficult to teach, involves the process of moving past the initial descriptive themes into the depth and richness of interpretation. Themes, therefore, are more of a tool along the way than the goal of analysis. While they may be useful in bringing some order into disparate material (see examples in Chapter Eight), it is the differences between participants at least as much as the similarities that may be productive in elucidating the complexity of the topic. Stated simply – in hermeneutics, one does not *end up* with themes but with interpretations.

Hermeneutic analysis is a very deliberate attempt to listen for particulars of experiences and thoughts that are not based on repetition to authenticate their authority to speak to the topic. Hermeneutic work, true to its phenomenological roots, encompasses a rich description of the phenomenon, but it must also complicate the description through highlighting exemplars, possible counter-exemplars, by exposing the phenomenon to contextual material, and by engaging in deconstruction, so that we are not simply imprisoned by our interpretations in our own standpoint. Interpretation in this work is a messy, difficult, complex, sophisticated endeavour that is honed and developed over time and through practice. It is both deconstructive and reconstructive, questioning how things, such as schools and hospitals, have come to be what they are, but also bringing to light new possibilities for better practice. In this chapter, we articulate ways to embark on deep interpretive practice, mindful of the intentions of it to enliven and deepen understanding of the subject matter.

Role of the Researcher in Interpretation

The role of researcher takes a particular place in hermeneutic work, based on views about objectivity and subjectivity in hermeneutic philosophy. Our strengths, as hermeneutic researchers, lie in a belief in the interpretability of the world and in a willingness to allow ourselves to be read back to us. Hermeneutics demands that we proceed delicately and yet wholeheartedly, and as a result of what we study, we carry ourselves differently, and we live differently. We are situated in the work but the work is not an autoethnography or an autobiography. We are situated in a conversation with the topic. Smith (1991) reminded us that the writing is *by us*, but it is not *about us*, though in one sense all writing is autobiographical as it comes from us, and involves self-understanding. The point is not to remove subjectivity from the work, which is impossible, but to acknowledge how it allows us into the interpretive process. We can then take it up with a sense of responsibility in recognizing how it translates into the way we listen to participants, what we hear, what stands out to us, and how we interpret it. Returning to some of the ideas in Gadamer's philosophy discussed in Chapter Three, it is possible to see how they inform the work of data analysis as interpretation.

Forestructures and Prejudices

Gadamer did not see objectivity and subjectivity as opposites, as an either/or proposition, but as dialectically related aspects of human understanding. We cannot see the world but from within the horizon of our own experience, and yet our experience is not fully our own, separate from the world. We share in histories, communities, and languages to the extent that, "(t)he self-awareness of the individual is only a flickering in the closed circuits of historical life" (Gadamer, 1960/2004, p. 278). For the purposes of research, the significance of this insight is that subjectivity is a resource, to be handled carefully, but nonetheless available to the research process.

As mentioned in earlier chapters, one of the ways of describing the workings of the subjectivity/objectivity dialectic is through what Heidegger identified as forestructures, and Gadamer called prejudices. Heidegger (1927/1996) asserted that our understanding proceeds from our preunderstandings and forestructures. Contained in this preunderstanding lies what Gadamer (1960/1989) termed our "prejudices" or presuppositions, or our leanings toward what we are able to see. Gadamer described prejudices as prejudgments that exist or are rendered before all other situational elements are examined. Unlike the notion of bracketing, we do not hold our prejudices in abeyance but think *with* them and we situate them in our understandings. Our prejudices allow us to hear something we would not have heard otherwise, they determine what we can recognize, and they provide our access to the world. The criticism sometimes lobbied against hermeneutic work is that it is subjective and therefore something less than a removed, objective view. Davey offered the idea that "subjectivity is not a block to greater objectivity but rather a gateway to it" (Davey, 2006, pp. 18–19). In other words, we cannot know anything other than subjectively, and it is our prejudices that help in allowing us this particular view.

By the time the researcher arrives at data analysis, he or she should already have been working reflexively to consider "why this particular topic for this particular researcher," and should be able to articulate the angle of attention to the topic. For Laing studying cancer camps, for example, her discussion of her encounters with the camps as a student nurse outlines the way her "prejudices" actually enabled her to enter into her research in an informed and committed way. Prejudices mobilize the space of understanding between the researcher and the topic and are thus inherently contextual. It is important to bring them into data analysis, both in the initial stages and in the eventual writing of a finished report but this has a different emphasis to than kinds of declarations of identity sometimes seen in interpretive work. When researchers simply declare which categories of age, ethnicity, gender, or occupation they belong to, it often reflects a commitment to an ideological position around the importance of identity politics. While that is one kind of statement of positioning, it forgets that prejudices and positions are there to be tested as well, to sort the good from the bad, as Gadamer would say. We argue that it is better hermeneutic practice to position oneself as an individual in relation to the topic, rather than as a representative of broad categories.

The Hermeneutic Circle

Interpretive data analysis demonstrates the hermeneutic circle as a metaphorical way of conceptualizing understanding and the process of interpretation in which we participate, and to which we belong, are situated in, and living through. It is not a method for uncovering meaning, but rather a description of how human understanding can be created from a stance of focused curiosity and reflexive attention to different standpoints and ways of seeing a topic. It also describes, after Heidegger, the relationship between self and other, between what is familiar and what is strange in experience, so it has an existential as well as conceptual aspect to it.

The hermeneutic circle is the generative recursion between the whole and the part. *Entering* the circle is accomplished by responding or listening to the call of the topic. *Staying in* the circle requires discipline and creativity, rigor and responsiveness. There is an inherent process of becoming immersed in, and engaging in a dynamic and evolving interaction with the data as a whole (the topic) and the data in part (a particular instance), through extensive readings, re-readings, reflection, writing, and conversation. In this process, there is a focus on recognizing the particular, isolating understandings, dialoguing with others about interpretations, making explicit the possibilities for being and doing that are implicit in the data and, eventually finding the appropriate language to clearly describe the understanding of the topic generated in the process.

On Conserving Stories and "Representing" Participants

The dynamic play between part and whole has particular implications for research application. Abram, a phenomenologist and deep ecologist, used a lyrical description of a bowl to show how we perceive an object in a flow of changing perspectives, each of which is partial at a given moment:

> The clay bowl resting on the table in front of me meets my eyes with its curved and grainy surface. Yet, I can only see one side of that surface – the other side of the bowl is invisible, hidden by the side that faces me. In order to view that other side, I must pick up the bowl and turn it around in my hands, or else walk around the wooden table. Yet, having done so, I can no longer see the first side of the bowl. Surely I know

that it still exists; I can even feel the presence of those aspects which the bowl now presents to the lamp on the far side of the table. Yet, I myself am simply unable to see the whole of this bowl all at once.

To take the bowl apart to learn more about it would be to lose the object as such:

> If I break it into pieces, in hopes of discovering these interior patterns or the delicate structure of its molecular dimensions, I will have destroyed its integrity as a bowl; far from coming to know it completely, I will simply have wrecked any possibility of coming to know it further, having traded the relation between myself and the bowl for a relation to a collection of fragments. (Abram, 1996, p. 51)

Data analysis as interpretation involves looking at the topic one aspect at a time, asking questions of it, being attentive to what the questions reveal, and yet it is not about breaking it apart or "cleaning the data," with the thought that any one story, statement, theme, or opinion is separable from the vital complexity of the topic. When we consider a "part," it is always with the knowledge that our attention is not on any other part, but that the larger world of the topic is implied in any particular aspect. Likewise, think-ing of the "whole" in relation to the parts, does not mean a presumption of knowing everything there is to know about a topic, but rather generating an awareness that there is more to be said, and that topics need to have bound-aries, for the moment at least, to come into view and be speakable, or able to be described.

The principle of part-whole interchange, expressed in the hermeneutic circle, applies to the treatment of participants' stories as data. Hermeneu-tics differs from other methodologies such as ethnography, grounded theory, narrative inquiry, or phenomenology that attempt to give an account of the participants, and whose researchers sometimes return to the participant for member checks to authenticate and substantiate how well they were repre-sented (Smith, 1991). The purpose in hermeneutic research is to bring un-derstanding around the topic; the participants in the study are not the topic but are chosen to bring their knowledge about, and to, the topic. Therefore, the goal is not to describe the participants fully, nor to conserve their stories and experiences intact, but rather to listen to what participants have to say for that which will cast new light on the topic and expand our understanding of the phenomenon we are attending to in the conversation. Therefore, an interpretation made by a researcher does not need to be authenticated by the participant. Rather, its authentication comes from the fact that it has opened up new possibilities for seeing and doing; it has "enlivened" practice. Allen (1995) suggested that "the strategy of returning to the subjects for validation is often based in a mirror epistemology in which the goal is to copy or reproduce the original meaning of the subjects' responses. This is questioned in hermeneutics" (p. 179). This is not to say that the researcher disregards the participant's perception, rather that the researcher is reliant on what has been said to reach strong interpretations, that is, new understanding of the topic. There are occasions where the researcher returns to the participants to clarify something that is questionable, or provocative, or to ask further questions that may have arisen from insights generated during the analysis, but this is very different in intent, process, and outcome than member checking. Hermeneutics does not report on meaning, but creates it. Its intent is to generate new understanding, not simply affirm what is already known. Through careful attention to, selection, and crafting of participant contributions, which is the responsibility of the researcher, the topic is illuminated further, and stands enriched beyond the initial horizons of either the researcher or the participants.

This does not mean to imply that participants' stories do not matter. They matter immensely, or rather their subject matter − how they address the topic and what they reveal − matters and, without them, the research could not occur. Embedded in their stories are invitations to understanding the topics, events of experience that *are* the topic. This work is not an autobiography of the researcher; it has a topic other than the researcher's life, and for this reason, it is also not a biography of the participants' lives. Frequently, for this reason, individual participant quotes will not be named, as it matters less who it came from than what it has to say about the topic. Quotes then are often arranged around the interpretations rather than the persons. Participants know of their experiences intimately; they know something of the topic. However, our intent is not to re-create participants, psychoanalyze them, or "correctly" portray them, but to generate insight derived from their unique knowledge and contribution.

The Analysis-Interpretation Process

...the term data implies separated objects of knowledge with analysis as a distanced examination of them. The hermeneutic understanding of language as interpretive instead demands an attention to aesthetics and expressive fluidity...Through this interpretive writing reflexivity once more emerges as one of the signatures of philosophical hermeneutics. Reflexivity is not the same as subjectivity − the researcher does not redraw the topic on a whim but rather commits to the play of the topic. (McCaffrey et al., 2012, p. 221)

Divergence, as a principle of interpretive work, makes particular demands on the researcher at the stage of data analysis. There is a freedom that comes with opening up pathways of understanding and seeking out illuminating associations in relation to the transcript data. The risk of too much freedom, however, is a chaotic pursuit of connections that distract and lead away from the data and the topic. Hermeneutics owes a great deal to aesthetic understanding, which is a helpful way of thinking about the researcher's approach to data. Davey (2013) wrote that, "aesthetic attentiveness demonstrates that the receptiveness associated with aesthetic reception is not grounded in subjective preference but in subjects' participation in enabling cultural horizons that shape their being" (p. 66). There is rationality in aesthetic understanding, an ordering and meaning-making whereby the art object – or research interpretation – takes its place in the world. There is, in Gadamer's (1960/2004) phrase, a "transformation into structure" (p. 110).

Preparing and Reading Transcripts

Interpretation is the dynamic of hermeneutic research, running throughout the course of a project (and even before and after in the historical life of a topic). Thus, interpretation is, in a sense, already going on during the interviews – in the selection of lines of inquiry, the wording of questions, and the decision when to finish. The audio recording and written transcript of the interview, however, become the focus for sustained and repeated analysis. Transcription is time consuming, but can bring closeness to the particulars of the material through careful moment-by-moment attention, listening not only to what was said but also to the pauses, hesitations, and silences.

In this kind of work, transcripts are designed in a line-by-line numbering format with a wide right-hand margin for notes. The transcript becomes a working document, to be read and re-read, written on, marked and remarked, so that it becomes a concrete work of dialogue between researcher and text. Working with transcripts in this way generates possible future directions for interpretive lines of inquiry. The text is read not only sequentially, as the representation of the linear interview, but also in terms of parts and wholes, looking at similarities or dissonances within a single interview, or between multiple interviews and, most importantly, for that which makes a difference. Researchers read for ideas that stand out, raise questions, provoke curiosity, answer questions, catch our attention and, most importantly, call our present understanding into question.

Writing Interpretive Conjectures

Alongside listening to the recordings and reading and annotating the transcripts, interpretive writing can take the form of noting beginning ideas and conjectures of possible meanings in a style that may form future writing. Keeping notes serves the practical purpose of tracking ideas and being able to retrieve them later on, both for the researcher's own use, as part of the unfolding story of doing the research that needs to be told and, importantly, as an audit trail to demonstrate rigor in the research. These beginning conjectures also support the practice of interpretive writing, and they provide a strategy for testing out emergent ideas, associations, and new ways of seeing things. At this early stage of writing, there is plenty of room for trial and error, to follow ideas to see where they lead. Writing, in turn, often leads to further reading, thinking, and searching back for an evocative quotation that suddenly finds a home, or looking for new material to support a fresh angle on the topic that is provoked by the data. Writing interpretive musings regularly throughout the data analysis is a practice that helps to generate possible interpretations. Over time, as a transformation into structure happens, there have to be reasoned choices made and articulated about the most useful, fitting, and interesting interpretations that generate new understanding. The writing informs the choices made, but also retains the possibilities held in the conjectures that may not make it into the final report. There may be ideas, or parts of ideas, phrases, or references that can be incorporated into other contexts. Nothing is ever wasted at this stage of developing interpretations – it is often marked by a creative superfluity and excess which will leave traces in finished interpretive writing.

Developing Interpretations

Hermeneutic interpretation is pluralist because it entails attention to the particular instance, which retains its particularity even next to other similar instances. Commitment to the idea of *Lebenswelt* has the effect that we are aware both of our unique, incommensurable experience of the world, and of our shared experience of a shared world. Thus, in working out interpretations from the data, there is recognition of similarity-in-difference and difference-in-similarity. There is no need for individual experiences to be subsumed into themes under the rubric of the same, but neither is any individual experience wholly separate from the fabric of understanding. Resistance to thematic reductionism as a goal of analysis is one of the hallmarks of hermeneutics. It flexibly allows for the recognition of extraordinary occurrences and exceptional views in the data while also seeking out points of affinity and relationship. This double movement can be seen in the exchange between part and whole in the hermeneutic circle, and in the tension between self and other that results in a kind of estrangement or distance from topic, necessary by Gadamer's account in *Truth and Method* for seeing the truth in the topic. The topic of research is the whole (in the sense of being a certain distinguishable aspect of the world, not as a discrete separate entity) to which data is related back through interpretation. There is a centrifugal and centripetal movement to interpretation (Davey, 2006): outwards by way of the unique insights afforded by each participant, and back inwards toward the topic, and toward the self, necessitating a transformation – "the transformation of structure that allows a subject to see its world differently and to become different to itself also sets the hermeneutic subject at a distance from itself" (Davey, 2006, p. 135). Thus, the imaginative, creative, associative forces in hermeneutics are balanced by the worldliness of the topic itself.

For example, while exploring a topic such as grief, bereaved people may often speak about guilt; they may not necessarily name it as guilt but the substance of what they are discussing may sound like the experience of guilt that can happen frequently in grief. Clinical work in the area of bereavement counseling bears this out (Moules & Amundson, 1997). The interpretive possibilities of the theme of guilt are revealed in the depth to which guilt then is unpacked and expressed as opposed to just a naming of it and a description of it. That is the distinction between arriving at a theme as part of a defining statement and using a theme as a jumping off point for interpretation. Within the theme in the latter sense, there may be many examples given from multiple participants who spoke of guilt and yet any of them could inflect the interpretive discussion by its difference or unique expression. Guilt would thus be taken up with a suspicious curiosity, ready to question prevailing assumptions, or to make original connections that introduced new perspectives. Interpretation involves some degree of confidence to try out ideas, but also humility in relation to one's ideas, which will hopefully be illuminating and useful but never the last, final, or total word. In this example, guilt, as understood and interpreted, becomes a layer in the understanding of grief as an entire experience that is contextual, nuanced, and particular. A finer, different sense of one's own guilt and grief would emerge from the interpretation as well. Thus, it is that interpretation is always in relation to the topic, and in relation to the self, as a movement of the part-whole dialectic, and a movement on the part of the subjectivity of the researcher, who must be careful and aware of his or her prejudices to stay open to the potential interplay of multiple perspectives, and the development of self-understanding.

Interpretation does not have to emerge from some aspect of the topic that, as with guilt and grief, is already a recognized dimension. Sometimes a particular word or turn of phrase, in the context of an interview transcript, might be enough to suggest that there is potential for reflection, questioning, and elaboration. For an example of something that can catch one's attention, in the interview offered in the previous chapter, one might be struck by the comment made by one of the participants that "parents' relationships *should* be put on hold while a child has cancer and that there must be trust that they will endure." From this statement, one could begin to work out an interpretation of "being on hold" and what that means. How is being on hold experienced; what are its costs and requirements? How does one understand trust, and what does one trust? It is not just about describing what it means to be on hold or to trust, but to dig deeply, with hermeneutic sleuthing, into the complexity of this idea. These kinds of questions would then open a portal for the interpreter to enter and begin the process of taking these ideas to life in language.

The reflexivity of the research process means that interpretation might also be sparked by apparently incidental events that are not part of the data as such. One example of an interpretive conjecture that did not arise so much from the words spoken but from the process itself is as follows. A graduate student was examining the experiences of women who had suffered a serious depression and were currently living with the possibility of a return of the depression once they had been relieved of it. The student called the supervisor (Moules) in distress recounting that she had just completed one of her "best interviews yet." However, when the interview was over and she went to transcribe the interview, she realized her tape recorder had not worked and nothing was on tape. Moules asked her what happened in the interview, what was said, and why was it such a good interview. The student proceeded to explain that the participant was talking about her sense of being failed by the promise of medication, that she had held such hope that medication would cure her but instead it had immense and unlivable side effects. Her sense was that of having been let down by science and modern medicine's promise to cure or provide relief. After this recounting, Moules said to the student,

> Then you write about *that* and about the failure of technology to live up to its promise and you write in about the failure of your tape recorder as a mirror of technology's inability to always deliver as promised. And then you go to Heidegger and you read his quote "Everywhere we remain unfree and chained to technology, whether we passionately affirm or deny it. But we are delivered over to it in the worst possible way when we regard it as something neutral" (Heidegger, 1977, p. 4). And that's where you begin your interpretation.

Out of this beginning, the student developed a beautiful interpretation around Technology, Promises, Hopes, and Disappointments. It is clear from this example, too, that to get to the pathway of the interpretation, the researcher needed dialogue with someone else, in this case her supervisor, in order to see something, a connection, that she had not noticed in her preoccupation with the seemingly irrevocable loss of material.

Interpretation, as the example above shows, can be organized around an interruption of the anticipated narrative with its striking character of attention to the instance and the particular, rather than an effort to generalize or to smooth over that which presents as disruption (Moules, 2002). Thus, the process of interpretation engages in a deconstruction of data and a reconstruction of meaning. The idea of deconstruction, most often associated with Jacques Derrida, involves a process of questioning traditional assumptions and certainties, rather than accepting them as assumed truths.

> Far from being opposed to deconstruction, philosophical hermeneutics requires it. Without difference and without language's endless deferral of meaning, the achievement of new understanding would not be possible. Philosophical hermeneutics contends that the vitality of understanding actually depends on difference. (Davey, 2006, p. xii)

One of the consequences of this deconstructive movement is that interpretation need not rely on complete stories, or logical narratives as data. As with themes, there is no rule against narrative, but interpretation serves an understanding of the topic, not any particular narrative offered by a participant. Interpretation goes on with the sense of truth as *aletheia* – unconcealment. While the goal is to bring to life some aspect of the topic, to remember forgotten or neglected truths, and generate new possibilities for practice, it is always at the cost of letting go of other possibilities. Interpretation involves choice at every moment, requiring tact, ethical focus, and clear sense of purpose.

Interpretive Writing: Bringing the Topic to Life in Language

Experience is not really meaningful until is has found a home in language.
(Madison, 1988, p. 165)

As mentioned, analysis in interpretive work has no beginning point, but rather is an ongoing experience. In the shaping of words on paper, something miraculous happens.

> Nothing is so purely the trace of the mind as is writing but nothing is so dependent on the understanding mind either. In deciphering and interpreting it, a miracle takes place: the transformation of something alien and dead into total contemporaneity and familiarity…that is why the capacity to read, to understand what is written is like a secret art, even a magic that frees and binds us. (Gadamer, 1960/1989, p. 163)

Hermeneutics requires a "tragic, loving relationship with language" (Moules, 2000, p. 15), meaning that language is the thing that carries interpretation into being but language, as Gadamer (1960/1989) suggested, has a forgetfulness of itself. It expresses one thing while at the same time silences another thing, and it is unstable, constantly open to re-interpretation: "…understanding and the hermeneutic translation and transcendence it affords depend upon the vital instability of the 'word'" (Davey, 2006, p. xv). Writing also has to reveal the vulnerability of the writer to not knowing, of being struck by something beyond words and understanding, of not fully understanding the topic, and of only partially and provisionally knowing what things mean. We are, after all, human beings on the move, caught up in things on the move. Phenomena are fluid, ever changing in time, as are we. Thus, we can never fully understand, and our awareness of this needs to show in our writing. This is not an easy thing to accomplish—to say things with confidence that does not also betray the provisional character of life itself.

Language holds something open in its possibilities; it clears a space around it and hands it on through articulation. Articulation, however, needs to be done well and in a way that allows the topic to stand against the articulation and not be consumed, constrained, or contained by it. Things should not be captured in the writing, not imprisoned by it, but set free within it. Yet, the tragedy lies in the notion that whenever words and meanings are given, other words and meanings are denied. This is the work of aletheia – to simultaneously reveal one thing while concealing another. Aletheia, in its enlivening, remembering, and unconcealment, is the goal of interpretive writing. Yet, writing itself inherently preserves some of the concealedness of the topic, respecting that all things cannot be fully known and there remains a privacy, mystery, and unknownness of all topics. Articulation should not flatten something out, but infuse it with vitality, energy, image, and imagination, in such a way that the articulation itself disappears, and the topic shows itself, perhaps even allowing it to be read in a more generous way than it reads itself.

> There is undoubtedly a question of style involved in philosophical hermeneutic writing, a valuing of creative expression that goes against the grain of contemporary belief that technical...language [necessarily] betokens substance. This is one of the challenges of hermeneutic research, both because it is not easy to do and because style cannot be allowed to run away with sense and purpose. (McCaffrey et al., 2012, p. 221)

Hermeneutic writing does have a "discernable signature" (Davey, 2006, p. 18). It is imaginative, creative, engaging, poignant, and stimulating. It can also be, perhaps should also be, disconcerting and tragic, "a condition of exposure in which one's conceptual resources have been blown away by what one has encountered. In this event, one finds oneself radically situated with no place to hide" (Bruns, 1992, p. 184).

Hermeneutic writing often has the character of exaggeration in strengthening what it wants to be heard (Smith, 1991). This does not mean that researchers invent things but instead attempt to highlight them. Exaggeration occurs deliberately, purposefully designed to disrupt, find, and cultivate the familiar. Hermeneutic work has to be more than just a good description; it has to be carefully crafted versions that will bear up clinical descriptions and exemplars and expand them into rich and full descriptions of the understandings generated and created within the study. For this reason, interpretations must be supported by data to allow the reader some recognition of how the interpreter arrived at the interpretations and to show that they are not just "made up" but came out of somewhere, something, or someone.

"Let the data speak for themselves these scientists say. The trouble with that argument is, of course, that data never do speak for themselves" (Keller,

1985, cited in Lenzo, 1995, p. 17). Steeves (2000) wrote of the dilemma of sending manuscripts to journals for review and receiving comments from reviewers with the criticism that he had "gone beyond his data." After his initial frustration with reviewers' lack of understanding, he came to realize that is exactly what he is supposed to do in hermeneutic research.

> It is the obligation of the researcher to go beyond his or her data, but not in the sense of reaching conclusions unrelated to the data or unjustified by the data. I am using *going beyond the data* to mean thinking what the data might mean in a broader way or using the data as a means of thinking about the broader world. What is the point of doing this work, investigating human experience, if thinking about this human condition in its largest sense is not allowed? (Steeves, 2000, pp. 97–98)

Steeves continued suggesting that one needs to "think *with* the data" (p. 98). Thinking with the data then means to be in the dialectic that interpretation requires, the back and forth of conversation, thought, questions and answers, possibilities, and puzzles. Davey (2013) offered the idea that interpretation is always X=X+; there is always something more to be interpreted and thinking with the data means going beyond it.

Jardine (2008) suggested that "(i)f one pursues a hermeneutic study…it is not enough to write about different things…I must also write *differently*, in a way that acknowledges, attends, and waits upon the agency of the world. Hermeneutics is therefore akin to the opening up of 'animating possibilities presented by each event' (Hillman 1982, p. 177)" (Jardine, 2008, p. 110). Writing differently is difficult. What is even more difficult is maintaining the creative and generative spirit of interpretive writing while remaining scholarly, citatious, deliberate, and mindful. This kind of writing does have a certain kind of flair and flavor, and done well, it also holds a keen sense of scholarship that is recognizable, and a keen sense of the limitations of the scholarship. If data analysis in the beginning is about looking to deconstruct the obvious, and unpack the assumed, it can be thought of as White (1993, p. 35) described as "exoticizing the domestic" – taking what is just a "given" and seeing it with a new lens. Once exoticized though, interpretations cannot be simply left there to dangle in an exotic display but must be brought back into the world where the topic is located; one could think of this as domesticating the exotic, "making what was once exotic to be recognizable and 'true'" (Moules, 2002, p. 3). Deconstruction is always in play with reconstruction.

Metaphors

Two senses of metaphor are at work in hermeneutics: one that signals our fundamental relationship with the world, and the other is that which is at work in language to make it possible to give expression to the nuanced character of experience. Often, in interpretive writing, metaphor is used as a linguistic device that can express the interplay of familiar and other. Well-placed metaphors draw the reader in and an original metaphor suddenly throws open an unexpected insight. For that reason, metaphor is often found in hermeneutic writing but we offer the caveat that metaphor, as a means to communicate meaning, can be overused. Writing that is rife with metaphor after metaphor may be engagingly picturesque but lose its hold on the topic, which disappears behind the metaphors rather than let the metaphor illuminate the interpretation. The word metaphor means to carry beyond, carry over, transfer or to bear (Hoad, 1986; Neufeldt & Guralnik, 1988); "Metaphor is the way language carried itself past its own powers to enter new realms" (Hirshfield, 1997, p. 111).

> Metaphors provide a view of something from a viewpoint of another thing and yet they work to make one feel 'at home.' *'Yes, that is right; that is what it is like; I recognize that.'* Paradoxically, a metaphor simultaneously serves to remove us, while at the same time offering us a home in language and understanding…Metaphors perhaps offer something to grasp, something that can be pictured and understood as a place to rest the mystery of the profound, wordless, faceless experience of suffering. (Moules, Simonson, Prins, Angus, & Bell, 2004, p. 105)

Metaphors have the ability to carry and bear things while providing meaning and understanding (Lakoff & Johnson, 2003). Used judiciously, they are rich and relatable ways of conveying interpretations. For example, in a hermeneutic study on grief cited in the quote above, Moules et al. (2004) used the metaphor of the "uninvited houseguest" to describe the arrival of grief after the death of a loved one. Since the publication of that study, Moules has received much feedback from bereaved people who can "relate" to this description and the metaphor has "grab" (Glaser, 1978, p. 95), serving to offer language and give meaning to an experience that is often indescribable.

The art of using metaphors relies on creativity, fit, and discernment about when and why to use them. As mentioned, the overuse of many metaphors, mixed metaphors, or metaphors that contradict each other can only serve to muddle the interpretations rather than to bring them clarity. When metaphors are overused, they become signifiers of implied shared values and points of view – fostering complacency rather than questioning. One such metaphor that has been overused in research (and elsewhere) is that of "the journey." This is not to say that it cannot be used but it should be substantiated, and presented and argued cogently so that it does manage to bear and carry the interpretation forward in such a way that the topic is illuminated richly.

Etymological Tracings and Intoxications

As a part of deconstructing or unpacking topics, an often-used practice in hermeneutic work is to carefully dismantle the meanings of words and their etymological origins. This can be a useful exercise if, as in the case of metaphors, it is not overused so that the paper begins to read like a dictionary, or playing with words for its own sake. Etymological tracings are a linguistic example of the importance of history for hermeneutics. Past meanings of words, and meanings of root words in other languages present layers of potential meaning within a word. There is no presumptive original or definitive meaning, but rather the presence of multiple meanings opens up another way of entering into dialogue with tradition and finding a way of questioning contemporary taken-for-granted points of view (Nicholas Davey, personal communication, August 7, 2014). As mentioned though, there can be an overreliance of the use of etymology as an interpretive tool, what Gadamer referred to as "etymological intoxication" (1960/2004, p. 409), and this can begin to disrupt or interrupt the fullness and flow of the interpretation with a constant return to the etymological tracing of the word. When this happens, it begins to appear as if the researcher is using word definitions and histories of words as the only means to reach an interpretation; in some cases, it even begins to resemble what could be called an etymological "trickery" in the sense that the play on words becomes an end in itself and a distraction from a lack of interpretive substance.

Tracing words back to their origins can be useful in the service of understanding the topic, if in fact it does bring understanding to the topic. For example, if one is trying to look at the topic of suffering and compassion, understanding the meanings and history of these words is vital. To suffer means to undergo, endure, tolerate, allow. It is connected to the word passion which is tied to the word patient. Compassion means to suffer with and suffering together. These tracings then make an argument for an interpretation that says something about what being compassionate is in the face of suffering, an understanding that has direct implications for practice (see for e.g., Moules, 1999, in her interpretive analysis of *Suffering Together: Whose Words Were They?*). Understanding the historical use and evolution of words as well as their multiple meanings is helpful when it serves the topic with substance and when the researcher can explain the purpose of an etymological exploration.

Summary: The Strength and Challenge of Interpretation

Hermeneutics involves answering questions that could be differently answered with different interpretations.

> All interpretation works under the promise of truth…When we opt for a given inter-
> pretation, we do not do so because we know it to be true…but because we *believe* it to
> be the best, the one that offers the most promise and is the most likely to make the
> text intelligible and comprehensible for us. (Madison, 1988, p. 15)

In believing something, we also need to be convincing; interpretations must be well grounded, justified, and articulated but not presented as incontrovertible.

Interpretation does not simply end; it offers a plausible and prudent response to something, but it does not offer a final answer. "What are perceived as the weaknesses of philosophical hermeneutics – its inability to arrive at a final interpretation…are indeed its strengths" (Davey, 2006, p. xv). The strength lies in the difficulty and vitality of the work. Davey (2006, p. xiv, citing Vattimo [2002]) reminded us of "the ever-present difficulty of residing within the 'quietness of a single interpretation.'" Interpretations are not quiet; they are bold, robust, assertive claims of something, but it has to be remembered that they can silence other claims if they are not made carefully, thoughtfully, and with enough room to allow an invitation to dialogue.

In spite of the boldness of interpretations, we do not want to protect any hermeneutic work from re-interpretation. Kvale and Brinkmann (2009) addressed the issue of the critique of hermeneutic analysis that different interpreters will find different meanings in the text, saying that this demand for objectivity premises on a belief that there can be only one correct interpretation. They countered this claim in acknowledging that it is the gift of hermeneutics to allow for pluralities of meanings and interpretations. There is an experience of needing to give the work up, of letting it move out of our hands into the hands of others, when we have finished the work to the best of our abilities, satisfied that the interpretations are fitting, and ring true of something; there is a handing over and that is exactly the right thing to do. In one way, it is as though the interpretation cannot settle and rest in one's own hands for, if it does, it stops growing, it stops being generative and fertile. It settles into a reified version of something without experiencing the life force and generativity of others and of the topic that it needs to sustain it. When interpretations go out of our hands and into the hands of others, they situate themselves exactly where they are supposed to be – in movement and play, and we cannot even save the work from our own re-interpretations. This is the curse and the gift of this kind of work.

In hermeneutic interpretation, we do not seek consensus or even absolute agreement; difference is not something to be overcome in hermeneutics. We hope for the newness that comes to meet it, the invocation for different interpretations. We hope for responses, and that the writing evokes something in the reader, that the reader's interpretation might make it better. Caputo (1987) suggested that hermeneutics succeeds

> only if it brings to words what we have all along understood about ourselves but have thus far been more or less unable to say…it comes down to its ability to provoke in us the ultimate hermeneutic response: "*That* is what we are looking for. That puts into words what we have all along understood." (p. 81)

The measure then of the credibility of the interpretations lies in the ways it brings understanding to the topic.

> When you talk to me about my research, do not ask me what I have found; I found nothing. Ask me what I invented, what I made up from and out of my data…I am not confessing to telling any lies about the people or events in my stories…The proof for you is in the things I have made – how they look to your mind's eye, whether they satisfy your sense of style and craftsmanship, whether your believe them, and whether they appeal to your heart. (Sandelowski, 1994, p. 61)

We have not laid out a formula for analysis in interpretive work, as that would be antithetical to hermeneutics, however we offer guidelines, suggestions, philosophical groundings, and invocations to move into interpretive analysis and to take interpretations to writing. In the next chapter, we offer examples of interpretive writing – of "writing differently" while maintaining scholarship and integrity.

References

Abram, D. (1996). *The spell of the sensuous: Perception and language in a more than human world*. New York, NY: Vintage Books.

Allen, D.G. (1995). Hermeneutics: Philosophical traditions and nursing practice research. Nursing Science Quarterly, 8(4), 174–182.

Bruns, G. (1992). *Hermeneutics ancient and modern*. New Haven, CT: Yale University Press.

Caputo, J. (1987). *Radical hermeneutics*. Bloomington, IN: Indiana University Press.

Colaizzi, P. F. (1978). Psychological research as the phenomenologist views it. In R. S. Valle & M. King (Eds.), *Existential phenomenological alternatives for psychology* (pp. 48–71), New York, NY: Plenum.

Davey, N. (2006). *Unquiet understanding: Gadamer's philosophical hermeneutics*. Albany, NY: SUNY Press.

Davey, N. (2013). *Unfinished worlds: Hermeneutics, aesthetics and Gadamer*. Edinburgh, Scotland: Edinburgh University Press.

Fleming, V., Gladys, U., & Robb, Y. (2003). Hermeneutic research in nursing: Developing a Gadamerian-based research method. *Nursing Inquiry, 10*(2), 113–120.

Gadamer, H-G. (1960/1989). *Truth and method* (2nd rev. ed.) (J. Weinsheimer & D. G. Marshall, Trans.) New York, NY: Continuum.

Gadamer, H-G. (1960/2004). *Truth and method* (2nd rev. ed.) (J. Weinsheimer & D. G. Marshall, Trans.) New York, NY: Continuum.

Gadamer, H-G. (2007). *The Gadamer reader: A bouquet of later writings*. Evanston, IL: Northwestern University Press.

Giorgi, A. (1985). *Phenomenology and psychological research*. Pittsburgh, PA: Duquesne University Press.

Glaser, B. (1978). *Theoretical sensitivity*. Mill Valley, CA: Sociology Press.

Heidegger, M. (1927/1996). Being and time (J. Stambaugh, Trans.). Albany, NY: SUNY Press.

Heidegger, M. (1977). *The question concerning technology and other essays* (W. Lovitt, Trans.). New York, NY: Garland.

Hirshfield, J. (1996). *Nine gates: Entering the mind of poetry*. New York, NY: HarperCollins.

Hoad, T. F. (Ed.) (1986). *The concise Oxford dictionary of English etymology*. New York, NY: Oxford University Press.

Hoy, D. (1998). Heidegger and the hermeneutic turn. In C. Guignon (Ed.), *The Cambridge companion to Heidegger* (pp. 170–190). London, UK: Cambridge University Press.

Jardine, D. W. (2008). Because it shows us the way at night: On animism,writing, and the re-animation of Piagetian theory. In D. W. Jardine, S. Friesen, & P. Clifford, *Back to the basics of teaching and learning: Thinking the world together* (2nd ed.) (pp. 105–116). New York NY: Routledge.

Keller, E. F. (1985). *Reflections on gender and science*. New Haven, CT: Yale University Press.

Kvale, S., & Brinkmann, S. (2009). *InterViews: Learning the craft of qualitative research interviewing* (2nd ed.). Thousand Oaks, CA: SAGE.

Lakoff, G., & Johnson, M. (2003). *Metaphors we live by*. Chicago, IL: University of Chicago Press.

Lenzo, K. (1995). Validity and self-reflexivity meet poststructuralism: Scientific ethos and the transgressive self. *Educational Researcher, 24*, 17–24.

Madison, G. B. (1988). *The hermeneutics of postmodernity: Figures and themes*. Bloomington, IN: Indiana University Press.

McCaffrey, G., Raffin Bouchal, S., & Moules, N. J. (2012). Hermeneutics as a research approach: A reappraisal. *International Journal of Qualitative Methods, 11*(3), 213–229.

Moules, N. J. (1999). Suffering together: Whose words were they? *Journal of Family Nursing, 5*(3), 251–258.

Moules, N. J. (2002). Hermeneutic inquiry: Paying heed to history and Hermes. An ancestral, substantive, and methodological tale. *International Journal of Qualitative Methods, 1*(3), 1–21.

Moules, N. J., & Amundson, J. K. (1997). Grief – An invitation to inertia: A narrative approach to working with grief. *Journal of Family Nursing, 3*(4), 378–393.

Moules, N. J., Simonson, K., Prins, M., Angus, P., & Bell, J. M. (2004). Making room for grief: Walking backwards and living forward. *Nursing Inquiry, 11*(2), 99–107.

Neufeldt, V., & Guralnik, D. B. (Eds.). (1988). *Webster's new world dictionary of American English: Third college edition*. New York, NY: W. W. Norton.

Smith, D. (1991). Hermeneutic inquiry: The hermeneutic imagination and the pedagogic text. In E. Short (Ed.), *Forms of curriculum inquiry* (pp. 187–209). New York: SUNY Press.

Steeves, R. H. (2000). Writing the results. In M. Zichi Cohen, D. L. Kahn, & R. H. Steeves (Eds.). *Hermeneutic phenomenological research: A practical guide for nurse researchers* (pp. 93–99). Thousand Oaks, CA: Sage.

van Manen, M. (1984). Practicing phenomenological writing. *Phenomenology + Pedagogy, 2*(1), 36–69.

White, M. (1993). Deconstruction and therapy. In S. Gilligan & R. Price (Eds.), *Therapeutic conversations* (pp. 22–61). New York, NY: W. W. Norton.

· 8 ·

INTERPRETATION AS WRITING

Interpretive writing is at the heart of hermeneutic research and it is a learned and practiced art that is often difficult to discern and develop for beginning researchers. Sometimes the most helpful way to understand how to conduct hermeneutic research or explain interpretive writing is to look at work that has already been done. In fact, our experiences with those new to the hermeneutic tradition have shown that hermeneutics often "explains itself" when one is able to read a published manuscript or dissertation of a hermeneutic study.

In this chapter, we offer two examples of recently completed and published hermeneutic research. These two examples are not the only way in which one can write hermeneutically, however they offer ideas of how the address, being methodical and following leads, conducting interviews, and interpretive analysis might look as an end product, as something available for public consumption.

Example One: "It's Not Just Camp": Understanding the Meaning of Children's Cancer Camps for Children and Families (Laing, 2013)

This study was the doctoral research done by Laing (supervised by Moules). In this study, Laing, whose clinical background was as a nurse in the field of pediatric oncology, was following up on something that had "struck" her in her previous clinical work, and that was the importance of cancer camp for children with cancer and their families. She remembered how excited kids would get thinking about going to camp, and how vitally important it became for many of them. Her job, as a nurse, was to make sure they were healthy enough to attend, inform the camp nurses about what needed to be done (medically) for the kids while they were at camp, and make sure all the paperwork was in order, ready for them to go. She never understood *why* camp was such a big deal – "it's just camp" after all, she thought.

Laing's hermeneutic study was conducted with kids who attended cancer camp, and their families (families attend too), in the summer of 2012. She interviewed six families, as individual families, usually in their homes approximately two weeks after returning home from camp. She also interviewed five camp counselors in a focus group setting at camp. Additionally, she spent eight days at camp, over the course of four weeks, in order to further understand the setting, people, activities, and culture. This fieldwork proved invaluable, and ultimately set the stage for several chapters of her dissertation. From this study, five interpretive chapters were produced, each relating to *something* that came from the interpretive analysis. Excerpts from each chapter are provided below.

Excerpt One: From the Chapter "In Play, At Play"[1]

Situated in the middle of a beautiful nowhere lies 160 acres of land best described as God's country. Dense forest and rolling hills against the backdrop of a never-ending blue sky, Camp Kindle is not just beautiful; it is excessively, indulgently, indefensibly beautiful. Its newly renovated buildings and wide-open spaces invite possibilities and whisper of opportunities to those who stay within its boundaries. As I made my way across a newly sodded part of a field, a little girl of about eight ran to catch up with me. "Didn't you know you're not supposed to be walking here? It's new grass, you know – it needs time to grow. What's your name? Are you a counselor? Are you someone's mom?" she rapidly fired me with questions the way only a young child without the burden of ego can. Her approach made me giggle and we talked as we made our way toward the lodge, me grateful to have someone to show me where I was going on my first day at camp. I came to learn that Molly was in her third year of treatment for leukemia and was at camp with her older sister and parents. She had been to camp a lot she said, "too many times to count" in fact. She seemed curious about my purpose for being there and did not seem to accept my answer of "research." I decided to try a little harder: "I'm going to be talking to kids and families, and even the counselors, to see if I can understand what it is about camp that's so great." She contorted her face as if that was the stupidest thing she had ever heard, and blurted out, "THAT'S EASY! IT'S SO MUCH FUN!" I laughed at her distaste for my research topic, realizing this girl was not letting me off the hook, and debated with myself how much further I would persist. Molly quickly grew bored however, and instead launched into a new conversation with me about how lots of the kids at camp are bald you know, and she used to be bald but isn't anymore, and some kids are missing a leg or an arm, and some have scars, and her only scar is from where her port is, and do I have any scars, and oh! have I been on the giant swing because she's been on the giant swing and she used to be afraid of it but now she loves it…and I kept my mouth closed and smiled and just listened to the flood of enthusiasm she washed over me.

The word "play" is deceptively ordinary. It likely conjures images of children, games, or a dramatic performance, however almost 100 definitions and idioms exist in reference to this word. We can play and be played, something can be at play or come into play, we can watch a play, play with words, play around, make a play for, or play along. Play is "complex and slippery" (Brown, 1998, p. 243) because the more one looks into, under, and behind the word, the more one discovers its history, roots, uses, and meanings. As a noun, play is defined as the conduct, course, or action of a game, or a recreational activity (Merriam-Webster, 2012). As a verb, it means to engage in sport or recreation; to move aimlessly about; or, to perform music or to act in a dramatic production. Etymologically, the origins of play are unknown but thought to come from old English plegian (verb), to exercise, frolic, perform music, and plæga (noun), recreation, exercise, any brisk activity (Online Etymology Dictionary, 2012). Throughout its etymological history, "play" has been closely connected to the world of children and make believe, and has generally stayed true to its primary meaning.

Excerpt Two: From the Chapter "The Island of Misfit Toys"[2]

Counselor: Um...I know this sounds really weird but sometimes I think of camp as the Island of Misfit Toys cause there's all something...they're all damaged in some kind of way and then it's just amazing to see the kids...they're so proud of who they are when they come to camp. The camper that comes to mind is JU...he's just, I mean ah, he has his leg amputated and he calls his little stump Tiny Tim (laughs) I mean outtrip (an overnight outside camping experience), like he was just telling a story and showing off Tiny Tim to all the campers just cause they're all curious about it...he's just so proud of himself and I think it's just fantastic to see and it really inspires the other kids in the group. I noticed since he told his story other kids have come out of their shells and they're just, they're like, you know what it's ok to be who I am...something might not look quite right but it ok cause we're all here together.
...

Mother (talking about the kids at camp): There's a variety of different types of challenges and everybody just kind of accepts that that's where they are, they've got theirs you've got yours and it moves on. Everybody's got their issues, they're all quirky, they've all got their challenges, so what?
Father: But outside the general, you know, the outlook, um, it's a little different, it's a little more harsh, a little less acceptance. (Parents of a child with a brain tumor)

The Island of Misfit Toys indeed became a chapter in Laing's thesis and ultimately an independent published article. Had she been looking for themes in her analysis, for example, this would never have shown up; one counselor said it one time. However, it spoke to her in that moment, and right then and there she knew there was something to this idea. She began to form a beginning interpretation in that moment. The interpretation reads in part as follows:

Before further discussion a closer examination of the word misfit is warranted. Merriam-Webster (2012) defines misfit as "something that fits badly," or, "a person who is poorly adapted to a situation or environment." It is an interesting word from an etymological perspective, with "mis" meaning "in a changed manner," and with a root sense of "difference, change," and fit, coming from the early 15th century, meaning "suitable" (Etymonline, 2012). It is not my intention to dissect this word into infinitesimally small pieces, however I wish to draw attention to something important as sometimes deconstructing words such as this offers a different lens from which to understand, or at least challenge, the traditional meaning. When one separates "mis" from fit, and examines them as two distinct words, the word misfit can be understood differently. Misfit, from an etymological standpoint, can be understood as something, or someone, that is "differently suited" versus the traditional definition offered earlier of "a person who is poorly adapted to a situation or environment."

Cancer camp, like the Island of Misfit Toys, offers a "sanctuary" of sorts, a place of belonging, acceptance, and safety. There is no such thing as someone who does not fit in, in fact *"usually the quirky kids get pulled into the group the fastest"* (Counselor). Before examining this culture of acceptance and how these children are "differently suited," it is important to first look at how it is children with cancer stand out and often feel un-accepted in the "real world."

Most of the families who spoke about camp being a place of acceptance had a child with a visible or behavioral difference that distinguished them from their peers. From loss of hair due to chemotherapy, to brain tumors, radiation therapy, or unrelated concurrent illnesses or syndromes (e.g., Asperger's/autism, ADHD, etc.) most children who have experienced cancer have also experienced looking, or being, different from their healthy peers at some point along the cancer trajectory. They have experienced a mis-fit in the real world, and all of the accompanying challenges. We know from the literature that "peer relationships are an important index of a child's current social competence and psychosocial adjustment" (Vannatta, Gartstein, Zeller, & Noll, 2009, p. 303). Establishing relationships with peers is a major developmental task of preadolescence and adolescence (Sullivan, 1953) and provide an important context for learning social skills and mastering the complexities of cooperation and competition (Hartup, 1999; Rubin, Bukowski, & Parker, 2006). I offer that it is by being completely, unconditionally accepted at camp, that these children come to understand that they are *differently suited* to their environment.

Excerpt Three: From the Chapter "Grief – The Bleached Bones of the Story"[3]

I don't want to forget that that's what happened to us, cause he's not here so, it's, it's real and I don't want to hide it. There's some families that we have met that don't want to have anything to do with it [camp] and I…just don't want to do that. It's helped my kids grieve, it's helped us grieve, and, I don't know, it's comforting to know that you're not the only one who has suffered like we have suffered out there. So we can share how we cope, what we do, do we talk about our son, you know, what special memories do we do every year, how do we remember him, how do the kids feel, and do you go to therapy, do you not go to therapy, you know, what do you do? But camp is like our therapy, it's just rejuvenating – it brings you together as a family to do something that you would never get to do. (Bereaved parent)

There is an inherent interpretive nature to grief, as it is experienced and understood differently by everyone, as eluded to by the parent in the above quote. Heidegger (1927/1962) suggested that to be human is to interpret, and hermeneutics reminds us that understanding is always interpretation; in fact, understanding is *already* interpretation, the two inseparable and intimately linked (Gadamer, 1960/1989). It is this concept of the intertwined nature of understanding and interpretation that I wish to bring to the forefront for examination with respect to grief and camp. The McMahon family, their child and brother now six years deceased, spoke readily about camp being a place that has helped them grieve. More than that, the father spoke to the changing nature of their camp experiences:

> *I think there becomes a point too where it transitions from where you become a net beneficiary of what happens at camp, to a point where you recognize how much of a strength and a blessing it's been in your life, so you start to look for ways to reciprocate and give back to it, if that makes sense. (Father)*

I have puzzled about this change – from "net beneficiary" to reciprocator, as I felt this change was indicative of something important. It perhaps was representative of the natural progression of grief over the course of six years, but I feel it needs to be highlighted, acknowledged, and exaggerated, in order to understand how grief changes.

> *We have a neat ceremony at camp…the families made these little lanterns with a little base out of a chunk of wood off of one of the trees – camp trees – and then we made, um, and then we put popsicle sticks to hold up – makes me cry (getting tearful) – um, put sticks up, and then we did paper and we designed the paper and made it especially for our kids and we floated it at night with a little tea light on it…it was gorgeous. (Parent)*

> *The luminaries…they took a piece of driftwood, a circle disc of driftwood…they call it tree cookies…and they put a candle in it, but first you have to decorate it and write a memory of your somebody special that has cancer or passed away from cancer, and then you make the luminary around it. You glue it on top and then you put it in the water and you say a prayer or make a wish and you put it off into the pond, and it's dusk at that point and it's all lit… it's really beautiful. (Parent)*

Luminaries, described in the above two quotes, was the activity of this past family camp, in place to honor the children with cancer, both survivors and deceased. Every year, it is something different, families told me, offering the examples of flags and kites they have made for this purpose. Most families spoke of this event – making the luminaries – and for most of these families, even the retelling of the story was an emotional event; it was clear that it had had a profound impact. One of the parents described this as a "ceremony," however I offer that it is more than a ceremony: it is a ritual. Rituals are present in our everyday lives from birth to death, and humans have ritualized life events since the beginning of recorded history. The word ritual has a rather mechanistic, routine connotation. Its root word, "rite," means a ceremonial act or action (Merriam-Webster, 2012), and often is in reference to church or religious ceremonies. Ritual, then, is of or relating to, rites (Merriam-Webster, 2012), relating to that which is sacred (not unlike magic). It is from this – the association of ritual with that which is sacred – that I frame the remainder of this discussion, specifically with the suggestion of camp as ritual, and ritual, as a way of understanding how it is that children and families come to understand their grief differently, at camp.

Everything at camp – from the activities, to the counselors' names, to the games and songs at meals and campfires, to creating something in honor of the child with cancer – could be considered a ritual. McCaffrey (2012) wrote,

> Ritual is not inevitably mechanistic, but has the dimension of a living process by which the person who enters into the ritual brings it into being through its enactment, and is simultaneously acted upon to shape his or her way of being in-the-world. (p. 4)

This perspective, McCaffrey argued, recognizes the degree to which the mental and the physical are connected. Ritual theories assert that focused interaction is at the heart of all social dynamics, and "rituals generate group emotions that are linked to symbols, forming the basis for beliefs, thinking, morality, and culture" (Summers-Effler, 2006, p. 135). Ritual and emotion are intimately linked, and have been touted as the fundamental mechanism that holds a society together (Durkheim, 1912, cited in Summers-Effler, 2006). Durkheim described the emotion that is produced from ritual as collective effervescence – a heightened awareness of group membership, as well as a feeling that an outside force (i.e., the ritual) has powerful, even sacred, significance. Ritual is thought to be a window by which people make, and remake, their worlds (Bell, 1992) offered that beliefs and rituals are intertwined, as "beliefs could exist without rituals; rituals, however, could not exist without beliefs" (cited in Bell, 1992, p. 7). Ritual, as Benner (2000) noted, can be an effective healing catalyst. Rituals can provide direction and validation to the search for meaning amidst grief. Through rituals, the people who are grieving are confronted with a new way of knowing, and may come to understand the world differently. It is perhaps, then, because of the collective effervescence (Durkheim, 1912) – the feeling of a powerful, sacred, outside force experienced by these families at camp, these rituals combine to help families make and remake their world (Bell, 1992), and come to new ways of knowing their grief. These rituals, I suggest, help families understand their grief, by bringing it down to a space where they can actually feel and comprehend the enormity of what has happened, and begin to understand differently, forming a new relationship with grief.

Excerpt Four: From the Chapter "The Stories of Cancer – From Glitter to Gratitude"[4]

Children never get to the point,
They surround it.
The importance of the point
Is the landscape of it.
You begin discussing
"The Rainfall of Vancouver Island"
And somebody has an uncle who lives there.
And there is an uncle in Alberta
Who has a zillion cows,
Some chickens, and a horse
(We get to feed the chickens
and ride the horse),
Which brings us to an uncle
In Saskatchewan, who has a house where
Deer pass the kitchen window
Every morning (he take us out
And shows us where they go).
If there were no uncles on Vancouver Island
It would never rain there.
(Stevens, 1981, cited in Jardine & Clandinin, 1987, p. 477)

As I write this dissertation, my daughters are three and fourteen years old. Despite their age difference, they are not as different as it might seem, particularly when it comes to telling stories. I marvel at the roundabout way in which words fall out of their mouths, saying nothing and everything at once. I have learned the art, as every parent must, of teasing out "the point" of their stories, often hidden among the debris of half-sentences, and distracted observations. Stevens' poem, particularly the first four lines, has had me pause to consider "points" and "landscapes," of stories. With children, "the importance of the point is the landscape of it," and I am brought back to my feelings of anxiety I had during my research interviews, as I felt that most children were "only" telling me stories, usually about what they did, not about how they felt. Try as I might, I was unable to get the kids to engage in, what I considered, "meaningful" conversation, with powerful quotes that would end up in my dissertation. I realize now, I was neglecting the landscapes of their stories. Their points were in the landscapes of their stories, and it was my error to have expected anything different.

Storytelling is said to have been around since the development of language. It has been used for centuries as a vehicle of communication and a way of passing wisdom along through the generations (Koch, 1998). "Stories are how we learn. The progenitors of the world's religions understood this, handing down our great myths and legends from generation to generation" (Mooney & Holt, 1996, p. 7). They are an important form of communication through which individuals, communities, and society conveys important messages, entertainment, knowledge, and experience to others (Bowles, 1995). Stories assist with reaffirming our lives and experiences, helping us connect with our inner selves and others (Atkinson, 2002).

"Stories" and "narratives" are often used interchangeably in the literature (Riley & Hawe, 2005). People lead storied lives (Connelly & Clandinin, 1990), and Frank (2000) suggested that people convey and tell stories rather than narratives. Wiltshire (1995) defined stories as personal experiences, informally and subjectively recounted, while Rubin and Rubin (2005) offered that stories are purposeful, and have the ability to change. Narratives, conversely, have been defined as being more structured and formal (Wiltshire, 1995), a partial description of a larger story (Rubin & Rubin, 2005), and, with respect to research, structured and formal accounts containing researcher additions and omissions (East, Jackson, O'Brien, & Peters, 2010). While I appreciate the distinction between the terms, for the purposes of this discussion, I have chosen to use the term story, as I believe it best speaks to the nature of what it is children and families are doing – they are telling their stories.

Laing opened this chapter with a poem that was the inspiration for the interpretation. This is a perfect example of how "following leads" might lead you to discover little gems along the way that enhance, add to, or create an interpretation. In this example, Laing was looking into an article by Jardine and Clandinin (1987), which happened to contain this poem. After reading the poem, she knew she had found the words upon which to build her interpre-tation, particularly the lines "Children never get to the point, they surround it. The importance of the point is the landscape of it." These lines provided the framework from which she built much of her "case" about the important purpose that storytelling served at camp. Interpretations sometimes feel like you are, indeed, "making a case," and this is further evidenced in this excerpt where Laing differentiates between "narrative" and "story." When writing hermeneutically, one has to be aware of the audience to which the writing is directed. Who are you writing to? What group of scholars will be most interested in this? In this case, Laing knew that her audience would consist of people well-versed in the tradition of narrative inquiry, and therefore it was important to distinguish between narrative and story, and be clear about which concept she was using and why. Laing, in this excerpt, moves on appro-priately with another story.

When I interviewed the McMahon family the youngest child, Christina, nine years old, sat quietly at the end of the couch near her dad. I was aware of her watching me – constantly – but she said little, usually being drowned out by her more gregarious older sisters and brother. She was wearing her camp shirt signed by fellow campers and counselors, and when I commented on it she beamed with pride, clearly happy I noticed. Christina contributed little for the first two-thirds of the interview, and I got the impression she was happy to sit on the sidelines. Something happened, though, toward the end, and Christina all of a sudden dominated the interview. As I reviewed the transcript, I counted thirteen times she spoke in the last third of the in-terview, versus two times in the first two thirds. I offer the following section of transcript not for the content, specifically, but more for the "dynamic" of what was happening:

Christina:	Also one of the things that I really liked was um, we were doing these super skills and I was in the studio and I learned a different way of finger-netting and um, these other people wanted me to show them how to do it, then all the people wanted to do it.
CML (Interviewer):	So you got to teach everybody how to do it?
Christina:	Yeah, and well, I told one of the counselors how to do it and she, like, some people from my group, we added all ours together.
Older sister:	Tell her how long it was when you added it together.
Christina:	Um, well mine, it was like a square and I had different colors, red, purple, blue, and I could jump over it, and then a lot of people wanted me to make, help them make some, and then like, they had fun.

CML:	*So you got pretty good at that!*
Older sister:	*They like, linked all their finger-nettings together, it was from one goal post to the other goal post, it was long.*
Christina:	*(laughing) Yeah, it was long enough that like, a lot of people liked it, they had fun. And her group (pointing to older sister), they were doing face painting and they liked it.*
Older sister:	*Every day we would have a new theme so on the day of her show and tell we would have Diva faces…glitter everywhere…and we had flowers, we did a tiger, we did an old man face…*
Christina:	*Um, there were other super skill groups like…(everyone starts talking at once, can't make anything out).*

Christina was engaged with me and telling me a story, her story, of something she did at camp. I, frankly, had no idea what she was describing at the time (it took me listening, and re-listening to the recording several times to understand what she was talking about). She talked quickly, her body leaning toward me, her eyes locked on mine, willing me to stay with her story. It was the kind of story nine-year-olds tell, with ambiguous beginnings, middles, and endings – the kind of story you need to "peripherally" listen to, because you lose the point when you listen straight on. The "point," I realized, was about how she took a leadership role in her group, and taught others a skill she had mastered. The point for her, however, lay in the landscape of the story – the finger-netting, the colors, the fact that everyone had fun – not at all about mastery and leadership.

Christina's talkativeness was further punctuated after the interview was over and Christina and her mother were showing me pictures and mementos of Tanner, their child and brother who had died. Christina remained very talkative, telling me stories about how she would accompany her brother when he needed painful procedures, and how "*they didn't let anyone into the room, but they let me in because they knew I could help calm him down.*" At one point, her mother said, "*This is so unlike her. She never talks this much!*" and I wondered about this for many days afterwards. In order to understand what is happening when we tell our stories, it is important to look beyond just the words. The stories we tell are not to say what we know, but to find out what we know, and in telling stories, "we try to make sense of life, like we try to make sense of a text when we interpret it" (Widdershoven, 1993, p. 9). Stories of illness (in Christina's case, of her brother's illness) help make sense and give meaning to dramatic and confusing times of life (Abma, 2005; Bosticco & Thompson, 2005).

It is our opinion that the best hermeneutic work occurs when the writer listens to how the data wants to be written. This sounds like a very mysterious concept – how does one "listen to the data"? Listening to the data comes from the complete immersion in the topic, reading and rereading of transcripts, and a commitment to staying true to a viable and valuable interpretation. In the above excerpt, for example, Laing tried to stay true to her interpretation – storytelling – by telling a story, the best story she had from her data, in order to convey an understanding. She could have just as easily chosen to offer only a few quotes here and there, and to have heavily substantiated the concept of storytelling by way of research, however she approached it differently. This is an example of "listening to the data" and finding a way to convey it best.

Excerpt Five: From the Chapter "Community as *Sensus Communis*"[5]

It's different for everybody but for me, I think the experience of being in a place where people are all experiencing, or have experienced, the same thing…and the support that gives, especially for people who don't ever get a break…to be in a place where everybody's experienced the same or similar, and are supporting one another and being able to just be who you are. (Parent)

Gadamer (1960/1989) spoke of *sensus communis*, its literal translation from Latin meaning "common sense," however not in the regular, every day use of the phrase. *Sensus communis*, according to Gadamer, relates to the general sense – the "common" sense – of the community. It is a common sense not only because it is widely accepted, but also because it is genuinely, authentically, shared by a community (Gelfert, 2006). "The main thing for our purposes is that here *sensus communis* obviously does not mean only that general faculty in all men but the sense that founds community…hence, developing this communal sense is of decisive importance for living" (Gadamer, 1960/1989, p. 21). *Sensus communis* can help us contextualize and understand in different ways, and is rooted in a common way of being. It speaks of connectedness to others and a deep sense of belonging.

I believe one of the ways we might understand the profound connections and support that families offer one another simply by virtue of a shared diagnosis is through *sensus communis*. These families share a "common" sense with one another – a sense only acquired by those who share the experience of having a child with cancer. There is a privacy to this sense – even I, for example, having worked closely with these children and families for many years, can never share in this "common" sense. Knowledge exists within the *sensus communis* that cannot be taught. As much as I would like to think I know about this experience, I can never *really* know it, unless I have lived it.

> *One of the dad's said, "I can't take anymore time off work so I could only come out for a couple days, cause you know, being off for a year" and I said "Yeah," and he goes, "People here get that! My family doesn't get that!" And he kinda walks away and I'm laughing to myself, cause it was true, you know, we do get that, because all of a sudden you're not able to work, you're not able to do anything. (Parent)*

> *People don't show sympathy for you, they show empathy [at camp]. They understand – you don't have to explain…and so you get into camp, you don't have to explain chemo, you don't have to explain radiation…cause you've got this experience bottled up and who can you talk to? Well, you know what, cancer parents you can tell anything (laughs), we've seen everything – or feel like we have! (Parent)*

It struck me that there was a sense of relief among these families, at belonging to this community – the kind of relief that helps to shoulder the heavy weight of the burden of this disease, and that offers a break from the fear and despair so often experienced, particularly in families newly diagnosed. This sense of community, belonging – the *sensus communis* – is fostered by children's cancer camps. Camp brings these families together into its community, the physical community of camp, defined in the traditional sense of the word by its landscape and natural boundaries. Then, like good hermeneutic work (Moules, 2012), it disappears into the background and allows for the *sensus communis* to form. For many families, camp is the first time they are exposed to other cancer families and often, up until that point, have felt very alone and isolated.

> *And you know, the thing is, sometimes I think when you're in it and feel alone, yeah you go to the hospital and you see everybody else going through their stuff and you realize that you're not the only one, but you're not there to converse on a personal level, you know? And so yeah, it's probably few and far between conversations in the years since treatment that I've had this, been able to have these kinds of conversations with parents. (Parent)*

Excerpt Six: Thesis Summary Chapter
Ordo ab Chao – Order from Chaos

Camp seems chaotic. From the meals and activities, to the campfires and dances, it is loud, messy, and – to an outside observer – chaotic. There is order to this chaos, however, and what seems haphazard is purposeful, and hidden among the noise and chatter, lies a meaningfulness worthy of a second look, and a third. You cannot see or understand the meaning of camp simply by looking at it, or asking "what is camp like"; you have to feel it, taste it, experience it, talk to people, try things, participate, sit back and watch, and get dirt under your fingernails. It is an experiential event, addressing each of your senses, and with this comes a seductiveness because it makes you want it more, when you maybe did not even realize you wanted it in the first place.

Camp not only cares for the children with cancer and their families, it is also an incubator for the future generation of young adults that are leaders in the highest sense of the word – the counselors. These young men and women are our moral compasses, our lighthouses, our stars, and they are the people that are going to make profound differences in this world. I cannot emphasize enough how special these counselors are, and how they are truly there to help, and make a difference. They too, are loud, crazy, talented, and contribute to the chaos I observed, however, they are the backbone of camp, and without them, there would be no order from this chaos.

Cancer camp has reminded me that the more sophisticated the science of childhood cancer becomes, the more obvious it is that curing the disease is only half the battle. While a great deal of attention has been given to cure, more attention is needed in areas of care. As more and more children survive the disease, the pediatric oncology community is still discovering the long-term effects of treatment, and there are as many psychosocial long-term effects of therapy as there are physical effects. Understanding the meaning of cancer camps for the child and family can help healthcare professionals and organizations like Kids Cancer Care refine and improve upon programs and services offered to these children and families, thereby improving upon the quality of care they receive. It is my hope that research, like this, can also be utilized to further legitimize the camp experience as one of significant benefit to children and families.

Like war, there are physical wounds from childhood cancer, but sometimes more importantly, there are psychological wounds that never go away. As one parent, whose son had been off treatment for 12 years, told me, "when you're newly diagnosed you think that emotional pain will never go away...I started crying the minute I drove up [to camp] and I'll probably cry again." In some ways, camp is a reminder of the journey traveled, and a caution for those of us who care for these families to remember that because a child might be "cured" physically, does not mean they are "cured" mentally, psychologically, or spiritually. Gadamer (1960/1989) stated that "hermeneutic work is based on a polarity of familiarity and strangeness, and…the true locus of hermeneutics is this in-between" (p. 295). I have come to think of camp as a physical representation of this "in-between" to which Gadamer referred. "In-between" implies an openness, or space, and throughout many of my interpretations, the "space" at camp has played significantly into how to understand what was at play.

> We are no longer able to approach this like an object of knowledge, grasping, measuring and controlling. Rather than meeting us in our world, it is much more a world into which we ourselves are drawn. [It] possesses its own worldliness and, thus, the center of its own Being so long as it is not placed into the object world of producing and marketing. The Being of this thing cannot be accessed by objectively measuring and estimating; rather, the totality of a lived context has entered into and is present in the thing. And we belong to it as well. Our orientation to it is always something like our orientation to an inheritance that this thing belongs to, be it from a stranger's life or from our own. (Gadamer, 1960/1994, p. 192)

Camp is a vast, open, empty space that is full of possibilities for new understandings, diminished suffering, and the telling of stories. Its empty space becomes filled with words, stories, emotion, laughter and play, kinship, fit, and community, and often, pain and suffering can be left there, to echo through the trees.

Example 2: A Hermeneutic Reappraisal of Nurse Patient Relationships on Acute Mental Health Units, Using Buddhist Perspectives (McCaffrey, 2013)

The second set of examples of hermeneutic writing are taken from the doctoral dissertation by McCaffrey, on the topic of nurses' experiences working in therapeutic relationships with patients on acute, in-patient mental health units. He made a decision early in the research process to introduce ideas from Buddhist thought to seek fresh perspectives on a very well-established topic. Hermeneutics was a natural research approach precisely because it provided theoretical resources to explain and to support a dialogue between disparate traditions, namely mental health nursing and Buddhism. Thus, the work of interpretation had already begun in McCaffrey's extensive clinical experience as a mental health nurse, in his practice and reading in and around Zen Buddhism, and in his noticing affinities, echoes, kinships, and contrasts between the two. This approach, in the context of a doctoral dissertation, required extensive preparatory sections to establish and explicate meaningful connections between hermeneutics, relational practice in mental health nursing, and Buddhist thought. Hermeneutics tends to manifest itself explicitly in research writing since the philosophy, as a way of thinking and practicing, perfuses the research. Hermeneutics is not a method that supplies a set of procedures that remain separate from findings, but a set of practices that run through all stages of research.

The following excerpt comes from the third chapter of the dissertation, entitled "Hermeneutics and Intercultural work." The chapter is part of building a structure in which to understand the topic coherently. Hence, in the excerpt, McCaffrey took up an idea about otherness from the hermeneutic writer Richard Kearney and applied it to Western Buddhism to establish the idea of a tension between familiarity and difference.

Excerpt One: From the Chapter "Hermeneutics and Intercultural Work"

"A Stranger It Comes to Us, That Quickening Word" (Hölderlin, c.1800/2004, p. 475): Cultural Otherness

The second sense of otherness in my topic is the regard of the nurse-patient relationship from Buddhist perspectives. This already assumes, or at least expects to find, that the Buddhist tradition can provide different ways of seeing from those afforded by professional convention and Western philosophies. The earlier discussion of affinities between Buddhism and nursing has indicated that there is something to this claim. Beyond this, however, to use Kearney's (2003) image of holding open the play of the familiar and the foreign, there will be little point to this dialogue if either Buddhist concepts can be simply translated into Western terms and assimilated, or if they are so different as to be of only esoteric interest. If Buddhism is rendered either too familiar or too foreign it is not of much help to us in practice, whatever other kinds of value it may hold. Philosophical hermeneutics is useful at the outset in guiding dialogue and opening up space for this negotiation between familiarity and foreignness.

[There is a] social reality that over the past fifty years Buddhism has taken root in the West as religion, as practice, and as a body of thought (Batchelor, 1994). Buddhism in the West has to be seen in the context of globalization, which has features of both the nearly universal spread of the technology with which Heidegger was concerned, and of an unprecedented availability of material from different cultures and traditions around the world (Mc-Mahan, 2008). This is where the principles of philosophical hermeneutics are helpful in negotiating the phenomenon of Western Buddhism, not least in resisting the error that Buddhism is one trans-cultural object to be explained. For example, Wright (1998), in a penetrating discussion of Zen literature, employed Gadamerian hermeneutics to read back through the Romantic assumptions that he identified as permeating previous Western readings of Zen.

McCaffrey's choice of topic made particular demands of explication and required wide reading that in turn shaped the structure and writing of the final dissertation. The function of the chapter, and of these two paragraphs, was to explore ways of substantiating a productive engagement between the two traditions of hermeneutics and Buddhist thought. One aspect of the writing to note is the sources embedded within it: in the first paragraph, the contemporary hermeneutics of Richard Kearney and in the second, a range of works by Western authors about the phenomenon of "Western" Buddhism. Hermeneutic writing thrives on a rich range of sources, but only so long as they have a bearing on the topic at hand. One function of drawing out connections and associations is to establish that, although a piece of hermeneutic research may stem from an individual "address," it has to stand in the world as more than one person's scratching an intellectual itch. It is not just that McCaffrey happened to become interested in Zen Buddhism, but that in doing so he entered into an emergent branch of an ancient tradition with its own characteristics and effects within the wider culture.

Excerpt Two: From the Chapter "Buddhism and Nursing"[6]

The following excerpt comes from the next chapter in the dissertation, closing in from the broad principles of dialogue between traditions to examples of terms common to both. Catherine Laing in the first part of this chapter wrote about play, how it emerged as a focus in her topic, and how it was also present in hermeneutics as an image of a free, to-and-fro exchange. Play, in this sense of an open-ended dialectic, is often a characteristic of hermeneutic writing.

McCaffrey took up the notion of practice, which is valued both in nursing and Zen Buddhism. He began by drawing attention to the fact that the word "practice" is so well used, in order to try to create a reflective distance around the word, to soften it up for reconsideration.

Practice: Dogen's Instructions to the Tenzo [Head Cook]

One of the axioms of nursing is that it is a practice discipline. When a term becomes widely assumed and taken for granted, it starts to slip away from us, unnoticed in plain sight like a comfortable pair of shoes. Words start to accrue qualifiers in order to reintroduce differentiation, jump start meaning, or to remind us of their presence. Thus we have practice that can be advanced (or by inference, basic), it can be the best, or bad (or malpractice – the legalistic sting of that Latin prefix) – is there a worst practice, the evil twin of best practice? If clinical practice is the epicentre of nursing, then what kind of practice is it that I am engaged in writing this? The one thing we are unable to do – we would not even want to try – is to get rid of practice. The following extract lets us take the step back, as a Zen saying goes, in order to see practice from another angle.

The 13th-century Zen teacher, Eihei Dogen put the practice of sitting meditation at the centre of Zen activity. To this day, the invitation to attend to one's existence in the present moment in the silence of meditation is the hallmark of Zen practice. Dogen, however, also deployed meditation as a kind of template for understanding how the activities of everyday life are also practice. He particularly addressed the day-to-day realities of monastic life, and the exigencies of people living together in "just institutions" to use Ricoeur's phrase (1994, p. 194). Zen Buddhism is a practice both of meditation and of how one lives (Rizzetto, 2005; Tanahashi, 1995).

In the thesis chapter, McCaffrey went on to discuss a work by Dogen about practicing mindfully by doing the necessary, everyday work of cooking in an institutional kitchen. One thing is shown in the light of another – nursing practice in the light of, for example, how to look after vegetables in a Zen monastery. These kinds of cross connections need to be worked into hermeneutic writing carefully – to use a culinary metaphor, ingredients need to be added in the right proportions at the right time for the finished dish to taste good.

Excerpt Three: From the Chapter "Forms"[7]

The following excerpt is taken from one of the "interpretive chapters" of the dissertation, referring to the interpretation of interview data. It is a label of convenience insofar as it is clear from the previous sections quoted above that the work of interpretation is intrinsic to hermeneutic research and writing. Students sometimes talk about "getting to the interpretation" as if it is a form of analysis to be switched on at a certain point. Different types of content demand to be handled differently but the judicious use of interpretation is always available as a part of the writing.

In approaching interview data, McCaffrey went through a similar process to Laing, above, in reading and re-reading transcripts and beginning to pick out significant words, statements, points of view, stories – or even on occasion, non-verbal elements such as silences, hesitations, or abrupt changes of subject. He sketched out a series of thematic headings, which appeared to follow similar points of attention across the interviews (in this case, there were four participants). These headings provided a series of locations for interpretive discussion. The goal was not to define themes as such but to ground interpretation in the matter of the transcripts. The startling exception to what other participants said or a stand-out phrase is potentially as much a stimulus to productive interpretation as the density of shared meaning. Amidst apparent agreement, too, interpretive writing is also about teasing out differences among similar sounding experiences or opinions as well as registering commonality.

For McCaffrey, the chapters based on the interviews took shape around ideas from Buddhist thought. These were not arbitrary or pre-planned, however. Material from the interviews brought forward a response from the researcher and writer who was, in this case, steeped in a dialogue between Buddhism and nursing. There proved to be no shortage of creative, useful, and convincing connections.

The following excerpt came from a chapter about ritual, taking a cue from a Western writer about Zen, who noted that, "The key [to ritual] is the gradual, even imperceptible, scripting of character through mental and physical exercise" (Wright, 2008, p. 11). Interviewees had talked about the way they felt compelled to behave in certain ways in the social environment of mental health units, so Wright's comment, suggesting links between identity, physical activity, and ideas provided a thread of interpretive insight. Once the theme of ritual was identified, McCaffrey went back and did further reading on that topic and discovered the work of a religious studies scholar, Catherine Bell (2009), on ritualized behavior. This source proved to be highly valuable in bridging insights from Zen sources and the work of nurses within a well-defined social context. In the end, it was Bell's flexible framework of understanding ritualized behavior that provided the main theoretical basis for the chapter.

Forms

The next feature of ritualization in Bell's (2009) account is that of an open-ended dialectic of body and environment. I have already used the example of a Zen sesshin [intensive practice period] to show how the detailed organization of bodies and gestures in space and time is simultaneously demanded by the environment, and creates the environment. The critical additional point here is the element of belief system and power relations that underwrite ritualized activity. One would not for long put up with the finely regulated routine of a sesshin unless one had at least a basic sympathy toward the Zen tradition. In turn, power relations are expressed through "the production of a ritualized agent able to wield physically a scheme of subordination or insubordination" (Bell, 2009, p. 100). Thus, through participation in a ritualized activity, in a specific body-environment dialectic, one knows one's place, and this knowing is the expression of certain power relations (though recalling the characteristic of misrecognition, this is probably not construed by the participant at the time). "Hence, ritualization, as the production of a ritualized agent via the interaction of a body within a structured and structuring environment, always takes place within a larger and very immediate sociocultural situation" (Bell, 2009, p. 100). This can be illustrated by an experience one of the participants described of going to work on an acute mental health unit in another country.

> *I remember the first day that I turned up and the – it was like – it was a scene from One Flew Over the Cuckoo's Nest, the whitewashed walls, the grilles on the windows, and the nurses in white dresses with their hats and the male nurses in all white but just with little shorts and knee high socks and white trainers and the aesthetic just didn't work for me...so I thought "I can't work here." On top of which it was substantially gate keeping that the nurses were doing, there was no real therapeutic role for nurses in that kind of environment.*

This nurse worked on the unit for about two weeks, but by this account had the measure of the place at first glance. Clearly implicit in this description is a tradition and set of beliefs that spoke eloquently through the environment, including the nurses' dress, and the conditioned forms of nursing behavior. In a kind of lived Foucauldian (2009) flashback, the asylum, confinement, and psychiatric power are all present in the image of this particular unit.

The following excerpt, from later on in the same chapter, shows the payoff for providing an interpretive framework, a way of thinking in terms of ritualized behavior. The language afforded by Bell's work enabled the insight that it is at least as much nurses as patients who are bound by medication giving rituals on acute care mental health units.

The third common type of activity as part of the nurse's role is the administration of medications. This did not figure all that prominently in the interviews, perhaps because it is such a taken-for-granted way of relating with patients. Nurses have to follow clearly mandated steps, now computer based, in ensuring that patients are given (or at least offered) the correct medication at the correct time, and that this is accurately recorded. One nurse mentioned *"thinking about doing my meds for the whole day"* with the inference that this is one of the structuring routines of nursing time. Each shift is marked out by the medication schedule of the nurse's assigned patients for that day, which entails for example knowing that at breakfast time and lunchtime, there will be medications to give out. Nurses are as much bound to this ritual as the patients. It is not surprising, then that negotiation over medications can become one common scene of dialogue between nurse and patient. Participants identified different approaches to this on the part of nurses. One identified a kind of approach in which a nurse will say to a patient:

> *"You have to take this medication,"* and I think it's more the approach *and the way things are said. "You have to take this medication," well actually they don't – and you know, just, it's "I know what I'm doing, I'm the expert here and you're gonna do what I say," that authoritative kind of thing. Sometimes you have to say "You have to take the medication" but you know, a lot of times they don't want to and "No, you have to" instead of – "Can I ask if you're worried about something with the medication?," like I think it's the approach.*

Another nurse made a similar point about trying to understand the context of a patient's behavior before assuming that medication would be the best strategy to address the patient's situation at that moment:

> *…you have a patient who is schizophrenic and they're hallucinating and you can tell that they are distressed. So rather than saying like, sitting down and having that conversation or even walking beside them as they are pacing the hallway, "you seem to be getting a bit upset right now – is there something I can do to alleviate some of your discomfort or have I totally*

misread the situation?" And then it gives them the opportunity to say "Yeah, either I am totally upset or nah, I'm fine, don't worry about me I just want to pace." "Great, you know what, if you need anything let me know."

By contrast, she characterized a more perfunctory response, picturing the nurse sitting behind the long desk at the front of the unit, watching patients: *"Nursing from the desk, patient appears agitated. What's going to be the next response? Patient offered, you know, Ativan or Zyprexa."*
What these accounts suggest is the degree to which nurses are bound by the activity of giving psychotropic medications, and if they often feel that patients must take them, they certainly feel that they must give them. They also demonstrate, however, that this compulsory element of practice can be a space of sympathetic curiosity and support for patients when nurses are prepared to exercise judgment about what is most helpful in a specific situation.
The phrase "nursing from the desk" that one of the nurses used, quoted here, turned up at several points in the dissertation – it appears again in the next excerpt. It is beautifully, economically expressive of a whole style of nursing, that emphasizes observation, distance, and symptom-watching over engagement and attempting to understand the person's experience. When asked to give a succinct summary of the whole study, McCaffrey usually turns again to that phrase. In retrospect, it could easily have been a chapter by itself, or even part of the title of the whole study. There is no one way to write up the data – another researcher, given the same transcripts, would write them up from her or his own interpretive angle (not necessarily any more or less valuable) and the same researcher, going back to the transcripts (as a thought experiment!) would not write the same dissertation twice. The phrase itself is multivalent, so that it informed the interpretation of medication-giving, above, and another interpretation of nurse-patient roles, below. One of the pleasures of hermeneutic writing is in the recognition, contemplation, and utilization of such multivalence.

Excerpt Four: From the Chapter "Host and Guest"[8]

"Host and guest" was a metaphor that merited a chapter by itself, because it proved to be so rich in exploring the roles played by nurses and patients in relation to each other. It was prompted in part by a conversation McCaffrey had with a psychiatrist, while they were working together on a consultation liaison team, conducting mental health assessments on patients on medical and surgical units. Often we had to conduct interviews with patients in shared rooms where other people were present, and we pulled curtains around the bed for privacy. The psychiatrist pointed out how quickly patients became "trained" to collude in the fiction that a curtain somehow prevented other people from hearing, as well as seeing, what was going on. This prompted a question, "whose hospital is it?"

From there, McCaffrey brought the metaphor of host and guest into play. The chapter was divided into two sections, since both Zen tradition and contemporary deconstruction have made much of the dialectic of host and guest. Again, there was a series of interplays between transcripts and interpretation, between topic and method, and between philosophical traditions. What held them together was the experience from the transcripts of nurses knowing about a plurality of modes of relationship.

The following excerpt comes from the second part of the chapter, drawing on Derrida's (2002) and Kearney's (2003) discussion of the etymology of the word "host," and the ambivalence between associated terms "hospitality" and "hostility."

Host and Guest

Host and guest, then, are produced in how nurses regard themselves in relation to the physical space of a hospital unit, and in how they regard patients and others in relation to the space. Differing inflections of host and guest are audible in the interviews with nurses about acute care mental health units. One nurse said, "*I see a lot more nursing from the desk.*" This is a succinct spatial image for a style of nursing in which the nurse remains behind the desk of the unit, observing patients across a physical divide and making decisions about interventions based on visible behaviors without engaging with the patient's thoughts and feelings so as to gain some understanding of the meanings of behaviors for the individual. The nurse hinted at the hostility buried in this kind of Derridean "hospitality" (Derrida, 2002, p. 358):

> And it's very frustrating when you're like, when you say that you agitate a patient because you haven't heard anything that they said. You told them what they will be doing today. To me that would be very disempowering. I would be like "absolutely not, I won't do that" that gets into a screaming match, who is going to suffer the consequences of that?

If control is a question for patients, however, it is also a question for nurses. Nurses on acute units do not have any say about which strangers turn up on their doorstep. Decisions about admission are made by psychiatrists else-where, in the emergency department, or on a medical unit, or in a clinic. The nurse's task is then to admit the stranger who comes. One of Kearney's key arguments in *Strangers, Gods and Monsters* (2003) is for a diacritical hermeneutics that incorporates the need for discernment, based upon the recognition that one cannot know if the stranger is a friend or enemy, that ambivalence in the *hostis*. Kearney critiqued the unconditional welcome to the other enjoined by Levinas and Derrida in the name of a stickier, but more worldly, "kind of critical hermeneutics capable of distinguishing – however tentatively – between enabling and disabling forms of alterity" (Kearney, 2003, p. 67). The recognition of the risk inherent in admitting the stranger perhaps helps to understand why it is that nurses resort to strat-egies of control that include assumptions about knowing what the stranger is, and wants, by observation. Nevertheless, two features of a hermeneutics of discernment are curiosity and the openness to an exchange in which the stranger has a chance to become less strange. For example, one nurse talked about enjoying the process of admitting a patient:

> Well, even though there was – you followed a protocol and there were things that you had to ask – it was always a little bit of uncovering a mystery – for me it was a bit about how do you make sense of why this person at this time at this place?

There is an interesting play here between protocol and mystery, the com-pletely predictable, formulaic routine of admission and the completely un-known (as yet) patient who enters the unit. That is, of course, thinking of the patient who is coming to the unit for the first time. When a patient is being readmitted and is well known to the nurse, then the challenge for the nurse becomes remaining open to what might be new and resisting the temptation to assume too much familiarity and to render the event entirely routine.

The above passage represents nursing practice and re-presents nursing practice in the light of Kearney's analysis of the difficulty of meeting the other. His metaphorical schema of gods and monsters helps to illuminate the contrasting attitudes described in the quotations from transcripts – on the one hand, a wish at times to shut patients down and maintain control, and on the other a lively curiosity. Both are accounted for in the interpreta-tion that helps to discover them as possibilities inherent in the situation of the nurse in the acute care setting. This gets to the point and the purpose of hermeneutic writing: to open up – and keep open – diverse understandings.

Often mistaken for passive description, hermeneutic writing creates possibilities for choice by giving a sound account of what is happening in the first place beyond the limitations of institutional, moral, and self-serving assumptions.

Excerpt Five: From the Chapter "Implications for Practice"

The last excerpt comes from the final chapter of McCaffrey's dissertation, aside from the conclusion. In practice disciplines, there is invariably a need for research to prove its value through the presentation of concrete outcomes and recommendations for practice (see Chapter Ten for a more detailed discussion of this topic). Though challenging for interpretive research, the goal of which is new understanding, it is nonetheless a part of the discipline of hermeneutic writing to locate new understandings and fresh perspectives in the world of practice.

In the excerpt, McCaffrey places his work back into the tradition of nurse-patient therapeutic relationship in mental health nursing, whence it came at the outset. He used the word "implications" rather than "conclusions" or "recommendations" to continue the interpretive integrity of the research. What emerges is strongly connected to a strain of advocacy in mental health nursing for the therapeutic potential of relational practice. It recognizes at the same time, however, that this in itself is one interpretation of the nurse's role, and that there are other forces and traditions that have different effects on nurses' practice.

Implications for Practice

Paying attention to modes of individual development is one important way of addressing implications for practice. Returning to the point about how individual practice manifests within networks of relationships, however, it is perhaps more important to consider possibilities for institutional development. This emphasis has been discussed in nursing literature in terms of the interaction between social structure and individual agency (Nairn, 2009; Porter, 1993). Nairn, as a nurse researcher, identified that in many interpretive studies there was an over-emphasis on individual agency at the expense of identifying the influence of institutional and social structures. Porter wrote as a sociologist trying to make sense of the literature reporting about psychiatric nurses not interacting in therapeutic ways with patients. He outlined theoretical models that sought to overcome a dichotomy between accounting for this phenomenon either in terms of autonomous individual actions, or institutional determinism. A dialectical approach allowed him to "examine how the actions of nurses are constrained and enabled by the institutions within which they work, while at the same time identifying how their actions either maintain or transform the nature of those institutions" (Nairn, 2009, p. 1561).

The institutional dimension introduces many different forces and interests that shape nurses' ways of working. These include unions and management practices, political priorities at provincial and national levels, and other disciplines, primarily medical psychiatry in the mental health context. Without entering into a discussion of possible implications of any or all of these forces, it is sufficient to note that advocacy for relational practice is only one theme among many. It is ethically exemplary and prominent in standards for practice (Canadian Federation of Mental Health Nurses, 2006) but in healthcare realpolitik it is often subordinated to an ideology of managerial efficiency (Rankin & Campbell, 2006). One of my arguments from this research is, however, that relatively subtle shifts in routine practices may have significant effects in the formation of how nurses understand themselves and their patients. The essential ingredient is to create reflective spaces, on a ground of compassionate ethical intent. The Tidal Model (Barker & Buchanan-Barker, 2005), which one of the nurses had used in her practice, is one example of doing this by valuing the patient's narrative experience and creating conditions to hear it. I would simplify this structurally even further, to the nurse entertaining a curiosity about from where the patient has come, and to where the patient is going. A relatively simple practice such as an interdisciplinary care-planning meeting, preferably facilitated by a Clinical Nurse Specialist or equivalent, can work to draw attention to the patient's experience and foster communication among clinicians. (I have in mind something less formal and more individually focused than traditional ward rounds, which tend to be driven by the medical agenda).

One thing to note is that the conclusions themselves are not dramatic or original. Hermeneutics can be deployed to denounce whole systems, but it is then left with the tricky task of coming up with realistic proposals for an alternative. What hermeneutic work can do very well is to reveal a situation in its complexity and, by doing so, present a clear picture of the sometimes conflicting forces at play – conflicts that are not neatly separated between "good nurses" and "bad nurses" or between nurses and management, but are personal and institutional, strategic and intermittent. It may be less dramatic, but it is more realistic to then propose suggestions for actions that can take into account having to start from within a living world of practice.

A previous section of the chapter was about implications for practice of introducing Buddhist thought into the vocabulary of nursing. Part of the argument was about the language of interconnection, which is well understood and articulated in Buddhist traditions. Although not re-stated in the above passage, the perspective underlies the discussion of Nairn's and Porter's work. There is a theme throughout the dissertation (most overtly in the ritual chapter, discussed above) of the importance of seeing mutual connections and influences between individual nurses' style of practice and the cultural, social, and physical environments in which they work. The theme returns in the implications chapter so that the sociological interpretation takes its place within a network of understandings. In turn, the recommendations are not for entirely new forms of work organization, but for highlighting and valuing existing forms in a new way. Returning to a point made at the beginning of this section, interpretive writing takes on different tones for different purposes, but it is a seamless process throughout a complete work such as a dissertation.

Book Chapter Summary

Hermeneutics begins when we realize something is going on, something is happening. It is interested in things that happen to us – not only in what they might *mean*, but also of what might be true about them. It is through the transcription process, reading and re-reading of the transcripts, reviewing of field notes, reflection on the interviews, and the generation of interpretations, that data will be interpreted. The process of how one goes from a transcribed interview to an interpretation that brings value, furthers understanding of the topic, and is *true of something* is challenging to explain in some respects, given that hermeneutics does not offer a defined method of conducting research or analyzing data. Some of what constitutes life is not measurable or analyzable by empirical means, and to make a topic conform to the likes of a technical method makes the topic technical in nature. In order to understand and bring forth meaningful interpretations from the data collected, the concepts of fusion of horizons and the hermeneutic circle are of assistance. The fusion of horizons, or the coming together of two or more understandings of the topic, coupled with the genuine curiosity of the researcher and desire to understand the topic in a new way will help to further the understanding of the topic. The hermeneutic circle – the metaphorical representation of looking at the whole and the parts – invites the researcher to consider the particulars of the topic in the context of the familiar, and similarly, the familiar in the context of the particulars (Gadamer, 1960/1989; Moules, Jardine, McCaffrey, & Brown, 2013). This movement in and out of the data allows for consideration of that which might not have been initially visible, and enhances the understanding of the topic. In these two examples offered in this chapter, we see the scholarship, beauty, and poetics of writing interpretively along with the careful attention to be citatious, rigorous, and meaningful.

In the next chapter, we address these important components of "good" interpretive research: rigor, integrity, validity, veracity, trustworthiness, and ethical conduct.

Notes

1. This chapter has been published in the *Journal of Applied Hermeneutics* (see Laing, 2012 reference).
2. This chapter has been published in the *Journal of Applied Hermeneutics* (see Laing & Moules, 2013).
3. This chapter has been published in OMEGA: *Journal of Death and Dying* (see Laing & Moules (in press)).
4. This chapter has been published in the *Journal of Applied Hermeneutics* (see Laing & Moules, 2014).
5. This chapter has been published in the *Journal of Family Nursing* (see Laing & Moules, 2014).
6. A version of this excerpt appears in McCaffrey, G., Raffin Bouchal, S., & Moules, N. J. (2012). Buddhist thought and nursing: A hermeneutic exploration. *Nursing Philosophy, 13,* 87–97.
7. A version of this excerpt appears in McCaffrey, G. (2012). "The pure guidelines of the monastery are to be inscribed in your bones and mind": Mental health nurses' practices as ritualized behavior. *Journal of Applied Hermeneutics,* September 2012.
8. A version of this excerpt appears in McCaffrey, G. (2014). Host and guest: An applied hermeneutic study of mental health nurses' practices on inpatient units. *Nursing Inquiry* (online early view). doi: 10.1111/nin.12065

References

Abma, T. A. (2005). Struggling with the fragility of life: A relational-narrative approach to ethics in palliative nursing. *Nursing Ethics, 12*(4), 337–348.

Atkinson, R. (2002). The life story interview. In J. F. Gubrium & J. A. Holstein (Eds.), *Handbook of interview research: Context and method* (pp. 121–140). Thousand Oaks, CA: SAGE.

Barker, P., & Buchanan-Barker, P. (2005). *The Tidal Model: A guide for mental health professionals*. New York, NY: Brunner-Routledge.

Batchelor, S. (1994). *The awakening of the West: The encounter of Buddhism and western culture*. Berkeley, CA: Parallax Press.

Bell, C. (1992). *Ritual theory, ritual practice*. New York, NY: Oxford.

Bell, C. (2009). *Ritual theory, ritual practice*. New York, NY: Oxford.

Benner, P. (2000). The wisdom of our practice. *American Journal of Nursing, 100*(10), 99–105. Retrieved from http://www.jstor.org/stable/3522335

Bosticco, C., & Thompson, T. L. (2005). Narratives and storytelling in coping with grief and bereavement. *OMEGA: Journal of Death and Dying, 51*(1), 1–16.

Bowles, N. (1995). Storytelling: A search for meaning within nursing practice. *Nurse Education Today, 15*(5), 365–369. doi:10.1016/S0260-6917

Brown, S. (1998). Play as an organizing principle: Clinical evidence and personal observations. In M. Bekoff & J. A. Beyer (Eds.), *Animal play: Evolutionary, comparative, and ecological perspectives* (pp. 242–251). Boston, MA: Cambridge University Press.

Canadian Federation of Mental Health Nurses. (2006). *Standards of practice* (3rd ed.). Toronto, ON, Canada: CFMHN.

Connelly, F. M., & Clandinin, D. J. (1990). Stories of experience and narrative enquiry. *Educational Researcher, 19*(5), 2–14. Retrieved from http://www.jstor.org/stable/117600

Derrida, J. (2002). *Acts of religion*. New York, NY: Routledge.

East, L., Jackson, D., O'Brien, L., & Peters, K. (2010). Storytelling: An approach that can help to develop resilience. *Nurse Researcher, 17*(3), 17–25. Retrieved from http://nurseresearcher.rcnpublishing.co.uk

Foucault, M. (2009). *History of madness* (J. Murphy & J. Khalfa, Trans.). New York, NY: Routledge.

Frank, A. W. (2000). The standpoint of storyteller. *Qualitative Health Research, 10*(3), 354–365. doi:10.1177/104973200129118499

Gadamer, H. G. (1960/1989). *Truth and method* (2nd rev. ed.) (J. Weinsheimer & D. G. Marshall, Trans.). New York, NY: Continuum (Original work published 1960).

Gadamer, H-G. (1960/2004). Truth and method (2nd rev.ed.) (J. Weinsheimer & D.G. Marshall, Trans.). New York, NY: Continuum.

Gelfert, A. (2006). Kant on testimony. *British Journal for the History of Philosophy, 14*(4), 627–652. Retrieved from http://www.gelfert.net/People/Axel/axel.html

Hartup, W. W. (1999). Peer experience and its developmental significance. In M. Bennett (Ed.), *Developmental psychology: Achievements and prospects* (pp. 106–125). Philadelphia, PA: Psychology Press.

Heidegger, M. (1927/1962). *Being and time* (J. Macquarrie, & E. Robmson, Trans.) New York, NY: Harper and Row (Original work published 1927).

Hölderlin, F. (2004). *Poems and fragments* (M. Hamburger, trans.). London: Anvil.

Jardine, D. W., & Clandinin, D. J. (1987). Does it rain on Vancouver Island? Teaching as storytelling. *Curriculum Inquiry, 17*(4), 471–481. Retrieved from http://www. jstor.org.ezproxy. lib.ucalgary.ca/action/showPublication? journalCode=currinqu

Kearney, R. (2003). *Strangers, gods and monsters*. London, UK: Routledge.

Koch, T. (1998). Storytelling: Is it really research? *Journal of Advanced Nursing, 28*(6), 1182–1190. doi:10.1046/j.1365-2648.1998.00853.x

Laing, C. M. (2012). In play, at play. *Journal of Applied Hermeneutics*, Article 6. http://jah. synergiesprairies.ca/jah/index.php/jah/article/view/16/pdf

Laing, C. M. (2013). *"It's not just camp": Understanding the meaning of children's cancer camps for children and families* (Doctoral dissertation). Retrieved from http://hdl.handle. net/11023/558

Laing, C. M., & Moules, N. J. (2013). The island of misfit toys. *Journal of Applied Hermeneutics, August 5, 2013*, Article 8. http://hdl.handle.net/10515/sy5js9hq4

Laing, C. M., & Moules, N. J. (2014). Stories from cancer camp: Tales of glitter and gratitude. *Journal of Applied Hermeneutics, January 31, 2014*. Article 3. http://hdl.handle.net/10515/ sy5qf8k16

Laing, C. M., & Moules, N. J. (2014). Children's cancer camps: A sense of community, a sense of family. *Journal of Family Nursing, 20*(2), 185–203. doi: 10.1177/1074840714520717

Laing, C. M., & Moules, N. J. (in press). Children's cancer camps: A way to understand grief differently. *Omega: Journal of Death and Dying*.

McCaffrey, G. (2012). "The pure guidelines of the monastery are to be inscribed in your bones and mind," Dogen (2010, p. 42): Mental health nurses' practices as ritualized behavior. *Journal of Applied Hermeneutics, Article 11*. Retrieved from http://hdl.handle.net/10515/

McMahan, D. L. (2008). *The making of Buddhist modernism*. New York, NY: Oxford University Press.

Mooney, B., & Holt, D. (1996). *The storyteller's guide*. Little Rock, AR: August House.

Moules, N. J. (2012). Dr. David Jardine and the "Descartes Lecture": Twenty years of miraculous returns [Editorial]. *Journal of Applied Hermeneutics*. Retrieved from http://hdl.handle. net/10515/sy5th8c32

Moules, N. J., Jardine, D. W., McCaffrey, G., & Brown, C. (2013). "Isn't all oncology hermeneutic?" *Journal of Applied Hermeneutics, Article 3*. http://hdl.handle.net/10515/sy5w95141

Nairn, S. (2009). Social structure and nursing research. *Nursing Philosophy, 10*, 191–202. doi: 10.1111/j.1466-769X.2009.00403.x

Play. (n.d.). In *Merriam-Webster's online dictionary*. Retrieved from http://www.merriam-webster. com/dictionary/play

Play. (n.d.). In *Online etymology dictionary*. Retrieved from http://www.etymonline. com/index. php?allowed_in_frame=0&search=play&searchmode=none

Porter, S. (1993). The determinants of psychiatric nursing practice: A comparison of sociological perspectives. *Journal of Advanced Nursing, 18*, 1559–1566. doi: 10.1046/j.1365-2648.1993.18101559.x

Rankin, J., & Campbell, M. (2006). *Managing to nurse: Inside Canada's health care reform*. Toronto, ON, Canada: University of Toronto Press.

Ricoeur, P. (1992). *Oneself as another* (K. Blaney, Trans.). Chicago: University of Chicago.

Riley, T., & Hawe, P. (2005). Researching practice: The methodological case for narrative inquiry. *Health Education Research, 20*(2), 226–236. doi:10.1093/her/cyg122

Ritual. (n.d.). In *Merriam-Webster's online dictionary*. Retrieved from http://www.merriam-webster.com/dictionary/ritual

Rizzetto, D. E. (2005). *Waking up to what you do*. Boston, MA: Shambhala.

Rubin, H. J., & Rubin, I. S. (2005). *Qualitative interviewing: The art of hearing data* (2nd ed.). Thousand Oaks, CA: Sage.

Rubin, K. H., Bukowski, W. M., & Parker, J. G. (2006). Peer interactions, relationships, and groups. In N. Eisenberg, W. Damon, & R. M. Lerner (Eds.), *Handbook of child psychology: Social, emotional and personality development* (6th ed., Vol. 3, pp. 571–645). Hoboken, NJ: John Wiley & Sons.

Sullivan, H. S. (1953). *The interpersonal theory of psychiatry*. New York, NY: W. W. Norton.

Summers-Effler, E. (2006). Ritual theory. In J. E. Stets & J. H. Turner (Eds.), *The handbook of the sociology of emotions* (pp. 135–154). New York, NY: Springer.

Tanahashi, K. (1995). *Moon in a dewdrop: Writings of Zen master Dogen*. New York, NY: North Point Press.

Vannatta, K. Gartstein, M. A., Zeller, M., & Noll, R. B. (2009). Peer acceptance and social behavior during childhood and adolescence: How important are appearance, athleticism, and academic competence? *International Journal of Behavioral Development, 33*(4), 303–311.

Widdershoven, G. (1993). The story of life: Hermeneutic perspectives on the relationship between narrative and life history. In A. Lieblich & R. Josselson (Eds.), *The narrative study of lives* (pp. 1–20). Thousand Oaks, CA: Sage.

Wiltshire, J. (1995). Telling a story, writing a narrative: Terminology in health care. *Nursing Inquiry, 2*(2), 75–82. doi:10.1111/j.1440-1800.1995.tb00145.x

Wright, D. (1998). *Philosophical meditations on Zen Buddhism*. Cambridge, UK: Cambridge University Press.

Wright, D. S. (2008). Introduction: Rethinking ritual practice in Zen Buddhism. In S. Heine & D. S. Wright (Eds.), *Zen ritual: Studies of Zen Buddhist theory in practice*. New York, NY: Oxford.

· 9 ·

THE RIGOR AND INTEGRITY
OF HERMENEUTIC RESEARCH

Rigor is less about adherence to the letter of rules and procedures than it is about fidelity to the spirit...of the work. (Sandelowski, 1993, p. 2)

We work from the premise that hermeneutic research is difficult, sophisti-cated, rigorous, and, most importantly, credible and relevant. Hermeneutics, like many qualitative research methods, is frequently asked to live up to the ways, means, and methods of the natural sciences and is evaluated by the same criteria. This application of criteria of acceptability and soundness is flawed in that the value, legitimacy, and integrity of hermeneutic research must be re-conceptualized and discerned by different regards than is natural scientific inquiry. In this chapter, we examine the difficulty, importance, and obligation of speaking to, and demonstrating, rigor in hermeneutic research.

The word rigor is defined in Webster's dictionary as a strictness or inflex-ibility; exactness in precision or accuracy; or rigidity. In this consideration of the word, it cannot be applied to hermeneutic work, for hermeneutics is quite the opposite of strict, inflexible, precise, exact, or rigid. However, like many words, there are different definitions that apply. Another definition of rigor is the "quality of being careful" (Merriam-Webster, online). Rigor in hermeneutics is the careful attention to the treatment of topics such that the work engenders trustworthiness and believability. Rigor in this context does not show itself in a strict adherence to an inflexible method, or in absolute and precise findings that can be replicated to authenticate them, but rather in attention to a cohesive, comprehensive, cogent, and expansive contribution to understanding of the topic. Within criteria of rigor in research, the words validity, reliability, and veracity also arise.

Validity in Hermeneutic Work

Applied to interpretive work, the term validity has to be taken up divergently from its conventional, technical meaning in quantitative research. First and foremost, validity is regarded as a form of social construction that affirms a legitimization of knowledge claims. What is deemed to be valid and therefore meaningful comes from a community of acceptability. Webster's offers a first definition of validity as applying to that which cannot be objected to because it conforms to law, logic, or facts, and is therefore free of error. The word, though, is also defined as strong, powerful, well-grounded, cogent, convincing, robust, healthy, and telling. Hermeneutic work, when done well, *is* strong, powerful, well-grounded, cogent, convincing, robust, healthy, and telling, and these are qualities that a hermeneutic researcher strives for in interpretations. Hermeneutics is not about explanation but understanding, and understanding can only be shared when it is put forward in a convincing, understandable, and telling way.

To make something valid, in the traditional scientific sense, is to make it repeatable. In hermeneutics, however, to reproduce more of the same does not make it more real. Rather, we think of *re-production* as a form of discovery, recovery, and legitimization, a freeing of something from encased and enclosed truths of the past, to recover possibilities and free the topic for new conversation as well as to discover something new. "Validity is an experience of application; it does not arise out of the past but from the future, becoming something only in the way it is lived out" (Moules, 2002, p. 17).

Gadamer (1984) offered us two approaches to achieving validity – *rhetorica* and *critica:*

> Rhetorica is obviously based on common sense, on the probability of arguments insofar as they are well received and assured by appearances. On the other hand, the critical attitude stands against appearances, on the side of the new physics with its insistence on method. (p. 55)

Rhetoric is the ancient Greek art of persuasion, the art of an argument well presented, the tradition of persuasive presentation that invites the listener or reader to participate. It is another term that Gadamer revitalized by reading it against its contemporary conventional implication of hollow language. Gadamer (1984) recognized an inherent persuasiveness in language and suggested that rhetoric has a "deep inner convergence" with hermeneutics in that one needs rhetorical tradition to not only "give a good talk but also in order to *read* and understand extended argumentation" (p. 55). Persuasion, however, does not mean to convince someone of an unbending truth, such that other truths are given up, but to convince that what is being presented is credible and believable, that it makes "sense" and has echoes of recognizability.

Writing about qualitative research as such, Angen (2000) preferred to speak of validation rather than validity, and described it as intersubjective agreement within communities and researchers that the findings are productive; in other words they can be "lived out" (Moules, 2002, p. 17). This production or re-production is, as stated, something of both discovery and recovery. Within validation, Angen named processes of ethical validation and substantive validation. One measure of ethical validation is the appraisal of whether the research findings inform and transform our practices and assist us in doing things differently. Substantive validation is grounded in the ways that the research accounts for prior research and theory, self-reflexivity, and popular, political, and personal understandings – all of which have informed the research.

To borrow Angen's (2000) proposal of validation, then the validity of the work lies in the extent to which it is received and validated where it matters most. For example, a hermeneutic study on the impact of the death of a child on pediatric oncology nurses is validated and finds its validity by the community of nurses who work in this area. This is not always strictly the case, however, because it is not always the population studied that needs to offer validation of the findings. There may be others who are affected by this, for example, managers of pediatric nurses, physicians, or those who work in children's hospices. There are many instances where the findings might not hold as much interest to the participants as it does to other groups of end users. An example of this might be studying the work of bereavement therapists and interviewing clients who have been through this type of therapy to find out from them what was most useful and meaningful to them in their therapeutic encounters. These participants might offer validation of the findings but in many ways it is the target population of bereavement therapists who might be in a position of validation.

Kvale and Brinkmann (2009) suggested the there are some studies where the validity is forefront in the product, executed through its strength and power of presentation.

> Ideally, the quality of the craftsmanship results in products with knowledge claims that are so powerful and convincing in their own right that they, so to say, carry the validation with them, like a strong piece of art. In such cases, the research procedures would be transparent and the results evident, and the conclusions of a study intrinsically convincing as true, beautiful, and good. Valid research would in this sense be research that makes questions of validity superfluous. (p. 260)

Hermeneutics does not aim for this kind of completion or for the product and interpretations to leave no question in the mind of the reader. Alternatively, Lather (1993) saw validity as the "incitement to discourse" (p. 674) and proposed "the conditions of possibility for validity are also its conditions of impossibility" (p. 687). The best hermeneutic work raises questions rather than just convinces, but on the other hand there must be *something* convincing enough in the presentation to incite discourse, and often in this kind of work it is not only in the presentation but also in its application.

Veracity: A Return and Turn to Truth

The veracity of hermeneutic work, or in other words, its truth value and credibility, depends upon the power of interpretations to offer faithful and recognizable descriptions of the topic that ring "true" to others. "Everything comes down to our capacity to recognize ourselves in the finished account, in the 'story' of human existence which is recounted there" (Caputo, 1987, p. 80). Hermeneutics recognizes that human experience is always storied and "good hermeneutical research shows an ability to read those stories from the inside out and the outside in" (Smith, 1991, p. 201). We argue that it is not just the act of recognizing "ourselves in the finished account" – we may not recognize ourselves at all, but still recognize the "truth" in the account. To see that the work is true of something does not mean that we have had to experience it, but that it is presented so compellingly and persuasively that it is possible to see how it helps us understand. As stated previously, to recognize something as true *of something* does not mean that it closes off other truths but that it offers a possibility of understanding that is generative and open. If one were to read a research study about a topic area unknown to the reader, it ought to be clear how the interpretations are linked to the data and how they help the reader to arrive at an understanding of the topic.

Madison (1988) suggested that a more useful question than asking if an interpretation is true or not, is to consider the acceptability of the interpretation. One interpretation may be accepted over another because it is more:

> fruitful, more promising…it seems to make more and better sense…it opens up greater horizons of meaning…all interpretation works under the promise of truth…when we opt for a given interpretation, we do not do so because we *know* it to be true…but because we *believe* it to be the best…(p. 15)

All interpretations are competing in one sense and can be falsified, so the argumentation is for a relative and defensible credibility of the work. Rather than finding or claiming truth, we attempt to remain true *to* something (the topic) and to interpret in such a way that it is true *of* something (within the topic). We are true to our work when:

> in our rewritings and retellings we are able to preserve and to take up, in a more meaning-giving way, with greater subtlety of narrative, the "truth" of our past, i.e., all the data that we have already made use of and their interpretations…We are in the truth when we are able to…maintain the openness of the conversation and keep it going. (Madison, 1988, p. 169)

Credibility in this work is shown and sometimes enacted differently than in other methods of research. As for reasons explored in Chapter Seven, in hermeneutics as we practice it, it does not involve member checking or consulting the participants to have them validate the interpretations.

The process of generalizability is one that is often questioned in many qualitative research methods, a question of whether or not the findings of a study can be readily applied to other contexts. Kvale and Brinkmann (2009) made a distinction between forms of generalizing, ranging from formal and explicit statistical generalization to naturalistic generalization, which is personal and tacit, to analytical generalization, which "involves a reasoned judgment about the extent to which the findings of one study can be used as a guide to what might occur in another situation" (p. 262).

Generalizability in any case is not where we believe that truth lies in hermeneutic work. We are not seeking an exactly replicable application of findings across any and all domains, so therefore the idea of transferability sometimes has a better fit with hermeneutics. This occurs when the findings of the research can "fit into contexts outside the study situation and when its audience views its findings as meaningful and applicable in terms of their own experiences" (Sandelowski, 1986, p. 27).

However, beyond ideas of generalizability or transferability, Madison (1988) offered that more meaningful criteria of good hermeneutic work are those of suggestiveness and potential. They describe the extent to which the research raises more questions than are closed off, thereby demonstrating its capacity for extension of understanding. He proposed other criteria: coherence, comprehensiveness, penetration, thoroughness, appropriateness, contextuality, and agreement. According to Madison, *coherence* is the presentation of a picture of something without glaring contradictions. We understand this to mean that, although there might well be differences or seemingly opposite points of consideration or paradox present, the writing itself shows an awareness of these and makes coherent sense of the contradictions. *Comprehensiveness* is a search for adequacy in the work – does it speak to the topic enough that it extends understanding or does it fall short of digging deeply enough into it? *Penetration* refers to the capacity of the work to make an impact on the reader, to "sink in" and make sense, to be heard. *Thoroughness*, similar to comprehensiveness, is the evidence that the work addresses significant problems and questions that show up within the topic. "The real power of hermeneutical consciousness is our ability to see what is questionable" (Gadamer, 1977, p. 13). *Contextuality* is recognition that topics do not happen outside of context, nor should the work be written or read outside of an awareness of the context from which it arises and emerges. *Agreement* does not imply consensus, but rather that there is agreement within the work to make it coherent and harmonious. Madison wrote of *suggestiveness* in regard to the way that the work is fertile and fecund and "raises questions that stimulate further research and interpretation" (p. 30). Lastly, in *potential*, he argued that the "ultimate 'validation' of a true interpretation lies in the future" (p. 30). Madison was not, in presenting these terms, attempting to create rules for the conduct of hermeneutic research, but rather to articulate guidelines for conduct of hermeneutic research and criteria for appraisal of the rigor of the work.

> There can be no *science* of interpretation. This, however, does not mean that interpretation cannot be a rigorous (if not an exact) discipline, an art in the proper sense of the term, and that one cannot rationally *evaluate* interpretations. (Madison, 1988, p. 31)

Rigor in Ethical Conduct of Hermeneutic Research

Hermeneutic research happens within the same structures of ethical standards as any other kind of research involving humans. Researchers have the same obligations to treat participants with respect, do their best to ensure informed consent, confidentiality and privacy and so on. Hermeneutic philosophy does, however, have an ethical slant that lends an additional perspective for thinking about the ethical conduct of research.

Ethics boards are necessarily concerned with the management of research according to established ethical principles, and they work with researchers to anticipate potential threats to the ethical integrity of research. What they cannot do is be present during the conduct of research, in the face of shifting, nuanced, multifaceted circumstances. This is another instance when hermeneutics emphasizes the contingencies of practice under the aegis of methodological structures of anticipation. There is a general point here about research ethics, although types of research that involve less formally determined interviews are likely to be more open to the dynamics of human relationships.

Stewart and Amundson (1995) suggested that it is not enough to acknowledge and follow the steps of ethical decision making for we must realize that ethical dilemmas are personal dilemmas, composed of competing values, and capable of addressing us in ways that challenge our own beliefs and commitments. The ethical call is for us, as researchers, to make the best decisions we can. Ethical dilemmas will greet us in all research, from the moment of the address of the question, through the interviews, in the analysis, and dissemination of the work. Researchers are met with situations of asking delicate questions in interviews, deciding what is appropriate to ask and what might be potentially hurtful to the participant; deciding what information to include from the transcripts; discerning how to protect confidentiality and minimize the recognition of participants in the final reports; and deciding how to disseminate research that can easily be located in particular contexts. There is an ethical dimension to making decisions at all points in the research process so that they must be constantly negotiated with awareness and sensitivity.

From this view, ethical conduct in research is an example of phronesis, the practical judgment discussed in Chapter Three. Elements of phronesis appear in the nursing literature around relational ethics, which is another way of conceptualizing ethical practice. Although primarily concerned with clinical nurse-patient relationships, insights from this literature are also applicable to researchers. Gadow (2009) postulated a shift from universal and rational ethics toward a more engaged, relational version of ethics. In the latter case, "the situated self encompasses not only rationality but emotion, imagination, memory, language, the body, and even other selves. Individuals are intrinsically relational; existential subjectivity is intersubjectivity" (p. 575). This description fleshes out (pun intended) Aristotle's suggestion that practical judgment does make use of reason, but not only reason. This makes sense in the context of researcher-participant relationships in which there is an intermingling of proximity and professionalism, intimacy and distance. Engagement as a researcher is "personal responsiveness to the particular other" (Gadow, 2009, p. 575). Bergum and Dossetor (2005) similarly mapped out the ethical dimension of practice in the open, contingent, and uncertain relational space of nurses' work with patients. It is important to remember that this way of understanding practice is not arbitrary or merely relativistic. Relational ethics do not arise regardless of institutional structures of professional standards, policies, and codes of ethics. For the most part, good relational practice ought concretely to manifest those very structures. Relational ethics, however, is open to the possibility of the exception and the demands of the particular. Since relational ethics responds to the address of the particular situation, that response might also include an answering-back to, or a questioning of institutional structures. It implies a dynamic response to the conditions of practice, as well as to the specific moment of practice.

Caputo described one of the consequences of acknowledging ethical responsibility amidst contingency:

> The "ghost" of undecidability hovers over the decision, before, during, and after the decision. It haunts it, lingering like a spectre, even after the decision. We do not dispel the ghost by deciding. We do the best we can to be just, here and now, under the law, but we must live with the consequences. (Caputo, 1993, p. 104)

We live with the consequences of this work, responsibly and responsively. The character of ethics is relationship. People, particularities, differences, commitments, and obligations inhabit ethics. It is the relationship between these contingencies that converge to constitute and occupy the rigors of an ethical examination of hermeneutic research. Decision-making, beliefs, feelings, and actions are complexly woven together, fraught with consequences and ramifications, costs and benefits. The rigor in this attention to ethical comportment is a constant attention to the potential to do harm and the potential to make a difference that is a good difference, something that must be done with integrity and harmony.

Integrity and Harmony

We have grounded this book of the conduct of hermeneutic research on a philosophical foundation and one of the measures of rigor is to maintain that grounding. For example, if researchers base a study on Gadamer's philosophical hermeneutics and then describe how they have used software to count the number of times a particular theme arose and thus determined this as an interpretation, there is an apparent contradiction of Gadamer's honoring of the particular. Of course, Gadamer never addressed questions like whether or not to use software in research, but it would at the very least call for a reasoned explanation in terms of his philosophy.

As much as we have suggested that hermeneutics can have a charming, ebullient, and seemingly effortless face, this is not the case. The work must have literacy and scholarship. When something is not guided by a strict methodological procedure, its strength and credibility lies in good scholarly judgment, in being citatious and accountable. One characteristic of hermeneutic work is its embrace of plurality and difference, so that although agreement is not the goal, the credibility and integrity of the work do require a sense of cohesion. Gadamer (1960/1989) suggested that "the harmony of all details with the whole is the criterion of correct understanding…failure to achieve this harmony means that understanding has failed" (p. 291). We interpret this as meaning that research ought to have consistency between its philosophical assumptions, its conduct, and the expression of its conclusions. This is not to say that there cannot be contradiction, disagreement, or differences in terms of the content or findings – in fact we should look for the expression of complexity as hermeneutic research takes up a topic and, in Caputo's (1987) words, "restores [it] to its original difficulty" (p. 1).

Integrity, then, of the work lies in part in its ability to hold tension, to be "not quite this and not quite that," in recognizing that with every opening, there is a closing of something else, in knowing that openings are invitations and portals to understanding, not dark rabbit holes where the topic disappears. Integrity lies in the hermeneutic humility of knowing that truth is a flexible encounter with something that offers room for many views.

Limitations of Hermeneutic Research

> I'll argue the stubborn argument of the particular, right now, in the midst of things, *this* and *this*. (Wallace, 1987, p. 111)

A part of the integrity of any research lies in recognizing and acknowledging that no one method provides all the answers and every method has strengths and limitations. It is the nature of hermeneutics to allow a topic to show itself, while knowing that it will exceed any single interpretation. The very thing that adds merit to this kind of research is that which restricts it. Hermeneutics is a study and honoring of the particular, discovering how the particular lives in its connectedness in the world (Moules, Jardine, McCaffrey, & Brown, 2013). In every well-conducted hermeneutic study, there are rich, vibrant, and expansive opportunities for understanding. It is the depth of these particulars that offers the gifts and strengths that surround this kind of research, but it could be argued that hermeneutic research is sometimes constrained by its very openness that resists solid conclusion. A research study of this kind does not have "power" in the traditional, quantitative sense, so what power does it bring?

We would suggest that it is rooted in the power of the particular – in the recognition of one voice, one experience, one mattering of human life, one diminishment of suffering, one experience of healing, one moment of seeing education come alive in the classroom – that the practice professions have always found their "real" power. It is in the moment of being present at the death of one child; or watching one child "get it" while learning math; or the privilege of being present while one family makes peace in troubled relationships; *or* in watching a family learn to laugh and play while attending a cancer camp where their own child can no longer attend, as he is no longer alive. It is in the richness of the power of these individual, particular moments of grace, kinship, and human relationship that our human practices have always found their own graceful and powerful place – in the context of one human life, here and now, in *this*, and *this*, and *this*.

Summary

In this chapter, we have spoken to some of the complexity of accounting for and recognizing rigor in hermeneutic research. We have discussed some of the distinctive traits of rigor in hermeneutic research, as well as issues that are shared with all research in contemporary academic institutions. We offer an advocacy for the value of interpretive research, which is not defense or apology:

> It is as if, in our quasi-militaristic zeal to neutralize bias and defend our projects against threats to validity, we were more preoccupied with building fortifications against attack than with creating the evocative, true-to-life, and meaningful portraits, stories, and landscapes of human experience that constitute the best test of rigor in qualitative work. (Sandelowski, 1993, p. 1)

Although, as Nicholas Davey has written, "hermeneutics is not always its own best advocate" (2006, p. xi), researchers in the hermeneutic tradition need to and must advocate *for* it, persuasively without apology and with confidence in the integrity of the process and the outcome of conducting this work well. In the next chapter, we discuss the "so what?" issue that is often asked of hermeneutic research.

References

Angen, M. J. (2000). Evaluating interpretive inquiry: Reviewing the validity debate and opening the dialogue. *Qualitative Health Research, 10*(3), 378–395.

Bergum, V., & Dossetor, J. (2005). *Relational ethics: The full meaning of respect.* Hagerstown, MD: University Publishing Group.

Caputo, J. D. (1987). *Radical hermeneutics: Repetition, deconstruction and the hermeneutic project.* Bloomington, IN: Indiana University Press.

Caputo, J. D. (1993). *Against ethics: Contributions to a poetics of obligation with constant reference to deconstruction.* Bloomington, IN: Indiana University Press.

Davey, N. (2006). *Unquiet understanding: Gadamer's philosophical hermeneutics.* New York, NY: SUNY Press.

Gadamer, H-G. (1960/1989). *Truth and method* (2nd rev. ed.) (J. Weinsheimer & D. G. Marshall, Trans.). New York, NY: Continuum.

Gadamer, H-G. (1984). The hermeneutics of suspicion. In G. Shapiro & A. Sica (Eds.), *Hermeneutics: Questions and prospects* (pp. 54–65). Amherst, MA: University of Massachusetts.

Gadow, S. (2009). Relational narrative: The postmodern turn in nursing ethics. In P. Reed & N. Crawford-Shearer (Eds.), *Perspectives on nursing theory* (pp. 571–580). Philadelphia, PA: Lippincott Williams & Wilkins.

Gadamer, H-G. (1977). Philosophical hermeneutics (D.E. LInge, Trans.). Berkeley, CA: University of California Press.

Kvale, S., & Brinkmann, S. (2009). *InterViews: Learning the craft of qualitative research interviewing* (2nd ed.). Thousand Oaks, CA: SAGE.

Lather, P. (1993). Fertile obsession: Validity after poststructuralism. *The Sociological Quarterly,* *334*(4), 673–693.

Madison, G. B. (1988). *The hermeneutics of postmodernity: Figures and themes.* Bloomington, IN: Indiana University Press.

Moules, N.J. (2002). Hermeneutic inquiry: Paying heed to history and Hermes. An ancestral, substantive, and methodological tale. *International Journal of Qualitative Methods, 1*(3), 1–21.

Moules, N. J., Jardine, D. W., McCaffrey, G., & Brown, C. (2013). Isn't all of oncology hermeneutic? *Journal of Applied Hermeneutics,* Article 3. http://hdl.handle.net/10515/sy5w95141

Sandelowski, M. (1986). The problem of rigor in qualitative research. *Advances in Nursing Science, 8*(3), 27–37.

Sandelowski, M. (1993). Rigor or rigor mortis: The problem of rigor in qualitative research revisited. *Advances in Nursing Science, 16*(2), 1–8.

Smith, D. (1991). Hermeneutic inquiry: The hermeneutic imagination and the pedagogic text. In E. Short (Ed.), *Forms of curriculum inquiry* (pp. 187–209). New York, NY: SUNY Press.

Stewart, K., & Amundson, J. (1995). The ethical postmodernist: Or not everything is relative all at once. *Journal of Systemic Therapies, 14*(2), 70–78.

Wallace, B. (1987). Particulars. In B. Wallace, *The stubborn particulars of grace* (pp. 110–111). Toronto, ON, Canada: McClelland & Stewart.

· 1 0 ·

"SO WHAT?" — IMPLICATIONS
OF HERMENEUTIC RESEARCH

Understanding does not merely interpret the world but changes it.(Davey, 2006, p. xiv)

In 2011, Dr. Catherine Laing, a doctoral candidate at the time, presented to board members of a local children's cancer care foundation on her proposed study of children's cancer camps. She described her intent to study the particular cancer camp run by the foundation and her goal to attempt to reach some understanding of the meaning of the camp for children and families. The board members wholeheartedly supported this research but they asked what the findings would bring them to support their requests for individual and corporate donor contributions to the running of the camp. "Will you get evidence to prove that camp makes a difference?" "What kind of statistics will you get from your study that will convince people to donate?" Laing responded that she would not have statistics or the kind of data that they thought they needed to be convincing. A cancer researcher sitting at the table, who is currently the Scientific Director of the Canadian Institute of Health Research, Dr. Stephen Robbins, astutely asked the questions: "Do you really want those numbers, that kind of measurement? Because what if you measured and you found out that camp made NO difference in the trajectory of the cancer, or that it even increased the possibility of infection, and then compromised treatment? What if all you found out was that camp was fun and it diminished the kids' suffering a bit for one week?"

To these poignant questions, the room of people had no response *but hermeneutics does*. Hermeneutics is not about measuring, quantifying, explaining, providing proof, or answering once and for all the questions of how and why, or cause and effect. Instead, it offers an answer to a question that could have been answered differently, and it offers an answer that cannot be ignored.

A year later, Laing, having completed her PhD, returned to the foundation's board and presented her findings. In the room were healthcare professionals and very high-powered corporate leaders, well connected in the community. As the group listened, visibly moved, there was an awakening that what this study said was important and that, in it, was all the evidence they needed to convince people (i.e., donors) that camp matters and why it matters, and it is not numbers alone that convinces but rather the understanding that children have cancer, people go to camp, and camp does, in fact, as Dr. Robbins suggested, make a difference in suffering.

As mentioned at the end of our last chapter, hermeneutics is an honoring of the particular; it is not necessarily attentive to or interested in the aggregate. This by no means negates the fact that evidence provided through quantitative means is important and makes a relevant contribution to practice and knowledge. It in fact has, and continues to, save lives. This is not a competitive venture nor an either/or but a both/and. As cited earlier in Chapter Three, Gadamer reminded us that "what is established by statistics seems to be a language of facts, but which questions these facts answer and which facts would begin to speak if other questions are asked are hermeneutical questions" (Gadamer, 2007, p. 84). In this chapter, we discuss what it is that hermeneutic research can bring to practice – from "philosophy to research to practice," as the title of our book suggests.

The Utility of Hermeneutic Research Findings

In 2004, Margarete Sandelowski wrote a seminal paper about the "use" of qualitative research in general. In this paper, she offered an attempt to respond to the demand and urgency of end user communities about the utility or what she called the "actionability" (p. 1367) of qualitative research, an urgency driven by the call for "evidence-based practice." Hermeneutic research, along with its fellow qualitative research methods, is constantly being called to account for its utility and actionability, for how and in what ways it adds value, knowledge, and change directly to the practice professions in which it is located (at least in the context of this book). Writing theses and dissertations, grant proposals, or research reports all call for the answer to the questions of "So what does this research tell us? What are the implications for practice?"

Estabrooks (1999; 2001) offered a classification of levels of utilization that serves as way to examine what it is that hermeneutic research brings to practice. We borrow these categories to speak to the utility of hermeneutic work.

Instrumental Utility

Instrumental utilization refers to the concrete application of research findings in a very practical sense that is tangible and visible. Sandelowski (2004) offered the examples of "clinical guidelines, care standards, appraisal tools, pathways, intervention protocols, or algorithms" (p. 1371), which are all material forms that are directed to achieve particular outcomes. This kind of utilization is evident to both the users and the ends users (the practitioners and the recipients of the practice – patients, students, clients, etc.). Because of the outcome of this level of utilization, one can anticipate that it most often arises from forms of research that are quite empirical. However, we argue that hermeneutic research can have an instrumental utility as well.

An example of this is that, as a result of a hermeneutic study conducted by Moules (2002, 2003, 2009a, 2009b) on therapeutic letters (described earlier in Chapter Five), there was a tangible and instrumental change in the practice of writing letters. This change first happened in the practice unit from which the data arose, but as a result of dissemination through research publications, it accounted for changes in the practices of others, even in the practice of the originator of therapeutic letters (Epston, 2009).

In the same vein, Laing (2013a, 2013b, 2014a, 2014b) drew from her findings in her research on children's cancer camps, offering that camp should be viewed as a necessity, not a luxury. If, in fact, this recommendation were accepted by health authorities, it could evolve into a part of the treatment protocol for some children with cancer and this would be reflective of an instrumental utilization, therefore attesting to the instrumental utility of the hermeneutic research.

Symbolic Utility

Less tangible and visible, symbolic utilization is not necessarily about making changes in practice directly, but rather "the use of research findings as a persuasive or political tool to legitimate a position or practice" (Sandelowski, 2004, p. 1371). Sandelowski further claimed that the "actionability resides largely in talk" (p. 1371), though it may in fact ultimately lead to instrumental changes.

The persuasive power of hermeneutic research is part of its symbolic potential. Laing's study on children's cancer camps is one such example. As discussed at the beginning of this chapter, potential donors for the camps were "swayed," persuaded and convinced that camp matters, simply by listening to the stories and interpretations that came out of her research. This research legitimized camp as a healing and helpful intervention for children and families facing childhood cancer and therefore as a persuasive piece of research to present to potential donors.

Conceptual Utility

The utility of research findings at a purely conceptual level appears to evoke no observable changes at all, no changes in practices, policies, or positions. Instead, change happens at the level of thinking about something – about people, practices, problems, or relationships. It has been well documented in therapeutic fields, however, that changes in thinking and in beliefs result in changes in behavior. Wright and Bell (2009) argued that changes in behaviors and practices are not sustainable if there are not changes in the thinking or the beliefs practitioners hold. For example, if teachers, as a result of research evidence, change their teaching practices to something they do not really believe will work with students, it is inevitable that the practice will not be sustained and the teachers will come to see what they originally believed to be true, reverting back to old practices.

In the beginning, the change happens quietly, often internally and often...

in the user who is newly informed or enlightened, but this change in the user may not be obvious to anyone nor have any obvious impact on anyone or anything else. Indeed the users who experienced this change may be unable to articulate the change experience even to themselves. Yet, like symbolic utilization, conceptual utilization may be a precursor to instrumental utilization as users develop the capacity to articulate the change experience and to translate it into more observable or material form. (Sandelowski, 2004, p. 1372)

The study mentioned in earlier chapters on grandparents' experiences of childhood cancer stands as an example of hermeneutic research that can make changes at a conceptual level that leads to behavioral/practice changes.

The KT Challenge

How do I know what I think until I see what I say? (Forster, 1927)

Currently, there is a demand for research to live up to promises of actionability and no more so than in the recent focus on knowledge translation (KT). Knowledge translation movements evolved out of the acknowledgement that, although there is much happening in research, there is an evident gap between the research and the findings and what happens in practice. Goals of a KT focus include improving how research results are communicated, utilized, and have impact at various levels of end-users (Knowledge Translation Canada, http://ktclearinghouse.ca/ktcanada).

Doane and Varcoe (2008)[1] raised questions about the epistemological limits of KT as it is usually presented, under various related but effectively interchangeable terms such as "research utilization, knowledge transfer, research dissemination, research uptake, innovation diffusion, and so forth" and their similar focus on the use of knowledge with the goal of 'how to get knowledge used' and 'translated' into practice" (p. 284). These authors drew on "deconstructive hermeneutics" (p. 283) to highlight the absence in conventional KT of sensitivity to the multilayered contexts of how knowledge finds its way into practice. Inherent in this limitation is the privileging of empirically based findings with the simultaneous diminishment of knowledge that cannot be empirically verified, including the subjectivity of practitioners using knowledge within ideologically loaded institutional settings. When knowledge is developed to meet existing horizons of knowledge gaps, the restricted goal of knowledge is to "confirm and refine prediction and hypothesis" (Doane & Varcoe, 2008, p. 287).

We argue that hermeneutics is not focused on a pre-set horizon and a part of the difficulty of meeting KT expectations is because hermeneutics is in search of new horizons of knowledge and understanding: "it is possible, and sometimes necessary that the horizon undergo revision…a reorganization of the whole field of disciplinary activity" (Caputo, 2000, p. 164). By keeping open to what might arrive as new, we do not and cannot prescribe in advance how this new knowledge will be translated. That it should be translated into practice is not in debate, but rather the decision of when or how it is located might be at a different juncture than current KT directives dictate.

The KT focus is undeniably important, but it presents a unique challenge within hermeneutic work in the way that granting agencies are organized and focused. To apply for funding for research requires a declaring in advance of what the KT strategies will involve and how outcomes of results will be actualized in practice. This is difficult in hermeneutic studies in many ways. In hermeneutics, we attempt to remain open to the newness that comes to meet us; we do not attempt to hypothesize or anticipate in advance what the findings will be. It is therefore very difficult to declare in advance what our KT strategies will be in dissemination and utilization of the results. For example, Moules, Laing, and Field (and others) are currently studying the topic of sexuality in adolescents with cancer. One might speculate that KT strategies around this topic could include the development of an online resource for adolescents, a psychosocial educational tool, support groups, or any number of other strategies, but the problem arises in that these cannot be declared prior to hearing and understanding what it is that adolescents with cancer *think* and *want*, if anything, in addressing issues of their sexuality. Maybe the researchers will hear that adolescents want to be left alone in this private business of their own sexuality; maybe adolescents want to talk to each other without adult intervention, and maybe they already do.

Learning how to write grant applications that promise a plan for KT becomes then a juggling act of discussing possibilities while keeping the research itself open to what the findings have to teach the researcher. In this sense, the KT portions of grant applications need to be written tentatively, fleshing out potential strategies, but being clear that the strategies are only possibilities and will be determined by the findings of the study. In many ways, the focus in this part of the application needs to be on strategies for dissemination that are creative and inclusive and do not only target an academic audience. A decision cannot even be made in advance about who really is the end user of the research; in the example above, it may be adolescents; *and* it may be parents, health care professionals, or teachers; *and* it may be all of these people and even other ones not anticipated. Each of these audiences may require different dissemination strategies, and this can be discussed in advance of conducting the research, however, the specifics of this dissemination cannot be anticipated.

For hermeneutic research, we caution against the somewhat lazy practice of simplifying implications for practice, as a "catch all" of recommendations that basically say "requires further research on the topic." This is not to say that studies do not indicate the need for future research, but the researcher must dig deeper into the implications of the current study to understand how the interpretations do have something to say to practice and to articulate what that something might be. Another common claim of implications for practice is that of "education," which works under the assumption that if people just "knew more or were taught better" the problem will be solved. This assumption flies in the face of years of practice and research that asserts that instructive interaction (i.e., educational strategies) do not always (or more boldly stated – rarely!) equate to behavioral change. A clear example of this is the failure of the years of anti-smoking campaigns in schools and the recent increase in teen and young adult smoking rates (Farrelly, Niederdeppe, & Yarsevich, 2003; Paek & Gunther, 2007; University of Georgia, 2007).

Because hermeneutics is attuned to the need to deconstruct taken-for-granted assumptions about human experience and practices, researchers in this tradition are cautioned against falling prey to prescriptive and taken-for-granted prescriptions of implications for practice. Instead, there is constant vigilance for remaining attentive to "what is at stake" in the research and also a recognition that all any research can do is offer advice for better practice; it cannot guarantee it.

What Is at Stake? Research as a Giver of Advice

It is my belief that it is in the explanation, in the interpretation of events, in the way we use them in our personal lives that history begins to matter... (Wallace, 1992, p. 27)

If we listen carefully to the interpretations found in hermeneutic work, we hear invitations and, in some invitations, we might be beckoned by something that sounds like advice on how to proceed in our practices and lives. Advice can be audacious, bold, and certain, but it can also be subtle and embedded, couched within speculation and wonder – *and* it can also, always, be turned down.

One of the tasks of hermeneutics lies in making visible the value of symbolic and conceptual utility. Understanding is the imperative of hermeneutic research, not explanation. The persuasion of it lies in its ability to meaningfully convince others of the truth of it and how, within truth, there is usually utility and meaning to be found. As Davey (2006) asserted, hermeneutics is not aimed at simply understanding or interpreting events in the world, but as a result of such understanding, the world (or parts of it) are necessarily changed. Creating space for possibilities of change demands discernment in deciding what is at stake in the topic and the study. We study things that matter in human lives and in our disciplines' work. Articulating why it matters often serves to lead us to implications for practice. For example, it matters that we understand issues of integration of disabilities in schools because it has impact on human lives and requires one to "live well with and for others in just institutions" (Ricoeur, 1992, p. 172). This mattering, then, means that we have to think about why we do what we do in the school system around disabilities, and ask the question: do we need to re-think this and do it differently and better? When something is at stake, when something matters, the conceptual utility of research results cannot help but lead to instrumental and practical utility.

A central question in hermeneutic work is to consider if the results are useful and, if so, for what purpose and for whom. Once determined, the pragmatic decision is to make choices of the delivery method of the knowledge; in other words, how might the findings be best disseminated to the audience who most could use them? Greenhalgh (2002) suggested that what makes qualitative research (which includes hermeneutic research) distinctive, in part, is its ability to narrow the gap between understanding and action as well as making the connection between efficacy of what works in research with effectiveness, which is what works in practice. Producers of research and users of research have a relationship but the line is not as clear as these terms suggest. Producers also use research to inform future directions of research, and users of research "by virtue of their use alone, re-produce and re-create" the results of research (Sandelowski, 2004, p. 1380).

> Qualitative research...could improve as a knowledge producing social practice by not just being reflexive about what individual researchers bring to the research process... but also by being reflexive about what this social practice of knowledge production... presupposes about the human reality, and how it affects human reality. (Kvale & Brinkmann, 2009, p. 315)

Summary: Living in the World Differently

Hermeneutics is in search of understanding of human reality. Through under-standing, through interpretation that brings understanding of the complexity of human reality, invitations for change most often reside and this under-standing compels us. As Humberto Maturana, the Chilean neurobiologist, offered:

> The knowledge of knowledge compels. It compels us to adopt an attitude of perma-nent vigilance against the temptation of certainty. It compels us to recognize that certainty is not a proof of truth. It compels us to realize that the world everyone sees is not the world but *a* world we bring forth with others. It compels us to see that the world will be different only if we live differently. It compels us because, when we know that we know, we cannot deny (to ourselves or to others) that we know… (This) implies an ethics that we cannot evade…an ethics that springs from human reflection and puts human reflection right at the core as a constitutive social phe-nomenon. (Maturana & Varela, 1992, p. 245)

The "so what" of hermeneutic research is inherently a social endeavor. Though questions that guide hermeneutic research are vitally important, no less important is to answer these questions – tentatively, openly, and with the hermeneutic humility that recognizes that no one question can be answered definitively once and for all. Rather, hermeneutics "concentrates on the question of what happens to us when we 'understand'" (Davey, 2006, p. xi).

Hermeneutics compels us as researchers and users of research to live in the world differently, to realize that understanding is not, as Davey (2006) invoked, just about interpreting the world but also about changing it. Herein lies the "so what" of this work, premised on the insight that when we know what we know, we cannot deny that we know and we are ethically obligated to do something about it.

Note

1. They also touched on the idea of translation as a form of interpretation (p. 293) – there is a hermeneutic study to yet to be written about the difficulties and nuances of translation in terms of KT, where the term is used naively.

References

Caputo, J. D. (2000). *More radical hermeneutics: On not knowing who we are.* Bloomington, IN: Indiana University Press.

Davey, N. (2006). *Unquiet understanding: Gadamer's philosophical hermeneutics.* Albany, NY: SUNY Press.

Doane, G. H., & Varcoe, C. (2008). Knowledge translation in everyday nursing: From evidence-based to inquiry-based practice. *Advances in Nursing Science, 31*(4), 283–295.

Epston, D. (2009). The legacy of letter writing as a clinical practice: Introduction to the special issue on therapeutic letters. *Journal of Family Nursing, 15*(1), 3–5.

Estabrooks, C. A. (1999). The conceptual structure of research utilization. *Research in Nursing and Health, 22,* 203–216.

Estabrooks, C. A. (2001). Research utilization and qualitative research. In J. M. Morse, J. M. Swanson, & A. J. Kuzel (Eds.), *The nature of qualitative evidence* (pp. 275–298). Thousand Oaks, CA: SAGE.

Farrelly, M. C., Niederdeppe, J., & Yarsevich, J. (2003). Youth tobacco prevention mass media campaigns: Past, present, and future directions. *Tobacco Control, 12,* 35–47.

Forster, E. M. (1927). *Aspects of the novel.* London, UK. Penguin Group.

Gadamer, H-G. (2007). *The Gadamer reader: A bouquet of later writings* (R. E. Palmer, Ed. & Trans.). Evanston, IL: Northwestern University Press.

Greenhalgh, T. (2002). Integrating qualitative research into evidence based practice. *Endocrinology and Metabolism Clinics of North America, 31,* 583–601.

Kvale, S., & Brinkmann, S. (2009). *InterViews: Learning the craft of qualitative research interviewing* (2nd ed.). Thousand Oaks, CA: SAGE.

Laing, C. M. (2013a). *"It's not just camp": Understanding the meaning of children's cancer camps for children and families.* Unpublished doctoral research, University of Calgary, Calgary, AB, Canada.

Laing, C. M., & Moules, N. J. (2013b). The island of misfit toys. *Journal of Applied Hermeneutics, Article 8,* http://hdl.handle.net/10515/sy5js9hq4

Laing, C. M., & Moules, N. J. (2014a). Stories from cancer camp: Tales of glitter and gratitude. *Journal of Applied Hermeneutics, Article 3, http://hdl.handle.net/10515/sy5qf8k16*

Laing, C. M., & Moules, N. J. (2014b). Children's cancer camps: A sense of community, a sense of family. *Journal of Family Nursing, 20*(2), 185–203.

Maturana, H. R., & Varela, F. (1992). *The tree of knowledge: The biological roots of human understanding* (rev. ed.). Boston, MA: Shambhala.

Moules, N. J. (2002). Nursing on paper: Therapeutic letters in nursing practice. *Nursing Inquiry, 9*(2), 104–113.

Moules, N. J. (2003). Therapy on paper: Therapeutic letters and the tone of relationship. *Journal of Systemic Therapies, 22*(1), 33–49.

Moules, N. J. (2009a). Therapeutic letters in nursing: Examining the character and influence of the written word in clinical work with families experiencing illness. *Journal of Family Nursing, 15*(1), 31–49.

Moules, N. J. (2009b). The past and future of therapeutic letters: Family suffering and healing words. *Journal of Family Nursing, 15*(1), 102–111.

Paek, H-J., & Gunther, A. C. (2007). How peer proximity moderates indirect media influence on adolescent smoking. *Communication Research, 34*(4), 407–432.

Ricoeur, P. (1992). *Oneself as another.* Chicago, IL: University of Chicago Press.

Sandelowski, M. (2004). Using qualitative research. *Qualitative Health Research, 14*(10), 1366–1386.

University of Georgia. (2007). Why some anti-smoking ads succeed and others backfire. *ScienceDaily,* July 20, 2007. www.sciencedaily.com/releases/2007/07/070719170315.htm

Wallace, B. (1992). *Arguments with the world.* Kingston, ON, Canada: Quarry Press.

Wright, L. M., & Bell, J. M. (2009). *Beliefs and illness: A model for healing.* Calgary, AB, Canada: 4th Floor Press.

· 11 ·

CONCLUSION — FIRSTS AND LASTS

If there can be no last word in philosophical hermeneutics, there can be no first. The question is how and where to join a continuing "conversation." (Davey, 2006, p. xi)

We have joined an old, yet current and continuing conversation in a particular way, offering our interpretation of the historical philosophical tradition's influence on hermeneutics as a research method in applied disciplines. In this book, we have traced the German school of hermeneutic scholars leading to the work of Hans-Georg Gadamer's philosophical hermeneutics. From that standpoint, we examined the methodological dilemmas of proceeding with research in way that is consistent with the philosophy that guides it. We followed with an exploration of aspects of hermeneutic research including the address of the topic, the conduct of interviews, interpretation (data analysis) in hermeneutics, examples of interpretive writing of research findings, rigor and integrity of this kind of research, and ending with the call to be accountable to the research in terms of its utility and usefulness.

In this endeavor, we hope we have challenged the notion that hermeneutic research is an unguided research approach, and shown rather that it is a rigorous practice of attentiveness, openness, discernment, tact, discipline, and dis-position.

> ...hermeneutics does not constitute a "philosophical position" but a philosophical dis-position. It is a practice of disposing or orientating oneself toward the other and the different with the consequence of experiencing a dis-positioning of one's initial expectancies...If philosophical hermeneutics is a practice of attentiveness, then like all reflective and spiritual disciplines it inhabits and articulates a tense space, the space of being in between. Openness to the other requires a particular refinement: the skill of being critically distant while remaining involved, attentive, and caring. Hermeneutic practice is indeed difficult. It involves the testing discipline of not residing in the quietness of a single interpretation. (Davey, 2006, p. xvi)

Being in-between is a tension that requires the ability to suspend certain things while holding other things in attention. In disclosing and unconcealing in efforts to understand, it covers some things while exposing others. This is not an easy adventure and it is necessarily one navigated personally; "for everything that understanding mediates is mediated through ourselves" (Gadamer, 2007, p. 244). Gadamer (2007) suggested that "understanding is an adventure, and like any other adventure, is dangerous" (p. 243), but we offer that understanding *is the ultimate hermeneutic wager*: that understanding matters and will make a difference. When we practice hermeneutics as a research tradition, we do so with the conviction that what we come to understand through its conduct are matters of human consequence of living well in conditions where suffering often exists. Research that involves the practice professions of nursing, education, psychology, or social work as examples, is research that touches on human conditions of living: illness, schools, children, health, relationships, suffering, healing, and hope.

As mentioned in earlier chapters, Davey suggested that "(p)hilosophical hermeneutics is not always its own best advocate" (Davey, 2006, p. xi), however, in this book, we argue that hermeneutic researchers need to advocate for the rigor and integrity of this kind of research. Hermeneutic research is buoyed and guided by philosophy but it ends up becoming something much more practical, tethered to praxis and phronesis.

In this ongoing conversation that Davey invokes, the first voice of hermeneutics is not known and our fervent hope (and belief) is that ours will not be the last.

References

Davey, N. (2006). *Unquiet understanding: Gadamer's philosophical hermeneutics*. New York, NY: SUNY Press.

Gadamer, H-G. (2007). *The Gadamer reader: A bouquet of the later writings* (R. Palmer, Ed. & Trans). Evanston, IL: Northwestern University Press.

Editorial

Journal of Applied Hermeneutics
January 11, 2015
❤ The Author(s) 2015

CATCHING HERMENEUTICS
IN THE ACT

Nancy J. Moules[1] & Graham McCaffrey[1]

As 2014 came to a close, we sent to publication with Peter Lang publishers a book manuscript entitled *"Conducting Hermeneutic Research: From Philosophy to Practice"* (Moules, McCaffrey, Field, & Laing, in press). As we await publication, we have been reflecting on the very intense, important, and exceedingly difficult work of writing this particular book.

We had the privilege of Dr. John D. Caputo writing a foreword to the book and he offered this remarkable comment saying that the book…

> catches hermeneutics in the act. It brings home in the most vivid way just what hermeneutics really is – in the concrete. Its authors are concretely engaged and hermeneutically enlightened practitioners who are describing the difficult and delicate conditions under which concrete hermeneutical work takes place. (Caputo, in Moules et al., in press)

These are humbling words that could not more clearly elucidate the difficulties that writing the book held – it *was* difficult and delicate work and, at times, it was wordless work, a challenge when you are trying to write a book! Catching something is tricky business and especially tricky if what you are after is the exact opposite. We did not want to catch and entrap hermeneutics as a research "method" – we wanted to catch it "in the act" of the world – in the ways it allows things to act and exposes the action that is often just "lost to the work of simply getting by" (Wallace, 1987, p. 12).

Caputo's words go to the heart of the enterprise of *applied* hermeneutics and are an encouraging reminder of the newness and excitement of what that represents. Caputo, as well as Dr. Richard Kearney and Dr. Nicholas Davey, have come to the annual Canadian Hermeneutic Institute to share their expertise as hermeneutic philosophers, steeped in a long and profound tradition. In each case, they have told us that they approached the invitation with curiosity as to what scholars and practitioners in practice professions both wanted to hear from them, and what we could have to add to that tradition. Each time, they have shared their knowledge, ideas, and thinking with exceptional generosity and they have "*got it*" – they have quickly seen that the interpretation of human encounters in the context of practice professions is as much a fit object for hermeneutic study as an artwork, a poem, or a religious text. Having a glimpse of applied hermeneutics through the eyes of philosophical experts is at the same time gratifying and a stimulating reminder that we are working fresh ground, and it behooves us to keep working to be as exacting as we can about what we do. It is in this spirit that it felt timely to undertake to describe the work-in-progress that is applied hermeneutics in the fleshed-out form of a book.

We proposed the book because we believed that something had to be articulated about how hermeneutics, particularly Gadamerian philosophical hermeneutics (1960/1989), had something to say to practice professions about a way to approach research around human concerns. Four academics (three nurses and one educator) endeavored then to find language that was "concrete" enough to be understood but did not fall into the trap of offering a prescribed method of conducting hermeneutic research. In Chapter Four of the book, we took up this issue of method as, rather than a set prescription, it is instead an act of being methodical and following leads. In his foreword, Caputo reminds us of the etymological meaning of method: *meta* as making one's way along a particular path (*odos*). Gadamer (2007) suggested that "understanding is an adventure, and like any other adventure, is dangerous" (p. 243), but, in this book, we tried to suggest that understanding *is the ultimate hermeneutic wager*: that understanding matters and will make a difference in matters of human consequence of living well in conditions where suffering often exists. We tried to offer a prompt to conduct research that touches on human conditions of living: illness, schools, children, health, relationships, suffering, healing, and hope.

This was hard work. Balancing a description of how to conduct something without offering a map, guide, baton, or train engine conductor cap is challenging. In many ways, the work of hermeneutics as a research approach is somewhat intuitive, but we also believe it is something that can be taught, learned, and definitely practiced. Writing the chapter about conducting interviews was an act of trying to capture the complexity, contingency, and fluidity of the interview. It is deeply responsive – as is hermeneutics. There is no guide for an interview, no prior questions determined that will protect one from what is going to come in the interview. It is like describing art – here is how it appears right here and now, but if you turn to look at it from another angle or through another eye, its meaning changes. Conducting an interview in a responsive mode requires tact, discretion, discernment, and skill. It requires a turn of head and turn of eye and ear. It is not easy to do and even harder to describe or teach.

The chapter on analysis stopped us in our tracks. We know what we do when we are into the deep work of interpretation and we so often talk with students about how to begin this deep and involved work. Interpretation is skilled, complex, and exciting work. To find language, though, to describe this practice was very difficult. We needed language that was at once concrete and yet complex. Hermeneutic analysis (i.e., interpretation) is not easy; we could not sell it off as such, however we had to present it as something that is "doable" and something that can be learned and practiced.

Data analysis, like so much in hermeneutics, is most purely caught on the wing, in the intense back and forth of making sense of particular human situations. Beneath the dry research terminology of data are the stories, memories, thoughts, and feelings of people often recalling moments of extremity in their lives. We bear a responsibility to hold those data and make good use of them, transforming them without traducing them, in our interpretations. That is the ethical heart of hermeneutic work.

Approaching the chapter on rigor and integrity of hermeneutic research felt like a revisiting of every proposal we have ever written, every presentation to scientists, or die-hard quantitative researchers, and a recalling of trying to defend something without being defensive (see for e.g., Moules, Jardine, McCaffrey, & Brown, 2013). Writing it, finding the words though, despite the difficulty, proved to be particularly affirming. We were not simply arguing for the rigor but really seeing it and, for once, actually believing in it with a conviction we had been shy about before. The same happened in the "so what" chapter – the understandable demand that the work matters and addresses what is at stake. What surprised us was the discovery that what is really at stake in this work is that it compels us to live in the world differently:

> The knowledge of knowledge compels. It compels us to adopt an attitude of permanent vigilance against the temptation of certainty. It compels us to recognize that certainty is not a proof of truth. It compels us to realize that the world everyone sees is not the world but *a* world we bring forth with others. It compels us to see that the world will be different only if we live differently. It compels us because, when we know that we know, we cannot deny (to ourselves or to others) that we know... (This) implies an ethics that we cannot evade...an ethics that springs from human reflection and puts human reflection right at the core as a constitutive social phenomenon. (Maturana & Varela, 1992, p. 245)

> The "so what" of hermeneutic research is inherently a social endeavor. Though questions that guide hermeneutic research are vitally important, no less important is to answer these questions – tentatively, openly, and with the hermeneutic humility that recognizes that no one question can be answered definitively once and for all. Rather, hermeneutics "concentrates on the question of what happens to us when we 'understand'" (Davey, 2006, p. xi). Hermeneutics compels us as researchers and users of research to live in the world differently, to realize that understanding is not, as Davey (2006) invoked, just about interpreting the world but also about changing it. (Moules et al., in press)

Hermeneutic questions are hard questions; hermeneutic understanding is hard understanding. Yet, at the heart of it is the capacity to know and live differently – to find language that works. We believe this book will make a contribution to our practices but we also believe it made a difference to our thinking and what is yet to come. Applied hermeneutics, hermeneutics as a way of conducting research, is in one sense well established – there are many published studies, there are variant approaches in the literature (to which this book makes a substantial contribution), but set against the centuries-old traditions of interpretation of religious texts, or the philosophical development of hermeneutics, it is still a new adventure. Each publication in a practice discipline that stakes a claim as hermeneutic is still perceptibly defining the field. There is a degree of exposure in this – we have encountered scholars in the humanities who look askance at our travails in the world of hermeneutics, just as we are familiar with the objections of those who fetishize the scientific method in our own disciplines. It is only a hermeneutic truism, however, to say that there is more to learn, more to be done, and that even as we have tried to articulate how far we have come, the way ahead lies open.

In this book, we strived to conserve the human conditions and sensitivities of our topics and, according to Caputo, we offered "what the philosophers call the 'hermeneutic situation' in the concrete, glowing white hot and jumping off the pages of the philosophy books" (Caputo, in Moules et al., in press).

Note

1. University of Calgary, Faculty of Nursing, Corresponding Author: Nancy J. Moules, RN PhD Email: njmoules@ucalgary.ca

References

Caputo, J. D. (in press). Foreword: The wisdom of hermeneutics. In N. J. Moules, G. McCaffrey, J. C. Field, & C. M. Laing, *Conducting hermeneutic research: From philosophy to practice*. New York, NY: Peter Lang.

Davey, N. (2006). *Unquiet understanding: Gadamer's philosophical hermeneutics*. New York: SUNY Press.

Gadamer, H-G. (1960/1989). *Truth and method* (2nd rev. ed., J. Weinsheimer & D. G. Marshall, Trans.) New York, NY: Continuum.

Gadamer, H-G. (2007). *The Gadamer reader: A bouquet of the later writings* (R. Palmer, Ed. & Trans). Evanston, IL: Northwestern University Press.

Maturana, H. R., & Varela, F. (1992). *The tree of knowledge: The biological roots of human understanding* (rev. ed.). Boston, MA: Shambhala.

Moules, N. J., Jardine, D. W., McCaffrey, G., & Brown, C. B. (2013). "Isn't all oncology hermeneutic?" *Journal of Applied Hermeneutics*, Article 3. http://hdl.handle.net/10515/sy5w95141

Moules, N. J., McCaffrey, G., Field, J. C., & Laing, C. M. (in press). *Conducting hermeneutic research: From philosophy to practice*. New York, NY: Peter Lang.

Wallace, B. (1987). Appeal. In *The stubborn particulars of grace*. Toronto, ON, Canada: McClelland & Stewart.

INDEX

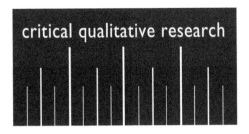

Shirley R. Steinberg and Gaile S. Cannella, *General Editors*

The Critical Qualitative Research series examines societal structures that oppress and exclude so that transformative actions can be generated. This transformed research is activist in orientation. Because the perspective accepts the notion that nothing is apolitical, research projects themselves are critically examined for power orientations, even as they are used to address curricular, educational, or societal issues.

This methodological work challenges modernist orientations and universalist impositions, asking critical questions like: Who/what is heard? Who/what is silenced? Who is privileged? Who is disqualified? How are forms of inclusion and exclusion being created? How are power relations constructed and managed? How do different forms of privilege and oppression intersect to affect educational, societal, and life possibilities for various individuals and groups?

We are particularly interested in manuscripts that offer critical examinations of curriculum, policy, public communities, and the ways in which language, discourse practices, and power relations prevent more just transformations.

For additional information about this series or for the submission of manuscripts, please contact:
Shirley R. Steinberg and Gaile S. Cannella
msgramsci@gmail.com | gaile.cannella@gmail.com

To order other books in this series, please contact our Customer Service Department:
(800) 770-LANG (within the U.S.)
(212) 647-7706 (outside the U.S.)
(212) 647-7707 FAX

Or browse online by series:
www.peterlang.com